TO PROMOTE THE
GENERAL WELFARE

TO PROMOTE THE GENERAL WELFARE

The Case for Big Government

EDITED BY STEVEN CONN

OXFORD
UNIVERSITY PRESS

OXFORD
UNIVERSITY PRESS

Oxford University Press is a department of the University of Oxford.
It furthers the University's objective of excellence in research, scholarship,
and education by publishing worldwide.

Oxford   New York
Auckland   Cape Town   Dar es Salaam   Hong Kong   Karachi
Kuala Lumpur   Madrid   Melbourne   Mexico City   Nairobi
New Delhi   Shanghai   Taipei   Toronto

With offices in
Argentina   Austria   Brazil   Chile   Czech Republic   France   Greece
Guatemala   Hungary   Italy   Japan   Poland   Portugal   Singapore
South Korea   Switzerland   Thailand   Turkey   Ukraine   Vietnam

Oxford is a registered trademark of Oxford University Press
in the UK and certain other countries.

Published in the United States of America by
Oxford University Press
198 Madison Avenue, New York, NY 10016

Library of Congress Cataloging-in-Publication Data
To promote the general welfare : the case for big government / edited by
    Steven Conn.
      p. cm.
    Includes bibliographical references and index.
    ISBN 978–0–19–985855–2 (pbk. : alk. paper) — ISBN 978–0–19–985853–8
    (hardcover : alk. paper)   1. United States—Social policy—19th
    century.   2. United States—Social policy—20th century.   3. United
    States—Politics and government—19th century.   4. United States—Politics and
    government—20th century.   5. United States—Politics and government—21st
    century.   I. Conn, Steven.
    HN57.T68 2012
    361.973—dc23   2011053397

ISBN 978–0–19–985855–2
ISBN 978–0–19–985853–8

9 8 7 6 5 4 3 2 1
Printed in the United States of America
on acid-free paper

To my friends and members of my family who work every day to make this a better country. I am lucky to know you.

Contents

Preface   ix
List of Contributors   xv

CHAPTER 1
Looking for Government in All the Wrong Places   1
Brian Balogh

CHAPTER 2
Transportation and the Uniting of the Nation   21
Zachary M. Schrag

CHAPTER 3
Uncle Sam at the Blackboard:
The Federal Government and American Education   44
Jonathan Zimmerman

CHAPTER 4
Banking on Government   65
Elizabeth Tandy Shermer

CHAPTER 5
Twenty-Nine Helmets:
Government Power and the Promise of Security   85
Kevin Boyle

CHAPTER 6
The Right to a Decent Home   102
Thomas J. Sugrue

CHAPTER 7
Solving the Nation's Number One Health Problem(s)   118
Karen Kruse Thomas

CHAPTER 8
Culture for the People:
How Government Has Fostered the
Arts and Culture   140
Steven Conn

CHAPTER 9
From Franklin to Facebook:
The Civic Mandate for Communications   156
Richard R. John

CHAPTER 10
From Endeavor to Achievement and Back Again:
Government's Greatest Hits in Peril   173
Paul C. Light

Notes   197
Index   227

CHAPTER 6

Preface

Not too long ago, my family and I went camping in the Four Corners region of the American Southwest. We camped at one magnificent national park after another. We drove to these places on extraordinary interstate highways that allowed us to travel over this once-difficult landscape at sixty-five miles per hour (okay, often faster). We passed reservoirs and irrigation projects built by the Army Corps of Engineers that provide water for agriculture and recreation for tourists.

And along the way we kept passing billboards denouncing "big government." Some of them supported particular candidates for office; others were more homemade screeds. They all seemed very, very angry.

At first we giggled at them—yet more amusing examples of the "keep your government hands off my Medicare" hypocrisy that has infected so much of our recent political debate.

But after a while and a few hundred miles, the joke began to wear off, and we genuinely began to wonder: don't these people see it? That so much of what enriches life in this part of the country has been made possible by one federal project after another?

After all, a trip like ours through the Southwest often takes you past enormous military installations, physical manifestations of an economy dependent on "big government" spending from the Pentagon. And it can take you past Indian reservations, which serve as sobering reminders that before this land was settled by the rugged individualists of American myth, it was cleared of its original inhabitants by federal troops.

So somewhere in southern Colorado, the idea for this book was hatched. Given the profound misunderstanding about the role the federal government has played in American life, I thought it might be useful to put together a collection of essays to review some of this history.

The essays you are about to read come from some of the leading academic experts in their fields. They range across topic and time—from transportation and public health to education and housing, and from Franklin to Facebook, to steal the title of one of them. They all demonstrate just how central the federal government has been in creating the kind of society Americans have wanted across the decades. As they make clear, those efforts have been far from perfect, nor do they suggest that the federal government is the answer to all our problems. But taken together, they make the case for "big government" by reminding us how seriously the federal government has taken its constitutional task: To Promote the General Welfare.

From the very beginnings of the nation, a substantial number of Americans have had a deep suspicion of strong centralized power, and those who rail against it usually offer three alternatives, in varying measure.[1] First, they argue that the private sector will do a better job at creating a prosperous society than government ever will; second, they want states, not Washington, DC, to be the most important source of governmental authority; third, they offer a gauzy nostalgia for the pioneer days when small communities took care of their own, and free individuals needed protection or support from no one.

The advocates of these positions usually make an appeal to the past: we used to be a nation of private enterprise, or states' rights, or rugged individualists. And then the federal government ruined it all.

The past, of course, is a little more complicated than that. So by way of introducing the essays that follow, let me review a few of the historical problems with each of these alternative views of how best to build and maintain our society.

Free market fundamentalism: The free market does a wonderful job of delivering goods and services at the best prices to consumers. It does a terrible job of things like building sewer systems, educating children, or keeping us healthy. Free market fundamentalists insist, however, that the private sector can solve all of our infrastructure, education, and health care problems, evidence notwithstanding.

This is an ideological position rather than a set of pragmatic solutions, and our history is littered with examples of what it can and cannot accomplish. But those failures do not constitute the biggest problem with this ideology. More significantly, the premise upon which it is built is wrong: the "free market" is a fiction. There is no genuinely "free market"—a place where purely rational economic actors are free to make choices without any government interference—except in the seminar-room exercises of some economists. What is more, there never has been.

Government structures the way any market will work by setting the rules of the game through the legal system and through regulatory mechanisms, among other ways. Ask anyone who has tried to do business in a country where contracts may or may not be worth the paper they are written on and where bribery substitutes for bureaucratic procedure. They can tell you about the value of these structures, and they will convince you that these government roles are essential. In addition, and as several of the essays here detail, government creates the infrastructure that makes the private market work better. Again, go to a country where the roads are not maintained, where the financial system is jerry-built, and where you may or may not be able to drink the water, and you quickly learn to appreciate the blessings of basic infrastructure.

So the question is not whether the government will play a role in the market, but how, on what terms, and for whose benefit.

During the Gilded Age, for example, the great industrial titans insisted that the government maintain a "laissez-faire" policy toward the economy. Then they lobbied for tariffs in order to eliminate competition from imported goods and they demanded that governors and presidents call out the National Guard when their workers went on strike. Laissez-faire when it suited them, government intervention when they needed it.

The fetish of states' rights: Those who insist that any power not specifically granted to the federal government in the Constitution must, ipso facto, belong to the states read the Tenth Amendment in the narrowest way. For these people, "states' rights" is both an article of faith and a rallying cry. Historically, however, the invocation of "states' rights" has been less about philosophical principle and more about situational ethics.

Southerners in the antebellum period insisted on their right to own slaves (and to secede from the Union to perpetuate that system of slavery) as a matter of "states' rights." Those same Southerners, of course, also insisted that the federal government enforce the Fugitive Slave Act, and they howled when they felt that federal law had been violated. Never mind that the act trampled on the "states' rights" of those northern states where slavery had been abolished.

Likewise, a century later when the federal government began to dismantle the southern system of segregation through court cases and legislation, white Southerners rose up in resistance to this infringement of "states' rights." At the same time, white southern politicians happily accepted the federal highway money that came pouring in to build the interstate system. No states' rights problems there.

Beginning in the 1980s, "states' rights" has been invoked as a way to deny women access to family planning, though why an American citizen should have less control over her reproductive health in Mississippi than in Massachusetts is more than a little difficult to defend. More recently, of course, "states' rights" has been the tool with which to deny gay couples the right to marry and to deny them all the benefits that come with marriage.

States can certainly serve as the "laboratories of democracy," in Louis Brandeis's memorable phrase, when they pioneer projects that then influence the rest of the nation. More often than not, however, states' rights constitutes less a theory of governance and more a façade to perpetuate traditions of bullying, bigotry, and oppression.

The myth of the Marlboro Man: Americans have had a century-long romance with the cowboy. He stands as the very symbol of libertarian independence, freedom, and self-reliance. President Reagan, for example—a middle-class kid from Illinois who made good in Hollywood—often had himself photographed riding horses on his ranch, looking like a cowboy. George W. Bush, scion of New England money and third-generation Yalie, also liked to portray himself as a Texas cowboy.

Everyone seems oblivious to the irony: historically, cowboys drove other people's cattle across the plains, usually working for wages as low-level employees of large companies. They may have slept under the stars around a campfire, but their livelihoods depended on railroad companies, meat processing plants, and the market for beef back in the big cities. And those pioneering homesteaders we also like to invoke? They farmed land that the federal government gave away for free.

The nouveau libertarian notion that we are a nation of autonomous cowboys and pioneers who are owed nothing and in return owe nothing to society resembles nothing so much as the teenager who thinks he deserves to drive Mom and Dad's car without paying for the gas or the insurance. We are all enmeshed in social obligations, networks, and relationships. To pretend otherwise is little more than an escapist fantasy. Benjamin Franklin had good advice for such people. In Franklin's view, the notion of private property extended only to the bare necessities, "but all property superfluous to such purposes, is the property of the public, who by their laws have created it, and who may, therefore by other laws dispose of it whenever the welfare of the public shall desire such disposition. He that does not like civil society on these terms, let him retire and live among savages." Few of us would go as far as Franklin did, but he reminds us that certain Founders had a collective rather than strictly individual conception of the "general welfare."

When Ronald Reagan announced in 1981 that "government is not the solution to our problems; government is the problem," he galvanized a generation of antigovernment activism. It was a great line, but it was, characteristically, wrong. Government is neither good nor bad—it is a tool with which citizens in a democratic society carry out our collective will. As Garry Wills put it nicely, this confusion leads to a strange patriotism in which we are asked to love our country by hating our government.[2]

Abraham Lincoln, also characteristically, had it right when he reminded the mourners at Gettysburg that ours is a "government of the people, by the people, for the people." Which is not to say that the federal government has always been effective or efficient or even just, as several of these essays also describe. Federal programs after World War II, for example, made homeownership a reality for millions of ordinary Americans, but they initially excluded African Americans from that dream. Our federal government is nothing more and nothing less than a collective reflection of ourselves, sometimes at our best, sometimes at our worst.

If we are, as our children pledge every morning, one nation indivisible, then as the essays in this collection ably demonstrate, the federal government deserves much of the credit for creating that nation and making it work. We hope you find them informative and useful and that they will spur you to think further about how Americans have put the federal government to work in the past, and how we might do so in the future.

As the editor of this collection, I have had genuine pleasure in working with all the authors who have contributed to it, and I thank them all for their enthusiasm for the book and for their willingness to write for it. A particular thanks to Jon Zimmerman and Brian Balogh, who helped me shape the volume. Thanks too to Angela Brintlinger, Peter Conn, Scott Sanders, and Jim Bach for various help big and small.

Contributors

BRIAN BALOGH is a professor in the University of Virginia's Department of History and chair of the National Fellowship Program at the Miller Center. He is also co host of the public radio show *Backstory with the American History Guys*. Balogh's latest book is *A Government Out of Sight: The Mystery of National Authority in Nineteenth-Century America* (2009).

KEVIN BOYLE teaches history at Ohio State University. He is the author of *The UAW and the Heyday of American Liberalism, 1945–1968* (1995) and *Arc of Justice: A Saga of Race, Civil Rights and Murder in the Jazz Age* (2004), coauthor of *Muddy Boots and Ragged Aprons: Images of Working-Class Detroit, 1900–1930* (1997), and editor of *Organized Labor and American Politics: The Labor-Liberal Alliance, 1894–1994* (1998).

STEVEN CONN is professor of history at Ohio State University, where he also directs public history initiatives. *To Promote the General Welfare* is his sixth book project. He has written regularly for newspapers around the country and is the founding editor of the online magazine *Origins: Current Events in Historical Perspective*.

RICHARD R. JOHN is a professor in the PhD program in communications at the Columbia School of Journalism, where he teaches courses on business, technology, communications, and political development. His publications include *Network Nation: Inventing American Telecommunications* (2010) and *Spreading the News: The American Postal System from Franklin to Morse* (1995).

PAUL C. LIGHT is the Paulette Goddard Professor of Public Service at NYU's Robert Wagner School of Public Service. He has previously been the Douglas Dillon Senior Fellow at the Brookings Institution, and the director of the Public Policy Program at the Pew Charitable Trusts. He is the author of numerous books including *Government's Greatest Achievements: From Civil Rights to Homeland Defense* (2002) and *A Government Ill Executed: The Decline of the Federal Service and How to Reverse It* (2008).

ZACHARY M. SCHRAG is associate professor of history at George Mason University. He is the author of *The Great Society Subway: A History of the Washington Metro* (2006) and *Ethical Imperialism: Institutional Review Boards and the Social Sciences, 1965–2009* (2010).

ELIZABETH TANDY SHERMER has published widely on the intersecting histories of labor, business, capitalism, policy, and politics, topics covered in her first book, *Creating the Sunbelt: Phoenix and the Political-Economy of Metropolitan Growth*. She is the Paul Mellon Fellow in American History at the University of Cambridge and an assistant professor of history at Loyola University Chicago.

THOMAS J. SUGRUE is David Boies Professor of History and Sociology and director of the Penn Social Science and Policy Forum. His books include *The Origins of the Urban Crisis* (1996); *The New Suburban History*, with Kevin M. Kruse (2005); *Sweet Land of Liberty: The Forgotten Struggle for Civil Rights in the North* (2008), and *Not Even Past: Barack Obama and the Burden of Race* (2010). He is writing a history of the real estate industry in modern America.

KAREN KRUSE THOMAS is a postdoctoral fellow at the Institute of the History of Medicine, Johns Hopkins School of Medicine.

She published *Deluxe Jim Crow: Civil Rights and American Health Policy, 1935–1954* (2011) and is currently completing a history of the Johns Hopkins School of Public Health.

JONATHAN ZIMMERMAN is professor of education and history at New York University. A former Peace Corps volunteer and high school teacher, Zimmerman is the author of *Small Wonder: The Little Red Schoolhouse in History and Memory* (2009) and three other books. He is also a frequent op-ed contributor to the *New York Times*, the *Philadelphia Inquirer*, and other popular newspapers and magazines.

TO PROMOTE THE
GENERAL WELFARE

CHAPTER 1

Looking for Government in All the Wrong Places

Brian Balogh

We know government when we see it, especially big government. And in case your eyesight is not what it used to be, just visit any conservative blog. Take the Heritage Foundation's recent "Morning Bell" post: "For most Americans, the idea of growing government at a time when deficits are sky high might seem preposterous. But for many on the left, it's the only way they can think of to get the economy moving again." "Their end goal? The continued rise of big government."[1]

The left is just as alarmist, often conjuring up a Dickensian world without government that conservatives are aching to impose. When the *Huffington Post* reported in 2010 that gubernatorial candidate Carl Paladino had proposed turning New York's prisons into dormitories for welfare recipients, one blogger shot back: "Combine this with Newt Gingrich's 90s proposal of reinstating orphanages, and we can return to the grandeur that was 1800s England."[2]

No question divides liberals and conservatives more starkly than the battle over the proper role of government. That debate structures the central narrative of our nation's history. It is the story of the continued growth of national authority powered largely by bursts of presidentially inspired reform that crested during the twentieth century through the New Deal and the Great Society. Progressives applaud these developments as welcome departures from the minimalist government of the nineteenth century. Conservatives do not dispute this interpretation of modern American politics. They do, however, question the premise that each growth spurt was beneficial for the nation. Oddly, both conservatives and progressives agree on one thing: nineteenth-century Americans embraced the free market and the principles of laissez-faire. Conservatives want to recapture that past; progressives celebrate America's liberation from it.

Neither ideological perspective takes seriously the possibility that Americans turned regularly to government throughout their history or that the public sector played a crucial role in shaping what Americans regard as the "natural" market. Nor does either side acknowledge the degree to which citizens who continue to bash big government have benefited from government largesse, even as they mobilize to stifle public programs that reward others. The historical premise underlying this debate is fundamentally flawed. Our failure to recognize the *ways* in which Americans have governed has distorted our understanding of the *extent* to which Americans have governed. As Suzanne Mettler recently documented, "Our government is integrally intertwined with everyday life from health care to housing, but in forms that often elude our vision: governance appears 'stateless' because it operates indirectly, through subsidizing private actors."[3]

Americans have always demanded a great deal from their government and often they have gotten what they asked for. But the shape that public authority took in America did not comport with the stereotypes of French gendarmes, Kafkaesque bureaucrats, or British civil servants. The United States governed *differently* from other industrialized contemporaries, but it did not necessarily govern *less*. Existing rules, routines, and structures of power governed nineteenth-century America—even at the national level. There were subsidies and mandates, especially at the state and local level. And those rules, subsidies, and mandates mattered. So too did American foreign policy, whether pursued in the service of opening up trade routes or securing territories across the continent.

These policies influenced the life chances of millions of Americans. They continued to do so through the twentieth century. The challenge to those who wish to understand politics today, then, is to discern how these governing patterns operated and to identify the ways in which they have endured and evolved.

In other words, those who want to cut government and advocates for expanding government have been looking for government in all the wrong places. It is time to help both sides with their search by revising the history of the way Americans have governed. A national government capable of mobilizing compatible resources in the private and voluntary sectors often produced more impressive results than unilateral state power. Historically, that is exactly the way Americans preferred it. Where no intermediate institutions stood between citizen and national government, Americans consistently advocated energetic governance when it came to trade, security, and economic development. Where local and state government was up to the task, or where voluntary and private groups might fulfill public purposes, Americans preferred that the national government enable rather than command.

Once we recognize the range of ways that Americans have governed we can move past the big government/small government stalemate. This will not be easy, especially because those who already enjoy extensive state-sponsored largesse are delighted to sustain this misguided debate in order to obscure the myriad ways in which they have benefited from public aid. Progressives should not make matters worse by ignoring the long history of the state working in association with private and voluntary partners.

We can embark on a far more meaningful discussion about who should benefit from government intervention in the lives of Americans and who should bear the cost once we acknowledge that government action in America is often most powerful when it is least visible. Indeed, obscuring the role of government has been crucial to the effective use of government for much of our history.

Once this and other long-standing patterns of governance are recognized, voters may begin to notice twenty-first-century iterations of these tendencies. That, in turn, will illuminate twenty-first-century government benefits that have helped millions of individuals succeed—altering popular (and plenty of scholarly) conceptions that lean heavily on heroic stories of market efficiency or individual initiative and hard work. The laws and tax expenditures that subsidize the so-called private world of pension and health care benefits today are a good example. Voters might well ask, for instance, whether federal subsidies to the employers of tens of millions of middle-class beneficiaries who receive employment-based health care should be classified as welfare and subjected to the same scrutiny as Medicaid benefits to the poor.

The essays in this collection illustrate the variety of ways in which Americans have governed. This introduction lays out five patterns of governance that have prevailed from the founding until today. First, however, it explores why Americans need to govern in such an indirect fashion. The modern-day Tea Party has reminded us of our founders' fears of distant, centralized government—especially if it threatened to tax patriots heavily. Forgotten in the mists of time, however, was the predisposition of those same citizens to act collectively to ensure their liberty in a dangerous world. The interaction of *both* these founding principles—fear of distant government *and* the creation of a state sufficiently powerful to ensure liberty—has yielded a vigorous state that is hidden in plain sight.

I conclude with a request: that progressives and conservatives get their history right. If they do, progressives will concede that

Americans have always preferred that the federal government operate indirectly, through state and local government when possible, and through the voluntary, even private sectors, when necessary. Progressives should operate in the same fashion to achieve their redistributive goals. Conservatives should acknowledge that their ideological predecessors have often been the first to turn to government to create and protect a national market or meet the challenges of national security. They should not take for granted the crucial role that government continues to play in these and other tasks.

Fearing Distant Polities but Trusting Your Own

Since the War of Independence, Americans have talked about government one way and behaved in another. That is because they sought to overthrow one regime yet quickly learned that the very liberties they sought to protect could only be secured by constructing another regime strong enough to safeguard their personal and economic rights in a dangerous world. It took a strong government to maintain the fiction that individuals could be free from government.

America was founded upon republican principles that challenged the British mercantile state. Great Britain had grown increasingly intrusive after the French and Indian War. Even before this, colonists worried that their fellow citizens would lose their independence—that they would fall prey to political influence and be manipulated by others.[4] By the 1770s, British North Americans burnished this "republican" ideology into an effective revolutionary weapon directed at British rule. They feared distant, centralized power. Their rhetoric resonated because it exposed the threat to liberty that arbitrary use of power and executive corruption posed at the very time that the Crown threatened the rights of all the colonists.

British North Americans countered distant power with citizen supervision and surveillance of executive authority. Only determined and wise political vigilance could preserve the republic, they believed.[5] This vigilance and antagonism to distant governance is a very real legacy of America's republican heritage. Modern-day progressives err in dismissing it and its champions, such as the contemporary Tea Party, as mere nostalgia or worse.

Yet there was more to the republican vision than fear of corruption and dependence. Many of today's Tea Partiers will be surprised to learn that republican thought also emphasized *energetic* governance. Indeed, the very same patriots who fought British taxation without representation did not distinguish between state and civil society or, for that matter, public and private roles for citizens. They imbibed a commonwealth tradition that thrived along with citizen vigilance. The commonwealth tradition stressed that the public good derived from placing the polity's interest ahead of the rights of individual citizens. Service to the republic disciplined self-interest in the cause of all citizens.[6] In the hands of such virtuous leaders, government could be trusted to do a great deal.

Leaders like George Washington worked tirelessly to preserve liberty, but they conceived of liberty as a corporate privilege to be shared by all of the republic's citizens. It was a blessing bestowed on the entire community rather than a privately held benefit distributed to rights-bearing individuals. Noted physician and Philadelphia reformer Benjamin Rush fashioned the boundary between public and private spheres in a manner that left little room for the latter. A citizen was "public property," Rush contended. As such, "his time and talents—his youth—his manhood—his old age—nay more, life, all belong to his country."[7] This too was the legacy of America's founding, the other half of republican thought that members of the *original* Tea Party embraced.

The most eloquent spokesman for a powerful federal government, Alexander Hamilton, certainly did not suggest hiding the national government's light under a bushel. Indeed, in *Federalist* 27, Hamilton pronounced that "A government continually at a distance and out of sight can hardly be expected to interest the sensations of the people. The inference is that the authority of the Union and the affections of the citizens toward it will be strengthened, rather than weakened, by the extension to what are called matters of internal concern." [8] Hamilton got it wrong.

Five Enduring Patterns

What Hamilton failed to anticipate was a national government that was often most powerful when it was hidden in plain sight. Even in those instances where the national government visibly entered the fray as a "Leviathan," as was the case in many of its wars against Indians, for instance, the memory of its influence was quickly displaced by sagas of heroic settlers fighting back savages. For good reason, Tocqueville noted, "In the United States, government authority seems anxiously bent on keeping out of sight." [9]

Over the course of the nineteenth century, Americans eschewed visible, centralized, national administration. That citizens resisted a national bureaucratic state does not mean that they did not ask the national government to do a lot for them. Combining national resources and private initiative proved to be a consistent formula for political success in policies ranging from land distribution to internal improvements. Subsidizing a communications system that provided access to newspapers in remote locations stimulated national political debate in a polity that was highly decentralized. Subsidizing roads, canals, and then railroads knit the nation together. State and local governments invested over $400 million in canals and railroads in the early nineteenth century. West Point trained many of the experts who surveyed, designed, and built these arteries. [10] The general government was instrumental in constructing a national market—a contribution soon washed from memory in a torrent of congratulations for America's exceptional stature among statist industrialized nations. During the Gilded

Age, the federal judiciary labored mightily to separate public from private action. It failed to do so, opening the door for the reintegration of public and private endeavors on a national scale in the twentieth century.[11]

Besides governing out of sight, four other patterns of governance endured. Americans consistently supported a more energetic, even bureaucratically empowered state, whenever they perceived their security to be threatened. The Civil War was the most pronounced example of this pattern—especially the Confederacy's Leviathan-like intervention into the private sphere. The Confederacy not only drafted men into the military but it also operated state-run factories and confiscated the private property of citizens deemed to be disloyal.[12] Similar consolidations of power were evident with the War of Independence and, to a lesser degree, the wars of 1812 and with Mexico. Americans were willing to grant the federal government even more power when Indians threatened security and economic development. The Trail of Tears was forged by an extraordinary mobilization of federal resources and the naked use of force.

A third pattern was the tendency to endorse unmediated national power when it was geographically removed from the locus of established authority. This was the case in the territories, which were governed directly by the national government until they became states. This was also true for territories acquired during the Spanish-American War. It was the pattern established through the programs aimed at western resource development, such as irrigation and forestry. The US Army proved to be a crucial resource here too. Americans who would never have tolerated this threat to their autonomy back East supported it when it was imposed on the West or in the Philippines. The army was also used to subdue Indians and police national forests. Eventually, an expanded civilian administration replaced the army, building dams and parceling out grazing rights in the West.

The key variable was the availability of intermediary institutions like state and local government, or voluntary organizations like churches, charities, interest groups, or professional societies. Once they existed, Americans preferred that they be used, rather than extending national authority directly. But the principle of empowering the central government at the periphery prevailed precisely because such intermediaries did not exist out West or abroad. Sustaining national authority in such remote regions required that intermediaries, starting with the basic building blocks of federalism, be nurtured to accommodate policies made in Washington, DC, to local needs.

A fourth pattern, closely related to the first, was resistance to visible forms of taxation. This, of course, was one of the reasons that Americans went to war against Great Britain. The threat of British functionaries violating the civil liberties of British North Americans was as unnerving to the colonists as the financial consequences of such taxes. Unable to avoid national taxation entirely, Americans settled uncomfortably on the tariff. The discomfort, however, had more to do with the inequitable distribution of costs and benefits from the tariff than the manner in which this tax was imposed. Almost all Americans agreed that this indirect form of taxation was preferable to direct taxes such as excise taxes, not to mention an income tax. The cost of the tariff to individuals was embedded in the price of imported goods and the government apparatus that collected tariffs from importers was literally located off shore. As Alexander Hamilton learned the hard way, this was a far preferable approach to collecting revenue than excise taxes like the one imposed on whiskey—which was far more visible and intrusive.

Use of judge-made law to shape the political economy constituted a fifth legacy of nineteenth-century governance. Like the tendency to rely upon intermediary institutions in order to stave off centralized control, reliance on courts allowed for national policy with little in the way of bureaucracy. And it provided a national language—a means of communicating central principles—that imposed common expectations and limitations on a sprawling nation. The language of "liberty of contract," for instance, resonated far beyond the courtroom in the nineteenth century. This judge-made law was originally intended to protect the rights of workers to the fruits of their own labor, but employers extrapolated from it to deny the most rudimentary attempts to ensure worker safety and economic well-being. Employers claimed that any collective safeguards, especially those imposed by the state, denied workers the right to bargain individually with their employer.[13]

Americans were willing to support powerful centralized institutions during crises that threatened their security or when these institutions operated far from population centers, where there were no intermediate institutions like states and localities to get the job done. For most day-to-day responsibilities, however, during normal times, indirect taxes supported a national government that sought to coordinate rather than command and that depended upon judge-made law to pave the way for a predictable national market inhabited by national corporations. Those corporations, for instance, were the first to capitalize (pun intended) on the due process clause of the Fourteenth Amendment. In a remarkable assertion of national authority (and judicial activism) the Supreme Court used this clause, intended to protect the rights of freedmen, to define corporations as "persons."

For the most part, the national government remained hidden in plain sight as it operated through judge-made law, subsidies, diplomacy, and partnerships with intermediaries ranging from local governments to private corporations. As the number of organizations that operated on a national scale grew during the Gilded Age, the possibilities for national associations between the federal government and these partners expanded.

The Transition to Twentieth-Century Governance

More effectively, albeit less boisterously than the high-profile battles fought between those who worked to expand the national bureaucratic state and their opponents, nineteenth-century patterns of interaction between state and society were advanced during the twentieth century through intermediaries working in conjunction with the federal government.

Some of these associations were public—states and local governments. Some were voluntary organizations like Blue Cross and Blue Shield. Some were religiously inspired. And some were profit-making corporations that ranged from defense contractors to the trade associations that served corporate masters. While the American Red Cross was unique in that it was chartered by the United States government in 1900, formalizing what would grow into a powerful working relationship between government and the voluntary sector in foreign affairs, most of these associations engaged national public policy in ways that strengthened their ties to the central government over the course of the twentieth century.[14]

Consolidated on a national scale over the course of the twentieth century, this associational order operated within the contours of political patterns established during the nineteenth century. State and local governments developed the capacity to act in concert on a national scale. Professions developed powerful national organizations, and universities emerged as national centers of expertise. Voluntary organizations adapted their agendas to national needs. Interest groups and trade associations flocked to Washington, DC. Corporate social policy competed with voluntary organizations and public agencies to promote welfare. By targeting their appeals through national organizations that worked in conjunction with the national government and often administered its policies, Americans demanded support and services from the national government at the same time that many continued to rail against big government. Filtered through the associational order, such federal support seemed less threatening—even traditional.[15] For many of the very constituents of these programs, it did not seem to exist at all.

With this set of nationally organized associations serving as intermediaries between national government and the individual,

Americans could preserve their sense of individual autonomy and personal control. Yet associations served collective ends, even though they hardly spoke for the entire nation. In the mass democracy that emerged by the middle of the twentieth century, claiming to speak for a major occupation, a key industry, the nation's states, or its universities was about as close as any institution or person could come to speaking for significant portions of the nation's citizens, bully pulpit aside. It was often a lot closer than the political parties came to voicing collective concerns.

The vast majority of these associations quickly learned to embrace some of the patterns of governance that I have already discussed. For instance, scholars have pulled back the curtain to reveal the "hidden" welfare regime, or the "contractual" national security regime.[16] A quick review of a few of these "hidden" networks of twentieth-century national authority underscores the continuity of nineteenth-century patterns of state-society relations, albeit increasingly projected onto a national, even international stage.

Governing Out of Sight

For decades, women were instrumental in forging voluntary networks that provided social services to the indigent, especially women and children. These women soon turned to state and local governments in the early twentieth century, and eventually, the national government—lobbying for the Sheppard-Towner Act in 1921—to finance these efforts. Ultimately, the Women's Bureau established a beachhead in the national government for programs directed at women and children. Whether financed at the local or the national level, however, many of the actual services were delivered by a diverse array of voluntary groups, making these programs more palatable to a broad range of Americans.

Once women gained the vote in 1920, they leveraged their ballots to hold elected officials accountable. True to a tradition that preferred the national government to play a supporting role, many women demanded that services be delivered through voluntary, state and local outlets, not directly by the national government. Thus, funding of health services in the states actually increased after the nationally legislated Sheppard-Towner Act expired.[17]

Universities also constituted a crucial intermediary between citizen and state. Perhaps their most important contribution was to create and certify professionals. Universities helped professions, like the medical profession, establish control over an exclusive body of esoteric knowledge that increased their authority and stature. Of equal importance, universities limited access to the professions, reducing competition within the profession itself. Through state licensing, professionals were granted a remarkable degree of autonomy over their own practices. Delegating life and death decisions on health care to groups like the American Medical Association had important public policy implications. The professions and universities soon dramatically increased their demand for support from all levels of government while retaining a great deal of their autonomy. Although state legislatures on occasion intervened in highly visible fashion, and even though the national government eventually demanded more accountability, for much of the twentieth century, vast sums of taxpayer money, public authority, and crucial policy choices were delegated to the professions and the universities that created and renewed these professions.[18]

Universities also served as coordinating mechanisms for state and federally sponsored public programs. The best example of this is the farm experiment stations and the extension service that worked hand in hand with them. The 1887 Hatch Experiment-Station Act provided federal funding for agricultural research at the state land-grant colleges (created by the Morrill Land Grant College Act of 1862). These laboratories were established to generate new knowledge, and more important, to apply that knowledge to the needs of farmers. Land-grant colleges created, and the national government eventually subsidized, an extension network that translated science into productive agricultural practice. That service was delivered, however, through familiar faces, well integrated into the community—much the way the mail had been delivered in the nineteenth century. Alternatively, the federal government rang the school bell for its newly acquired subjects overseas. In the Philippines, the number of Filipinos studying under the American flag ballooned to 2 million by 1940.[19] Once again, the national government delivered services directly to distant clients, when there were no other intermediaries to operate through.

Even when Americans were forced to construct new national bureaucracies in response to the economic crisis of the 1930s, long-established patterns prevailed. There is no better example of this tendency than the Social Security Act of 1935. There were highly visible and even intrusive elements of that social insurance program. President Franklin D. Roosevelt (FDR), for instance, worried that assigning numbers to working Americans would smack of totalitarian government—he was concerned that these numbers would be labeled "dog tags." Yet social insurance—which did assign social security numbers—was the *only* title of this omnibus legislation that was administered at the national level. Welfare, unemployment compensation, and several other key social programs included in the act were administered at the state and local levels. FDR was keen to spin off the administration of social insurance as well, but even his brain trust could not figure out a way, in an age before computers, to keep track of Americans who were likely to move between states over the course of a lifetime. Keeping track was essential because the Social Security Administration and the Democratic Party claimed that retirement benefits were akin to individualized savings accounts—linked to the contributions of each worker—not some one-size-fits-all government program.[20]

It was the contributory element of social insurance that Roosevelt liked most—even if it did require national administration. The program's supporters labored to maintain the image that what workers got back came from what they put in, even as the program itself became an engine for fiscal redistribution from younger generations to the elderly. It lifted several generations of the elderly out of poverty at the expense of future generations of retirees. Three-quarters of a century later, "Social Security" remains one of the few nationally administered income maintenance programs and is sharply distinguished from locally administered "welfare" programs by the perception that those collecting Social Security benefits are merely getting back what they contributed *individually*. The social insurance formula hit the trifecta in this regard: individuals felt that they had their own private accounts; contributions went to a trust fund that specified what these revenues could be spent on; and the government—as inconspicuously as possible—subsidized several generations of beneficiaries.[21] They did not complain.

As in the past, Americans empowered the national government to expand its administrative reach (and suspend civil liberties) when national security was threatened. World War II and the ensuing Cold War leap out as the most illustrative examples, although the most sweeping reorganization of the executive branch of the national government after the Cold War era occurred in the wake of the attack on the World Trade Center and Pentagon on September 11, 2001. Like British North Americans during the Revolutionary War or Americans in 1861, mid-twentieth-century Americans jettisoned their concerns about standing armies and quickly embraced a central government with considerably enhanced powers. During the Cold War, they went even farther, constructing a "prominis-trative" state that combined professional expertise with federal administrative capacity to wage this twilight struggle.[22] Even during the Cold War, however, Americans avoided what Harold D. Lasswell labeled the "garrison state." They constructed a "contract state" instead—taking a page out of the nineteenth-century US Postal Service and army procurement handbooks.

The military-industrial complex thrived by outsourcing to the private sector and to academia some of its most vital functions, ranging from weapons development to methods of psychological warfare. The federal government picked up the tab, but universities, like Stanford and Johns Hopkins, and contractors like Northrup Grumman did the research and development.[23]

The classified, contractual, national security state is merely one of several vast regimes that remain hidden, and consequently, insulated from careful scrutiny. The others do not rely on security clearances. Rather, they are hidden in plain sight, obscured only by our failure to appreciate long-standing patterns of American governance. Take, for instance, the federally subsidized infrastructure for suburban growth. As Tom Sugrue points out in "A Right to a Decent Home," investment in their homes is the major, and often only, asset that citizens possess. Those suburban castle/collateral accumulating fiefdoms epitomize the hard work, entrepreneurial skill, and independence of their owners. Just ask them. The story of the government financial regulation and tax policy, as Sugrue puts it, not to mention the highway programs and government jobs that fueled this growth, remains submerged, invisible, even to those who benefited the most.

Americans ignore the national government's influence when it is delivered in a manner that does not create visible national bureaucratic structures. This is how they prefer to govern. Indeed, Americans who have benefited the most from these patterns are precisely the group that desires such preferences to remain obscured.[24]

Conclusion

Many of the employees who worked at government-funded jobs, although not necessarily for the government, lived in suburbs that spread like crabgrass after World War II. These suburbanites were the beneficiaries of educations funded by the Servicemen's Readjustment Act (GI Bill), the same legislation that subsidized their mortgages.[25] Even before the GI Bill, white suburbanites had benefited from federal credit programs such as those of the Federal Housing Administration that standardized and popularized low-interest, long-term mortgages. Federally funded education benefits, federally backed mortgages, the tax incentives that went along with home ownership, and the public schools that owning a home in the suburbs entitled residents to were only a few of the public benefits that flowed disproportionately to white suburbanites.

Perhaps the most enduring contribution was the market rationale that accompanied this suite of government rewards. It submerged the government's role, leaving a story of market magic in its place. As historian David Freund noted, "the postwar 'free market' narrative—and its rationale for maintaining the color line—was popularized by many of the same federal interventions that were fueling economic growth and perpetuating inequality: namely the banking, monetary and credit programs that encouraged millions of Americans to finance new levels of consumption by going into debt."[26] Not only had the government intervened to make market mechanisms more forgiving to white suburbanites, but some of the very same government programs covered their tracks, crediting the market rather than federal intervention for these accomplishments.

Segments of the nation's health and welfare system were no more visible, despite massive federal investment. Management guru Peter Drucker, writing in the 1970s, referred to the proliferation of private pension plans that dotted the corporate landscape after World War II as an "unseen revolution." In Drucker's opinion, this was an "outstanding example of the efficacy of using the existing private, non-governmental institutions of our 'society of organizations' for the formulation and achievement of social goals and the satisfaction of social needs." Drucker got one thing wrong: the nongovernmental part (although he was correct to deny the presence of visible national institutions). As Jacob Hacker, one of the charter scholars of the "hidden welfare state" school put it, "Quite the opposite: Private pensions have been encouraged by public policy both directly and indirectly—through tax and labor law, through targeted regulatory interventions, and through the structure and reach of Social Security itself." Health care provision has traveled the same path—shaped by federal tax policy that subsidizes "private" health care benefits provided by employers. The taxes forgone (or expended) on pensions and health benefits neared $200 billion by 1999, approximating the cost of Medicare.[27] Success is often the federal government's worst enemy. As Karen Kruse notes in her review of federal health care policy, "the public health infrastructure of the nation—from research labs to hospitals to communication networks and immunization campaigns—stands as one of the triumphs of Federal policy over the last century, and one which most of us simply take for granted."[28]

The decision to govern indirectly has had significant consequences. Pensions and health care delivered through private mechanisms, regardless of the billions of federal dollars that subsidize them, are skewed toward the middle class and upward. While the United States spends no less on social provision than other industrialized nations, its benefits go disproportionately toward those who are most financially secure, and probably not coincidentally, most politically influential. No wonder that progressives are wary of hidden states.[29]

They should not be. In spite of a Herculean effort to distinguish sharply between public and private spheres in the Gilded Age, the long-standing nineteenth-century pattern of melding these two spheres persisted in America. In fact, this amalgam of public and private soon thrived at the national level like never before—aided by the emergence of an associative order and connective institutions like the American Farm Bureau Federation and the American Medical Association. Governing out of sight "works" because Americans accept it. Indeed, they demand it. Progressives should put this long-standing pattern of governing to work toward progressive ends.

The support for Medicare from some of the most vocal critics of big government provides a case that most progressives still fail to appreciate. During the heated town hall meetings on President Obama's health care reform proposal, one outraged citizen warned conservative Congressman Robert Inglis (R-SC) to "keep your government hands off my Medicare." Inglis responded, "Actually, sir, your health care is being provided by the government." "But he wasn't having any of it," Inglis told the *Washington Post*.

Progressive outlets were all over the story. *Slate*, for instance noted similar confusion between public and private benefits among Medicare recipients during the Clinton campaign for health care reform and vowed to keep a running tally of people who encourage "such nonsense." Bill Maher likened the statement to "driving cross country to protest highways."[30]

The phenomenon that Representative Inglis addressed was not new. Americans have been forgetting about the state since it was founded. Recognition of the role that the feds played is often the first casualty when historical narratives are constructed. The state has consistently been displaced by individual initiative and market mechanisms in personal and collective memory and scholarly interpretations as well.

Reorienting the contemporary debate from big versus small government to a discussion about how best to solve pressing problems through means that Americans historically have embraced offers a great opportunity to break a stalemate that generally has been resolved only during times of crisis. Conservatives should concede that Americans have always turned to the national government to solve problems. In fact, conservatives—whether Gilded Age jurists or businessmen eager to establish national markets—have often been the first to advocate energetic national governance.

For their part, progressives should break their lock-step assumption that cooperative partnerships between public and voluntary organizations are inherently regressive. Progressives should also master the art of turning the legal, regulatory, and fiscal resources of the national government toward redistributive ends. In short, they should learn how to make government work toward progressive ends through traditional means. Progressives should embrace the powerful belief that it is appropriate for the central government to serve as a catalyst for and coordinator of individual initiative or to fund programs through a range of more trusted intermediaries. That is precisely what FDR achieved with Social Security legislation, and President Lyndon B. Johnson (LBJ) achieved by building upon the conception of "individual contributions" to Medicare.

Which means that progressives should *celebrate* when Americans who fear big government insist that the government keep its hands off their "private" Medicare benefits. Progressives should learn how to achieve the kind of redistributive ends that Social Security, Medicare, and the Earned Income Tax Credit programs delivered through the kinds of mechanisms that allowed each of these successful programs to hide government in plain sight. While this is no easy task, it is far more promising than reverse engineering the mechanisms through which Americans have governed for much of their history.

CHAPTER 2

Transportation and the Uniting of the Nation

Zachary M. Schrag

Jack Cady was angry at the government.

It was November 1973, and the calamities of Vietnam, Watergate, and the oil embargo made many Americans question the nation's leadership. But Cady, a former trucker, steamed about something else: government interference in transportation. "I drove a truck in the Sixties when the state and federal regulations would push a lot," he explained. "I seriously doubt if I could drive one today because of the constant state, local, and federal regulations...bureaucrats steal more than money. They take a man's time, eat at his perception and life with hot little worms of red tape." After complaining some more about state regulators, the Department of Transportation, and the Interstate Commerce Commission, he concluded "that there is a new reason to be on the road. A man can for a while feel that he is running away from bureaucrats."[1]

That Cady experienced only the *feeling* of running away hints that he understood the truth: there is no escaping the reach of government even while on the road. Not only did bureaucrats regulate the fuel and equipment Cady used, the load he hauled, and the price he charged; along with elected officials they also had mapped the highways on which he drove, devised their finances, chosen the materials for the road surface, and even picked colors and typefaces for the signs. They had done comparable work for America's canals, harbors, railroads, and airports. And they had been doing so for as long as there had been a United States.

Big government involvement has not always been uncontroversial, efficient, or wise. The history of transportation policy has its share of blunders and crimes, some of which did lasting damage on a massive scale. What is remarkable, though, is the constancy of the involvement. Before the Civil War, when Americans fretted about states' rights and constitutional restrictions, the federal government still shaped transportation. During the Progressive Era and the 1920s, when Americans preached the values of free enterprise and voluntary cooperation, the government still shaped transportation. After World War II, when Americans called for reduced spending and fiscal responsibility, the government still shaped transportation.

Argue as they might about *how* government should shape transportation, Americans generally accepted a heavy government presence. They believed that good transportation would bring benefits to the community as a whole, thus justifying a larger investment than a private company might be willing to make. They embraced new technologies—from the steamboat to the jet airplane—as symbols of modernity. They saw in the federal government a way to limit the damages of transportation, from monopolistic pricing to environmental pollution.

Perhaps most compelling was the sense that transportation was inherently political, for the government depended on it. Only if they could physically gather could Americans build and defend the geographically extensive republic they desired. From the founding of the nation to the current debates over high-speed rail, Americans have regarded transportation as not merely another economic sector, but as the circulatory system of the body politic.

"Roads Will Everywhere Be Shortened"

We can start the story in 1784, on the Potomac River. Under its 1632 charter, Maryland claimed the entire river "unto the further Bank," which meant right up to the piers of the port of Alexandria, Virginia. Ship captains tying up there were using this clause to avoid paying duties to Virginia. Moreover, vessels on the Potomac—as well as the two states' other water boundaries, the Pocomoke River and the Chesapeake Bay—needed navigational aid and protection from pirates.[2] As they negotiated the issue at Mount Vernon, the home of George Washington, commissioners from the two states realized that the Potomac and Chesapeake debates were part of a larger problem.

At its founding, the United States was already one of the world's largest nations, with 900,000 square miles, or more than seven times the area of the British Isles.[3] How could such a vast territory be governed? How could settlers already streaming westward be persuaded to remain loyal to the new nation, rather than declaring their own independence? European powers still controlled the Mississippi and St. Lawrence ports downstream from American rivers; would not western farmers ally with those nations rather than the weak United States along the Atlantic coast? In other words, how to use interstate transportation to create a strong nation?

In part to answer these questions, the commissioners called for further meetings involving more states. Eventually, delegates from twelve of the thirteen states met in Philadelphia in the summer of 1787. They emerged with a new Constitution, designed—among other things—to "provide for the common defence [and] promote the general Welfare" by creating a much more powerful central government than existed under the Articles of Confederation. As delegates to state conventions pondered the prospects for such a union, some worried that the new nation was physically too large to be governed by a single, central government. To reassure them, James Madison penned *The Federalist* 14, arguing that better technology would make the republic effectively smaller:

> Intercourse throughout the Union will be facilitated by new improvements. Roads will everywhere be shortened, and kept in better order; accommodations for travelers will be multiplied and meliorated; an interior navigation on our eastern side will be opened throughout, or nearly throughout, the whole extent of the thirteen States. The communication between the Western and Atlantic districts, and between different parts of each, will be rendered more and more easy by those numerous canals with which the beneficence of nature has intersected our country, and which art finds it so little difficult to connect and complete.[4]

Such arguments helped persuade the state conventions to ratify the Constitution, and under the new charter, presidents and Congress began thinking about truly national transportation needs. The most dramatic action came in an effort to serve the farmers in the newly settled lands west of the Appalachians. Lacking roads to the east, they had little choice in selling their produce except to float it downstream on rivers that led to the Mississippi River, and ultimately to New Orleans—which was then in French hands. To give them an American route, in 1802 President Thomas Jefferson instructed his representatives in Paris to ask about buying the city of New Orleans, and the rest of the east bank of the Mississippi. The following year, the French responded with a startling offer to sell all of the Louisiana territory, which Jefferson's delegates quickly accepted. Thus, in order to address a single transportation problem, the new nation almost doubled in size.

But if the Louisiana Purchase solved one transportation challenge, it created many more. The vast lands would be useless until transportation routes could be mapped. Private enterprise, represented by such outfits as John Jacob Astor's American Fur Company, did some of this work, and Americans could borrow or steal additional information from European explorers and geographers. But big government had a hand as well, as when President Jefferson dispatched army officers Meriwether Lewis, William Clark, and Zebulon Pike to explore the vast Louisiana territory.

Back east, Congress began, with little controversy, building federal lighthouses and buoys. Spread along the coastline, such navigational aids cost little and did not favor one region over another.[5] But roads or canals were bound to be more expensive, and that meant picking winners and losers.

The challenge was to connect the seaboard to the territories north of the Ohio River. Anglo-Americans had been gazing at these lands since the end of the French and Indian War in 1763, and their settlement was one of the objectives of the Revolution. Building a road to the Ohio appeared so important that even Thomas Jefferson, with all his scruples about limited government, endorsed the idea in 1802, as Congress prepared to carve the new state of Ohio out of national lands. And in 1806, Congress authorized this "national road" to be built from Cumberland, Maryland, to the border of the new state.

Seeing the chance to get federal funds for local projects, boosters began petitioning Congress for aid with all manner of canals, piers, roads, and ports. In an effort to allocate funds in a way that would most benefit national, rather than local, interests, Albert Gallatin prepared his *Report of the Secretary of the Treasury on the Subject of Roads and Canals*.[6] This offered a startlingly ambitious plan, including a turnpike along the east coast, canals to cut through narrow necks of land (such as Cape Cod) that jutted into the ocean, improvements in major rivers, and roads to carry people and freight over the crest of the mountains where canals could not reach.

Gallatin's plan proved unworkable for three reasons. First, it would have been very expensive, costing $20 million over ten years, at a time when total annual federal expenditures were only about $10 million. Tensions and eventually war with

Great Britain absorbed those funds that could have gone into road making.[7] Second, even the plan's supporters doubted that the Constitution empowered Congress to build the projects. Gallatin himself noted, "It is evident that the United States cannot under the constitution open any road or canal, without the consent of the state through which such road or canal must pass."[8] Both presidents Jefferson and Madison called for constitutional amendments to remedy this flaw. Third, and perhaps more seriously, Gallatin's plan depended on Americans' willingness to put national priorities above local and regional interests. Perhaps some true nationalists—like Henry Clay and John Calhoun—could, but most politicians of the day (and since) remained loyal to the districts or states that elected them. These latter factors destroyed Calhoun's effort in 1817 to establish a permanent federal fund for internal improvements. Congress amended his bill in ways that left real planning power in the hands of state governments, and then Madison vetoed it on constitutional grounds.[9]

Ambitious politicians kept trying to find ways to have the federal government finance a network of internal improvements, yet they could never overcome this combination of sectional rivalries and constitutional concerns. Finally, in the spring of 1830, Gallatin's vision collapsed completely. First, Congress rejected a bill calling for the federal government to build roads from Washington, DC, to Buffalo and New Orleans. Then President Andrew Jackson vetoed as unconstitutional a bill offering federal funds for the paving of the Maysville Road within Kentucky. Neither grand schemes nor small components of a national system could make it into law.

Yet the failure of a national program hardly left the business of transportation to private enterprise. For one thing, state governments invested heavily in improvements. The completion of the Erie Canal by New York state in 1825 led other states, notably Pennsylvania and Ohio, to follow suit. (Congress joined to a small degree, buying stock in the Chesapeake & Ohio and the Chesapeake and Delaware canals.) Then, in the late 1820s, British and American engineers demonstrated the reliability of the steam locomotive, leading to a railroad boom. While much of the capital came from private investors, state governments often provided a roughly equal share, as was the case with the Baltimore & Ohio and Pennsylvania railroads.[10] All told, state and local governments invested more than $400 million in railroads and canals in the early nineteenth century, the equivalent of at least $1.3 *trillion* today.[11]

And the federal government remained a key player. In 1824, having found that the US Military Academy at West Point was producing more trained engineers than the army could use, Congress authorized the president to lend army engineers to civilian projects. Starting in 1827 with the Baltimore & Ohio, army engineers worked on dozens of railroads. These officers surveyed routes, searching for even grades that would allow for cheap operation in the future. (In the 1840s, the navy would likewise assign officers to help design and command oceangoing mail steamers, so they could gain experience with the new technology.)[12]

Even after Andrew Jackson abolished the army-railroad program and closed off possibilities for major projects within the states, the federal government continued to fund coastal projects and roads through federal territory not yet organized into states. Thus, during Jackson's presidency, the federal government spent more on internal improvements than it had under all previous presidents combined.[13] Finally, and crucially, starting in the 1820s, the federal government began granting sections of federally owned land to states, which would then sell the land or use it as collateral on bonds to build roads, canals, and eventually railroads. Amounting to tens of millions of acres of land, these grants allowed Congress to finance transportation without directly giving handouts to private companies.[14]

There is no denying the vitality of the antebellum transportation revolution. Americans had completed marvels of civil and mechanical engineering, inventing some new technologies—such as the steamboat—and adapting others, like the steam locomotive, in ways unknown to their European counterparts. By 1855, the United States possessed more than half the world's railroad mileage, along with thousands of miles of canals.[15] Although the system had not been guided from Washington as Gallatin had wished, big government—federal and state—had made this possible.

And an even heavier hand might have produced a more efficient network. Thanks to the defeat of repeated proposals for a greater federal role, the antebellum system was overbuilt in some areas, underbuilt in others. State governments actively discouraged railroads from providing connections to other states, and local investors sought mainly to serve their own cities.[16] The result was a transportation network no more unified or coordinated than the nation—which was on its way to civil war. Thirty thousand miles of railroad lines were built on a variety of gauges, in some cases deliberately chosen to prevent easy connections to other cities.[17] In the North, competing lines provided redundant service, while the South lagged behind. And most ominously, the network lacked railroad bridges across the Potomac and Ohio rivers, foreshadowing a North-South split that would tear the country apart.

"Bind Us More Indissolubly Together"

Just as Madison had counted on improved transportation to allow all the land east of the Mississippi to function as a single republic, so later generations of Americans hoped that newer technologies would allow that republic to grow to the Pacific Coast and beyond. As Congressman Israel Washburn Jr. remarked in 1854, the annexation of Louisiana and Texas had succeeded thanks to steamboats and railroads, and those technologies—and perhaps new ones—would allow even Hawaii to be incorporated into the nation. Such facilities, he assured his colleagues, "bind us more indissolubly together. We can not fly apart."[18] Washburn was overly optimistic. In fact, railroad politics helped tear the nation asunder as the sectional crisis reached its climax in the 1850s.

The trouble began soon after the end of the Mexican War in 1848, which forced Mexico to surrender roughly half of its territory in exchange for $15 million. Along with the earlier settlement of the boundary between Oregon and British territory, and with the annexation of Texas, this treaty extended the United States to the Pacific. Only two years later, in 1850, California joined the Union as the first state ever admitted that did not adjoin another state. Indeed, it was a good 1,500 miles to the borders of Texas or Iowa, the nearest states.[19]

If American citizens were to settle this new state—as well as the other newly acquired territory—and still remain part of the republic, they would need passenger, freight, and mail service to the East Coast. In 1848, the navy and the Post Office began subsidizing steamer service between New York, New Orleans, and the Caribbean coast of Panama (then part of Colombia), and between the Pacific coasts of Panama, California, and Oregon. At first, passengers making the trip between the coasts traveled by canoe, steamboat, and mule, but in 1855 American investors completed a railroad line across the isthmus. Though Congress declined to subsidize the building of the line, it did provide mail contracts worth hundreds of thousands of dollars annually to both the steamship and railroad companies.[20]

While this route was quite good for some purposes, most politicians and boosters assumed that the nation ought to build a railroad across its own territory, connecting the settled areas east of the Missouri to the new American settlements on the Pacific.[21] Not only did they hope to boost settlement along the route, but they pointed to the military advantages of being able to move troops to meet a coastal challenge from Great Britain, France, or Russia.[22]

The question was where to route the line. Southerners wanted a southern route, to Memphis, Vicksburg, or New Orleans.

Northerners hoped for routes pointing toward Chicago or St. Louis.[23] In an effort to win southern support for a northern route, Senator Stephen Douglas of Illinois advocated a repeal of the Missouri Compromise, which had for decades delineated the border between slavery and freedom. The prospect of the spread of slavery in turn heightened sectional differences, helping bring on the Civil War in 1861.[24]

Only with the secession of the southern states—and the absence of their representatives from Congress—could a railroad bill proceed. In 1862, the rump Congress passed the Pacific Railroad Act, authorizing the construction of a single trunk line from San Francisco to a point somewhere between the Republican and Platte rivers, in present-day Nebraska. Even then, to satisfy boosters from Minnesota to Missouri, Congress had to allow at least the possibility of branches serving towns along the Missouri from Sioux City in the north to Kansas City in the south.[25]

To finance the railroad—and later, parallel routes—Congress extended the system of land grants it had begun in the 1820s, but on a scale previously unknown. As historian Richard White notes, "the federal grant to the Union Pacific [established by the railroad act] roughly equaled the square mileage of New Hampshire and New Jersey combined . . . the land grant railroads east and west of the Mississippi received 131,230,358 acres from the United States. If all these federal land grants had been concentrated into a single state, call it Railroadiana, it would now rank third, behind Alaska and Texas, in size."[26]

In giving such generous grants to private corporations, Congress had managed to combine the worst features of big government and big business. As one congressman complained, the system allowed private enterprises to build railroads "on government credit without making them the property of the Government when built. If there be profit, the corporations may take it; if there be loss, the Government must bear it."[27]

Nor was that all. The corporations that built the western railroads cheated their shareholders, overcharged their customers, and abused their workers. In the absence of any guidance from above, they competed ruthlessly, building parallel lines far in excess of demand.[28] And their shaky finances helped bring about depressions in 1873 and 1893, while corporations controlling almost half the railroad mileage in the country went into receivership at one point or another.[29] A relatively unregulated market, it seems, produced not efficiency and rationality but fabulous wealth for a few and misery for a great many. Charles Francis Adams, the reformist president of the Union Pacific, remarked that "our method of doing business is founded upon lying, cheating and stealing:—all bad things."[30] By the 1880s, Americans who appreciated railroads as a technology despised them as corporations.

So Americans turned to regulation. In 1869, Massachusetts established the first state railroad commission, and other states followed suit. Midwestern states were particularly eager to regulate railroad rates to end the discrimination against intraregional traffic. And the Supreme Court approved, judging railroads to be "affected with a public interest" and therefore subject to legislative power.[31] Finally, in 1887, Congress passed the Interstate Commerce Act, establishing the Interstate Commerce Commission (ICC) and forbidding railroads to charge more for short hauls to towns without alternatives than they did for long hauls to cities where they competed with other railroads. The railroads did not put up too much of a fight; executives themselves saw advantages in the predictability of a regulated market. As one explained, "a large majority of the railroads in the United States would be delighted if a railroad commission or any other power could make rates upon their traffic which would insure them six per cent dividends, and I have no doubt, with such a guarantee, they would be very glad to come under the direct supervision and operation of the National Government."[32]

At first, this system worked reasonably well. Rates did rise along the most competitive routes between New York City and Chicago, but they also became more predictable, a benefit for railroads and shippers alike.[33] Beyond setting rates, government—both state and federal—helped make rail travel safer and more efficient. In some cases, railroads acted in response to the threat of state action; for example, they adopted a uniform signal code and standard time (the basis of today's time zones) only when they saw they might be forced to do so.[34] In other cases, the government did act. In 1889, moved by statistics collected by the ICC and by a petition signed by nearly 10,000 brakemen, President Benjamin Harrison declared, "It is a reproach to our civilization that any class of American workmen should in the pursuit of a necessary and useful vocation be subjected to a peril of life and limb as great as that of a soldier in time of war."[35] In 1893, Congress passed the Safety Appliance Act, requiring the use of self-couplers and air brakes. And in 1900, the ICC began inspecting freight cars, uncovering many defects. These measures were hardly panaceas, for technical fixes could only address some of the many kinds of accidents that killed and injured workers and passengers.[36] And in later years, Congress ignored calls from the ICC's Signal Board for more safety requirements.[37]

Meanwhile, in 1897 a series of Supreme Court rulings gutted the ICC's power to fix rates, approve cartels, and stop most railroads from charging more for short-haul freight than for long-haul.[38] Over the next two decades, Congress tinkered with railroad regulation, passing a series of bills that reshaped the ICC's authority.

Then, with the outbreak of World War I in Europe in 1914, the nation received a dramatic reminder of railroads' national importance. Midwestern farms and factories sent their products to eastern ports en route to Great Britain and France. But the volume overwhelmed the railroads and was exacerbated by bad winters and German submarines, which kept ships in harbor.[39] After enduring months of jams, in December 1917 President Woodrow Wilson declared presidential control of all the nation's railroads. Though remaining privately owned, the railroads would be operated by a US Railroad Administration with the power to direct freight movements, order the sharing of equipment, limit passenger travel, and set wage rates. Once again, the needs of the republic trumped any commitment to market competition.

Though federal control ended in March 1920, the railroad industry never really recovered. The railroads of the late nineteenth century had so abused their customers and so defrauded their investors that Congress wanted the ICC to set rates based on the "fair value" of railroad property. But that meant counting and appraising "every rail, spike, building, acre of land, and machine" in the country. And since the railroads did not trust the purportedly objective experts employed by the government, they set their own experts to conduct a parallel evaluation. Both teams kept working into the 1930s, with the ICC spending $45 million to compile its forty-seven volumes of findings, and the railroads spending $138 million on their version.[40] Meanwhile, the ICC collected tens of thousands of pages of testimony about the rates charged for grain, cottonseed, and other commodities.[41]

Such micromanagement undoubtedly hurt the railroads. But so did the relatively weak state of the ICC after 1920, which left it unable to affect a national consolidation plan. In the absence of strong government, railroad executives returned to their old ways, borrowing heavily to finance mergers in an attempt to ruin their rivals.[42] During the Depression of the 1930s, only the lending of $1 billion by the Reconstruction Finance Corporation—created by Herbert Hoover and maintained by FDR—spared the nation another round of railroad bankruptcies like those that had come with the depressions of the 1870s and 1890s.[43]

There is no doubt that some of the federal efforts to tame the railroads did more harm than good. But they must be understood as the response to the failures of the free market to provide Americans with a vital service—railroad transportation—in a way that served national needs and appeared fair to shippers, passengers, and cities along their routes. Big government regulation was not pretty, but it was prettier than the more laissez-faire alternative that had been tried in the 1870s and the 1920s. Perhaps even heavier intervention would have been better.[44]

As it was, throughout the twentieth century, the railroads would continue to pay for the sins of their nineteenth-century predecessors. And in addition to regulation, government would tame them by championing new technologies.

"The Very Name We Bear—United States"

Some of the railroad's rivals were old. Since the 1850s, Americans (as well as Europeans) had been pondering the possibilities of a canal across the Central American isthmus. Railroads—whether across Panama or the United States—could transport freight and passengers, but they could not transport warships. After the United States' two-ocean war against Spain in 1898, American imperialists renewed their efforts. In 1903, President Theodore Roosevelt helped engineer the secession of Panama from Colombia, along with a treaty giving the United States quasi-sovereign rights over a ten-mile-wide Canal Zone across the country. In other words, an entirely new sovereign country had been created simply to meet America's perceived transportation needs.[45]

Other technologies were new. Though the federal government did not invent the airplane, it did try. In 1886, Samuel Pierpont Langley, secretary of the Smithsonian Institution, began to investigate the possibilities of mechanical flight. Using Smithsonian funds, he constructed a series of models, achieving an impressive test in 1896. Then, in 1898, he received $50,000 from the army to build a craft large enough to carry a person. But in October and December 1903, Langley's Aerodrome crashed on launch.[46] Nine days after Langley's second failure, the Wright brothers (who had benefited from the pamphlets they had received from the Smithsonian) flew successfully at Kitty Hawk.

Though it had not given birth to this infant technology, the federal government suckled it. Entrepreneurs and investors would not be able to turn aviation into an industry without a new generation of aircraft, pilots to fly them, airports from which to take off, navigational beacons to guide their way, and a steady revenue stream. Government supplied them all.

Local governments often built the airports, albeit with significant prodding from the army and the Post Office.[47] Most of the other assistance came from the federal government itself. From the Wright brothers' first contract with the army in 1908, military contracts proved crucial to the development of aircraft.[48] The armed forces also trained thousands of pilots, many of whom went on to careers in civil aviation.[49] The National Advisory Committee for Aeronautics, established by Congress in 1915, developed key technological innovations that shaped both military and commercial aircraft.[50] Starting in the 1920s, the Department of Commerce licensed pilots and certified aircraft, and in the 1930s it took over air traffic control as well.

The agency most responsible for building the aviation industry was the Post Office. The first regular airmail service began in 1918, and by 1925 airmail had become the most successful—perhaps the only successful—form of civil aviation in the country, pioneering such technologies as electric beacons for nighttime navigation.[51] As postmaster general under President Herbert Hoover, Walter Folger Brown sought to rationalize an industry as chaotic as the railroads had been in the previous century.

Since no airline could realize a profit without an airmail contract, he had enormous leverage. Like Gallatin before him, he sought to create "a logical map," only with airways rather than turnpikes and canals. So he pressured airlines into mergers and awarded contracts to carriers that met his liking until, by 1931, he had established an oligopoly of airlines that would carry both mail and—at a loss—passengers.[52] All of this cost tens of millions of dollars in public funds; as late as 1959 almost half of airline revenue came from subsidy.[53]

Even more significant was the government's support for highways. With the rise of the railroad, the federal government had largely dropped out of the road-building business, and even states displayed little interest, seeing roads as a local matter. That began to change in the 1880s, as Americans took to bicycling and demanded better roads for their hobby. In 1893, Massachusetts established the first state highway department, and Congress provided $10,000 to the US Department of Agriculture for road research, which led to the establishment of the Office of Road Inquiry. Later renamed the Bureau of Public Roads and, later still, the Federal Highway Administration, this modest office would become a major factor in the expansion of federal authority over transportation.

At first, the small office emphasized best practices, building short stretches of model highway around the country to show what could be done. Money flowed faster after 1916, when Congress passed the first Federal-Aid Highway Act, which authorized $75 million in federal funds for states that would improve their rural post roads. President Woodrow Wilson later explained his support in national terms: "Wherever you have not got a good road you have created a provincial and sectional population. Wherever you have a good road, you have tied a thong between that community and the nation to which it belongs. And that is my interest in good roads, for, my fellow citizens, my present interest is chiefly in the nationalization of America."[54] Along these lines, in 1922, General John Pershing sketched a national highway system that would serve both commercial and military needs—the first version of a network that would eventually be realized as the Interstate Highway System.[55] In subsequent decades, the states relied on 50 percent federal funding to build a national system of primary and secondary roads, the former comprising what are now known as the US numbered highways, such as Route 66 from Chicago to Los Angeles.

This expansion of federal involvement into a new transportation sector did provoke some grumbling. In 1914, Senator

William Borah warned that the head of the Bureau of Public Roads could become "the practical dictator of road matters throughout the United States," and in 1921, Congressman Sam Rayburn complained that he was "sick and tired of the federal government's everlasting sticking its hand into the affairs of my state. I am against any building of more bureaucracies in Washington to reach out into the states and tell the people what they shall do and what they shall not do."[56] Even signage could be an issue, with Southerners objecting to the words "United States" on signs designating roads that had been built by the states—though with federal aid.[57]

Yet most Americans—state officials included—approved of the new federal aid for roads. As head of the Bureau of Public Roads from 1918 to 1953, Thomas McDonald enjoyed significant power. In 1935, for example, he withdrew certification of Georgia's highway department—freezing $19 million—because he judged that the governor had appointed a highway commission based on politics rather than expertise. For the most part, however, he won friends in the states and in Congress by making the bureau the undisputed leader in technical matters of road planning and construction.[58]

Equally important, Americans saw highways as an alternative to monopolistic railroads. As new technologies came on line, railroads experimented with them, operating their own trucks and buses and partnering with airlines to move people and freight in new ways. Though experts applauded the move, Congress remained fearful of the railroads and limited railroad companies' ability to invest in road, water, and air transport and to remake themselves as integrated transportation companies.[59]

The great expansion of federal road building came after World War II. For years, the Bureau of Public Roads had resisted calls—from groups like the Lincoln Highway Association—for highways built primarily for long-distance, even transcontinental, travel. But expressways built in Germany, Italy, New York, and Pennsylvania proved popular, leading some federal officials—including President Franklin Roosevelt—to ask for a reconsideration. In 1944, the presidentially appointed National Interregional Highway Committee recommended building a system of 33,900 miles of interstate highways. Over the next twelve years, officials in the executive branch and members of Congress debated what kinds of roads these should be, where they would go, and how they would be paid for. In 1955, President Dwight Eisenhower endorsed the program as essential to national identity. "The uniting forces of our communication and transportation systems are dynamic elements in the very name we bear—United States," he told Congress. "Without them, we would be a mere alliance of many separate parts."[60] Finally, in 1956, Congress funded construction of the National System of Interstate and Defense Highways, a 41,000-mile system of high-speed, limited-access highways. The act established a Highway Trust Fund—financed with federal fuel and tire taxes—to pay 90 percent of the cost of the system, then projected at $25 billion.[61]

Given the magnitude of its eventual impact, the interstate system was surprisingly uncontroversial. The proposal was hardly an expression of market choices. Congress did not let the market decide whether it wanted superhighways, conventional two-lane roads, railroads, or something else entirely. Nor did it give the states the option of using this unprecedented federal largesse for other projects—railroads, buses, schools, or sewers. It abandoned the market-based principles of the existing state turnpikes, whose dependence on tolls might limit superhighways to routes where drivers and shippers wanted them enough to pay out of pocket. Instead, expensive superhighways would be built across plains and deserts, and through downtowns and neighborhoods, with no market cue to signal when supply was outpacing demand.

Only a few observers were shocked by the decision. "When the American people, through their Congress, voted last year for a twenty-six-billion-dollar highway program, the most charitable thing to assume about this action is that they hadn't the faintest notion of what they were doing," lamented critic and urbanist Lewis Mumford, condemning an "ill-conceived and absurdly unbalanced program."[62] Indeed, by the late 1960s, residents of cities across the country were protesting the demolition of waterfronts, historic districts, and homes to make room for federally financed urban expressways. Meanwhile, the billion-dollar highways encouraged commuters to abandon mass transit, leading to the collapse of that industry. Eventually the protests got so loud, and the projected costs of the expressways so great, that the US Department of Transportation cancelled many planned roads, allowing states and cities to redirect the funds to mass transit.[63]

"No State Lives in Isolation"

Indeed, much of transportation policy since 1956 has been an effort to rebalance the national system in the wake of the highway act. In particular, the new highways competed with the railroads for both passengers and freight. The railroads were not sorry to abandon passenger service, which as early as 1946 was losing half a billion dollars each year.[64] Ridership continued to decline, and the Post Office stopped sending first-class mail by passenger train, cutting a vital subsidy. Only the Interstate Commerce Commission's insistence that railroads maintain select intercity routes kept any passenger rail going. Finally, in 1970, Congress created the National Railroad Passenger Corporation to take over the intercity routes that remained and combine them into a single system: Amtrak. But the new system inherited many woes of the old railroads, and—like the highways—had to serve parts of the country that offered few paying passengers but which were represented by powerful members of Congress.[65] The federal government did try to keep the railroads in the freight business, which had suffered as trucking firms took advantage of the new interstate highways to offer faster, more flexible (though far more fuel-intensive) freight service.[66] Permitting mergers at first seemed a failure; the bankruptcy of Penn Central in 1970 led to the creation of a massive, subsidized freight railroad—Conrail—in 1973. This kept freight rail alive until a series of mergers left the nation with a small number of large, and financially viable, railroads—a goal that policy makers had pursued since 1920.[67]

In recent decades, Congress has tried not to put all its transportation investments into any one mode. In 1991, it passed the Intermodal Surface Transportation Efficiency Act (ISTEA), which more or less ended construction of the Interstate Highway System. Instead, the new law emphasized flexibility; federal funds could go to road and bridge maintenance, transit, safety, and even bicycles and carpools. Thus, the federal government became the savior of intercity rail, commuter rail, and local mass transit. But with greater flexibility came less coordination. Rather than completing portions of a national map, states and cities would get to choose their own priorities for many of the funds.[68]

Advocates of smaller government ask why the national government should be supporting projects not of a national scope.[69] The cynical answer is that Americans enjoy getting subsidies for transportation projects they want, and members of Congress enjoy securing pork-barrel projects for their districts, like Alaska's infamous proposed "bridge to nowhere."[70] Less cynically, local aid can be seen as a means of adjusting the national system. Massive federal investment in superhighways in the mid-twentieth century unbalanced the national transportation system as much as the overbuilding of railroads in the nineteenth. The post-1960 aid to other modes is both an effort to rebalance the system and to relieve congestion at key points.

As the federal government offered more flexible subsidies, it also deregulated much interstate transport. Since the 1950s, presidents had sought some form of deregulation of rates and routes, but transportation firms and unions were comfortable with the way things were, and relatively few people complained.[71] By the 1970s, however, the regulation of tariffs and fares had become so calcified that such diverse leaders as presidents Gerald Ford and Jimmy Carter and Senator Edward Kennedy could all support deregulation in some form. Between 1978 and 1980, large majorities in both houses of Congress deregulated air, truck, and finally railroad transportation.

As hoped, market pressure dramatically decreased fares and tariffs paid by passengers and shippers, and it led transportation firms to embrace new technologies and business methods, such as the computer reservation systems now ubiquitous in air travel. But it also led to bankruptcies, layoffs, slashed wages, and—for smaller markets and smaller shippers—diminished service or higher rates.[72] And since the deregulation was only partial—the government continues to subsidize air service to towns and cities that might otherwise lose it—economists continue to debate what the effects have been and would be had the effort been more complete.[73] To complicate things further, state governments have been exploring projects that blur the boundaries between public and private, like the eighty-year contract between the Commonwealth of Virginia and a private company to build $1.9 billion worth of high-occupancy/toll lanes along a stretch of the Capital Beltway outside Washington, DC.[74]

Yet the idea of a national map did not disappear. The Intermodal Surface Transportation Efficiency Act required the US Department of Transportation to designate a National Highway System of around 155,000 miles, to include not only the interstates but high-priority corridors, principal arterials, strategic highways, and connectors to major military installations. And when Transportation Secretary Federico Peña unveiled a draft map in 1993, he called for something even more ambitious: a National Transportation System that would include "all of American's transportation systems—not just roads, but air and waterways, ports, pipelines, rail and urban transit."[75]

His successor, Rodney Slater, later emphasized the need for national planning:

> We should not be pulling apart, program by program, into a loose confederation of states that lacks the ability to deliver to the American people the benefits that we can only realize as a Nation. No state lives in isolation.... The challenges before us are national in scope; and the solutions require national involvement.[76]

Most recently, in his 2011 State of the Union address, President Barack Obama called for high-speed passenger railroads worthy of "the nation that built the transcontinental railroad, brought electricity to rural communities, constructed the Interstate Highway System." Like American leaders since the Revolution, Obama saw government investment in transportation as vital to "winning the future."[77]

Conclusion

The point here is not to defend all or even most transportation policy over the centuries as wise or just. For example, historian William Childs describes the relationship between state and federal railroad regulators in the late nineteenth and early twentieth centuries as one of "pragmatic federalism." "Because pragmatic federalism was a messy political process," he writes, "it was often rife with contradictions and paradoxes, not always logical in its development or successful in its implementation."[78] Messy, political, contradictory, and paradoxical are all good adjectives to keep in mind when thinking about the history of transportation policy in any age. The adjective *corrupt* is often useful as well. Indeed, these adjectives are likely to apply to any policy crafted by contentious democratic politics, especially in a complex, federal system.

There is a kind of logic that runs through the history of big government transportation policy: the same logic articulated by

James Madison in 1787, mapped by Albert Gallatin in 1808, and expanded in big government projects by Abraham Lincoln, Theodore Roosevelt, Woodrow Wilson, Walter Folger Brown, and Dwight Eisenhower in later generations. It is the logic that weighs social, political, and military considerations against mere economic efficiency. The country started out big, got bigger, and—even in the age of jet travel—remains big. And it may take big government investment in and coordination of transportation to make that big country function as a single republic, to make the states united.

CHAPTER 3

Uncle Sam at the Blackboard

The Federal Government and American Education

Jonathan Zimmerman

I owe my graduate education—and, by extension, my present-day livelihood—to the federal government. In 1988, as a young public school teacher in Baltimore, I applied to study for a PhD in history at the Johns Hopkins University. I was admitted, with a fellowship that covered only part of my tuition. To pay the rest—as well as my rent—I had to look elsewhere.

Like millions of other Americans, I looked to Uncle Sam. I took out a federally subsidized student loan for my first year, with terms much friendlier than anything I could have obtained in the private market. Midway through that year, I also applied for a Jacob K. Javits Fellowship from the United States Department of Education. I was hugely fortunate to receive this generous scholarship, which paid for the remaining four years of my graduate studies. When I was awarded my PhD in 1993, I only had to pay back a few thousand dollars in loans; the rest was free. And so was I.

Not everyone has been so lucky, of course. But all of us have benefited from federal largesse in education, in ways large and small. Did you attend a big centralized high school in the American countryside? It was probably erected or refurbished by the Works Project Administration or another New Deal agency, which overhauled the nation's school buildings in the 1930s. Did your father or grandfather attend college after serving in World War II? He almost certainly got a scholarship under the GI Bill, operated by the Veterans Administration (VA). Did you receive part of your graduate education overseas? You're most likely a beneficiary of the State Department's Fulbright Program, our chief public sponsor of study abroad. And is your local elementary or secondary school wired for the Internet? Then thank the E-Rate Program of the Federal Communications Commission (FCC), which has provided discounted services and connections to tens of thousands of American schools.

Or let's say you were on a women's sports team, in high school or college. Then you're a daughter of Title IX, a 1972 federal law that spurred gender equity in sports; before the government got into *that* game, very few women were allowed to play. Perhaps you have dyslexia, attention deficit disorder, or another type of disability. Thanks to a 1975 federal law, your schools have been required to provide you with special services and instruction. Maybe you're an immigrant, who came to America in the past forty years speaking little to no English. Then you probably received some kind of bilingual education, a federal initiative dating to the same era. Or perhaps you were simply born into poverty here in the United States, where roughly one out of five children have the same ill fortune. Then you have surely received a wide range of federally subsidized services, from tutoring and counseling to free breakfast and lunch.

That doesn't mean the services have always worked, of course. Bilingual and special education programs have mixed records, stemming in part from inadequate funding but also from our own limited understanding: despite many years of research, we really don't know what "works" in these realms. And in our efforts to overcome the educational effects of poverty, especially, we have scant evidence that federal laws and dollars have made much of a difference at all. Indeed, many observers believe that the most recent federal education law—the 2002 No Child Left Behind Act—has made things *worse* for America's poorest children, by encouraging rigid test preparation over imagination and exploration in the classroom. Yet federal action has shone a bright light on our dismal educational inequalities and deficiencies, which is surely a necessary condition—if not a sufficient one—for addressing them. Most of all, the federal government has helped promote the now-consensual American ideal that all children have both the right and the ability to be educated. Like all ideals, it is imperfectly realized. But the ideal itself is of surprisingly recent vintage, and we owe it—in large part—to federal initiatives.

Finally, as my own biography illustrates, the federal government has also provided a myriad of educational benefits to a broad swath of middle-class and even wealthy Americans. When conservatives say that federal efforts to assist the least privileged via education haven't succeeded, they're mostly correct. But the same critics often overlook the many ways that federal education programs have helped the rest of us. Many of the benefits have not come from an "educational" agency, per se, so it's easy to miss them: consider the GI Bill and the E-Rate Program, which have been run by the VA and the FCC, respectively. Or, like subsidized lunches, federal aid is so deeply woven into the fabric of our schools that we forget who is picking up the tab. Over the past two centuries—and, especially, over the past five decades—the federal government has evolved from a bit player into a major actor in our shared educational drama. It's time we all woke up to that fact, instead of sleeping through the show.

The most important fact about American education is that it is primarily a local and state endeavor. The next most important fact is that it has never been only that; the federal government has always been involved. From its inception, America's new national government subsidized education by granting land for it. Under the Northwest Ordinance of 1787, which passed the same year that the Constitution was ratified, federal territories were required to set aside one-sixteenth of every township to support public schools. "Religion, morality and knowledge, being necessary to good government and the happiness of mankind, schools and the means of education shall forever be encouraged," the Ordinance declared. So while the Constitution itself does not mention education, as conservatives correctly point out, it's simply false to say that the founders of the nation did not envision a federal role in schools. (The Constitution doesn't mention Social Security or a space program, either, but almost nobody questions federal spending in those realms.) The land grants were not reserved for school buildings per se; instead, revenue on their rental or sale was devoted to education. Over the next century, Congress ceded over 77 million acres for this purpose. By the late 1800s, most states west of the Mississippi received over 10 percent of their school revenue from income on federal land grants.[1]

The federal government used land grants to promote higher education, too. Most famously, the Morrill Act of 1862 distributed 17 million acres for colleges and universities that would provide instruction in "agriculture and the mechanic arts" (or "A and M," as it became known). Each state received 30,000 acres per each member of its congressional delegation. Again, the land would be sold or rented; each state decided how best to use the resulting revenue. Some of them added land-grant programs to existing colleges like MIT and Cornell, which developed agriculture and engineering degrees. Others created entirely new universities, fostering a feisty rivalry with their flagship state institutions. In Michigan, the established university in Ann Arbor found itself under challenge from Michigan State, the new land-grant school in Lansing; in Oregon, the upstart state university in Corvallis competed with the older institution in Eugene. Nor did all the land-grant money support "A and M" programs: in California, for example, the state legislature used its land-grant funds to create a liberal arts institution in Berkeley, modeled after New England colleges. All told, the 1862 Morrill Act spawned sixty-eight new colleges and universities. A second Morrill Act in 1890 generated more new schools—including seventeen black colleges in the South—and also extended funding to older universities below the Mason-Dixon Line that had not been eligible in 1862, when the Confederate states were in rebellion.[2]

Then, as now, critics of these measures insisted that education should remain a state and local affair rather than a federal one. A pre-secession version of the first Morrill Act was actually vetoed in 1859 by James Buchanan, who claimed it was unconstitutional. Defenders of the bill pointed out that Congress had already doled out individualized grants for higher education to seventeen different states since 1796, including a whopping 100,000 acres to Tennessee. They also noted that George Washington had lobbied for a federal university in the nation's capital—he even willed fifty shares of stock for that purpose— and that Congress had established a military academy at West Point (1802) and a naval one at Annapolis (1845). Both institutions provided key manpower not just for national defense but for also for domestic improvements, especially in engineering and other technical fields: as Brown University president Francis Wayland observed in 1850, nearly every new bridge or highway in the nation seemed to have been constructed under the direction of a West Point graduate. After the Civil War and into the twentieth century, the federal government also took charge of education for Native Americans and for the nation's new subjects in its burgeoning overseas empire, particularly in the Philippines. By 1923, 1.2 million Filipinos—or 12 percent of the colony's population—were enrolled in public schools; by comparison, just 2 percent of people in British India and 4 percent in Dutch Java went to school. The number of Filipino students would swell to 2 million by the start of World War II, making their school system the third largest under the American flag. Only the systems in New York and Pennsylvania were bigger.[3]

On America's own shores, meanwhile, the New Deal of the 1930s would mark the first real surge of direct federal engagement in education. The reason was simple: amid the greatest economic crisis in national history, local districts could no longer support their schools. So Franklin D. Roosevelt's "alphabet agencies" stepped into the breach. The Federal Emergency Relief Administration (FERA) provided funds to employ teachers who had been laid off and also to pay those whose salaries were overdue. Southern states were the poorest, so they also received the most aid: in Arkansas alone, FERA funds allowed authorities to keep open 4,000 rural schools serving 150,000 children. All told, about 1 million students were enabled to stay in school because of emergency federal relief. To make sure they remained there, meanwhile, the National Youth Agency (NYA) also provided them with part-time work. Between 1935 and 1943, 1.5 million high school students and another 620,000 college students got paid jobs from the NYA; without this income, many of them would have been forced to quit school. Finally, New Deal agencies also improved or replaced the schools themselves. The Public Works Administration (PWA) helped build or upgrade almost 7,000 schools; the Works Project Administration constructed over 3,000 new schools and repaired more than 21,000. School districts received a total of $1 billion in building and maintenance aid from the federal government, which assisted 70 percent of all new school construction between 1933 and 1939.[4]

But the New Deal did more than simply keep America's schools afloat; it also introduced several long-lasting educational innovations. The most important were public nursery schools, introduced by the WPA's Emergency Education Program (EEP). In 1933, America had only 300 public nurseries; ten years later, thanks to the EEP, they numbered 3,000. Congress also began purchasing surplus agricultural commodities to provide school lunches, which had formerly been served only by private charities or select school districts. By 1941, the WPA was funding school lunches for 2 million children; the following year, the number skyrocketed to 6 million. The WPA also employed over 64,000 people—almost all of them women—to prepare and serve the lunches. Finally, the Department of Agriculture contracted with dairy providers to sell milk in American schools at 1 cent per half pint. Like school lunches, this "Penny Milk Program" killed two birds with one stone: taking surplus food off the market, which stabilized prices, it also provided valuable nutrition for hungry American children.[5]

Both new programs would continue during and after World War II, but with a different rationale: national defense. When the WPA expired in 1943, many of its nurseries remained open under a new congressional measure—the Lanham Act—that provided special federal aid for education in so-called war-impacted areas—that is, in communities where large numbers of women had joined the paid workforce to replace men who were serving in the military. At their height, these "Lanham Act Nurseries" took in over 130,000 children; over the course of their existence, they would enroll over half a million. After the war, meanwhile, national security concerns spawned the nation's first official National School Lunch Program (NSLP, in 1946). Like its New Deal antecedents, the NSLP used food surpluses to feed the nation's students; even more, supporters said, it would also shore up the country's depleted armed forces. As the director of the Selective Service System told Congress, in a plea for the school lunch program, 155,000 American casualties in World War II had been "directly related to malnutrition." With the specter of another totalitarian enemy haunting America, some critics of the NSLP suggested that it was socialist or even communist in spirit. Nonsense, replied its advocates: for a tired nation just emerging from war, hot lunches would dampen the appeal of "Red" alternatives instead of promoting an appetite for them.[6]

But the most important war-related educational measure was the "GI Bill of Rights" (1946), known colloquially as the GI Bill. The law provided federal assistance for returning veterans to purchase homes and also to attend colleges and universities, which had formerly been reserved for a fairly elite sector of America. By 1947, just a year after the GI bill passed, veterans already made up nearly half of all college students; by 1950, 2.2 million of 14 million eligible veterans had chosen to enroll in postsecondary education under the GI Bill. In so doing, they altered American education—and, eventually, American society—forever. To serve the massive influx of veterans, universities had to construct thousands of new dormitories, laboratories, and classrooms. Most of all, though, they had to accommodate a much more diverse population—including working-class, married, and disabled students—than America's educational leaders had imagined. At Harvard, president James B. Conant worried that the veterans would dilute academic standards; and at the University of Chicago, Robert Hutchins warned that they would turn American colleges into "educational hobo jungles." The concerns were unfounded. Veterans acquitted themselves well in the classroom, demonstrating that less-privileged citizens could benefit from higher education. Indeed, through the GI Bill of Rights, they made higher education into a right of democratic citizenship itself. By 1964, GI Bill beneficiaries included 450,000 engineers, 360,000 teachers, 243,000 accountants, and 150,000 scientists.[7]

As America's fight against fascism gave way to a Cold War against communism, national security anxieties spawned a new round of federal educational initiatives. The key measure was the National Defense Education Act (NDEA, in 1958), which passed in the wake of the USSR's Sputnik satellite launch the previous year. Fearing that America had fallen behind its global rival, especially in scientific and technological domains, the NDEA funded college loans, graduate fellowships, and laboratory equipment in defense-related areas. These subjects included not just the hard sciences and engineering but also foreign-language study: in the new Cold War environment, Americans' poor proficiency in non-English languages was regarded as a national security threat as well as an international embarrassment. Thanks mostly to NDEA aid, the number of language laboratories in the United States rose from just forty-six in 1958 to 7,000 in 1965. All in all, by 1968, the NDEA had provided loans to 1.5 million undergraduates and scholarships for 15,000 PhD students. Unlike aid under the GI Bill, which was theoretically available to any returning veteran, NDEA assistance was explicitly targeted at "students with outstanding aptitudes," as the law said. To recruit them, the law required states to develop testing and vocational guidance programs in their public schools. Using NDEA funds, one California school district even produced a guidance film called *The Butcher, the Baker, the Missile Maker.* It didn't take a rocket scientist to figure out which choice the strongest students were supposed to make.[8]

A similar "best and brightest" elitism marked the federal government's other major educational initiative during this era: university-based research. Federal funding for research at American universities skyrocketed from $254 million to $1.57 billion—a sixfold increase—in the decade following *Sputnik*; by 1963, federal dollars already accounted for 70 percent of academic research. But over half of this sum went to just six universities, while almost 80 percent of it went to only twenty institutions. "In the advance of science...there is no substitute for first-class men," explained the redoubtable James B. Conant. "Ten second-rate scientists or engineers cannot do the work of one who is the first rank." As time went on, however, a wider array of universities dipped into the federal research till. By 1966, for example, the thirteen most favored targets of the National Institutes of Health (NIH) received just 32 percent of its grants; and eighty-eight different institutions received over $1 million each from the NIH, which had already supplanted the Department of Defense as the largest single sponsor of university research. Other key patrons included the National Science Foundation and the National Aeronautics and Space Administration, which accounted for nearly 10 percent of all research payments to universities in 1965. By this time, several large public universities—including Michigan and UC-Berkeley—received more money for annual operations from federal sources than they did from their own state legislatures.[9]

Meanwhile, the federal government embarked on its first broad, need-based effort to help Americans pay for college: the Higher Education Act (HEA) of 1965. The GI Bill's aid packages had established higher education as a right, but only for veterans; the NDEA extended assistance to special subject areas, and to skilled students within them; but the HEA, signed by President Lyndon B. Johnson, aimed to allow *anyone* to obtain a college education. "Every child must be encouraged to get as much education as he has the ability to take," Johnson declared. "Higher education is no longer a luxury, but a necessity." The HEA and other federal initiatives provided 2 million grants and loans over the next five years, reaching one out of every four college students. The 1972 Pell Grant program provided even more aid, loosening the income restrictions for participants and expanding the packages they received. Thanks in large part to federal largesse, the fraction of eighteen- to twenty-four-year-olds attending college rose from 17.8 percent in 1955 to 33.5 percent in 1974. As in the era of the GI Bill, meanwhile, institutions had to expand their physical plants to accommodate the new student populations. The biggest growth occurred among community colleges, which shot up from 400 colleges serving 325,000 students in 1955 to 973 colleges enrolling 3.4 million students in 1974. Aided by the Higher Education Facilities Act (1963), one community college was opening every week by the late 1960s. Just as Lyndon Johnson had envisioned, almost any high school graduate could find a way to go to college.[10]

But the news from the schools themselves was not nearly as rosy, as Johnson also realized. From the early 1960s, a wealth of social science data demonstrated that K–12 schools were underserving the poor. As in the 1930s, then, the federal government would try to bridge the gap. Whereas Franklin D. Roosevelt's New Deal focused mainly on improving school buildings and preventing teacher layoffs in poor communities, Johnson's "War on Poverty" resolved to change the day-to-day education that the poor received. On April 11, 1965, Johnson traveled to the one-room schoolhouse he had attended as a child in Texas to sign the Elementary and Secondary Education Act (ESEA), the first broad-based, federal effort to influence teaching and learning in American classrooms. Its centerpiece was Title I, which appropriated about $1 billion to meet "the special educational needs of educationally deprived children," as the law said. Thanks mostly to Title I, the federal share of American K–12 spending rose from 3 percent in 1958 to 10 percent in 1968, where it has hovered ever since. To Johnson, who had also taught poor Mexican American children at a school near the Rio Grande, educational inequality was simply inconsistent with America's promise of democracy. "By passing this bill, we bridge the gap between helplessness and hope for more than 5 million educationally deprived children," Johnson told his one-room school audience, repeating the language of the law. "As the son of a tenant farmer I know that education is the only valid passport from poverty."[11]

Unfortunately, educational inequality proved much more intractable than Johnson imagined. ESEA has provided poor school districts with books, curricula, classroom equipment, teacher training, and a host of other goods and services. Yet almost fifty years—and many billions of dollars—later, scholars have found "limited, if any, consistent and lasting benefits of those interventions for the most disadvantaged," as historian Maris Vinovskis summarized in 2007. But the law did benefit *advantaged* Americans, in ways they rarely recognized or appreciated. Although the lion's share of money went to Title I, which was targeted at high-poverty areas, ESEA also included several programs for districts across the board. Most notably, Title II of ESEA allocated $100 million for school libraries, textbooks, and periodicals; Title III provided another $100 million for educational television, mobile libraries, and laboratories. At the time, fully half of American schools did not have a centralized library; among elementary schools, two-thirds lacked one. By 1967, just two years after ESEA was signed, 3,600 new school libraries had opened, serving 1.5 million children; while some of the recipients were poor, to be sure, most were probably not. Ditto for the students who enjoyed educational TV programs or revised textbooks, both hallmarks of ESEA. Before then, even well-to-do districts used history texts that concluded at World War I or physics books that omitted the atomic revolution.[12]

Finally, even money that was designated for the poor sometimes went to districts and children that were in no way impoverished. Under Title I's complex distribution formula, every congressional district in the country—and 95 percent of its counties—received federal aid. Although Title I was supposed to help the "educationally deprived," states and localities were free to decide how to do so. Inevitably, then, they diverted Title I money away from its intended target and into their own pet projects. Some well-off districts used Title I dollars to build swimming pools; others updated their audio-visual equipment. At the same time, however, the formula helped guarantee the political viability of ESEA. In 1965, just 26 percent of Republicans in the House of Representatives voted for the measure. By 1974, however, 74 percent of GOP (Republican) members backed its reauthorization; four years later, 90 percent did the same. That would never have happened if the law had served *only* the poor. As legislators and their constituents correctly perceived, it assisted the broad middle class as well.[13]

It also added new programs and benefits, over successive reauthorizations, which increased both its scope and its popularity. In 1965, ESEA had only five titles (that is, sections) and a dozen programs. Thirteen years later it had swelled to thirteen titles and over 100 different federal programs, ranging from arts education and environmental education to programs promoting ethnic heritage and equality for women. As per the Washington norm, each new program was backed by a professional organization or another special interest group; this lobby would in turn forge alliances with the relevant congressional committees and with bureaucrats in the new federal Department of Education, which became a full-fledged cabinet-level agency in 1979. But the process also fostered strange-bedfellow coalitions across party lines, belying the polarization that affected so much of national politics in the 1970s and beyond. A good example was Title VII, the Bilingual Education Act of 1968. Having spanked children for speaking Spanish in the Texas school where he taught, Lyndon Johnson was lukewarm about the measure. But it was eagerly embraced by Richard Nixon, who saw bilingual education as a good way to lure Hispanics into the GOP fold. Nixon's lawyers pressed for the strictest possible interpretation of the bilingual education measure, insisting that it required each school district to make special provisions for second-language English learners. Twenty years later, with anti-immigrant sentiment surging through the country, many Republicans would turn against bilingual education. By then, however, it was too deeply inscribed in American schools—and in American society—to undo altogether.[14]

No such controversy has dogged so-called handicapped or special education, which has drawn almost uninterrupted bipartisan support for the past half century. Several ESEA amendments in the late 1960s and early 1970s increased federal spending on educational services for the handicapped, but did not require states to provide these services. That mandate awaited passage of the Education for All Handicapped Children Act (1975), which obliged school districts to provide all children with a "free, appropriate public education" in the "least restrictive" setting. Over the next twenty-five years, the number of children identified as disabled in American public schools rose from 3.7

million to 6.3 million, or 13 percent of total K–12 enrollment. The volume of litigation over special education also doubled during this period, as parents and educators—and, of course, their lawyers—struggled to interpret the meaning of the 1975 statute. What *was* an "appropriate" education, for a child with severe disabilities? And what constituted a "restrictive" setting for him or her? No matter how one answered these questions, the Education for All Handicapped Children Act—now known as the Individuals with Disabilities Education Act—clearly signaled a sea change in the way that Americans thought about the issue. Into the 1950s, many states and school districts saw no reason to educate children whose IQ scores deemed them "idiots," "morons," or "cretins." Many of these youth were committed to institutions for the so-called feeble-minded, which aimed mainly to protect them from others—and from themselves. That seems light-years from the situation today, when middle- and upper-middle-class parents often plead with schools to *declare* their children disabled, which in turn qualifies them for special services under federal law.[15]

Last, millions of American girls and women—of every class and background—have also benefited from federal gender equity measures in education. The watershed legislation was Title IX (1972), which barred public schools and colleges from discriminating on the basis of sex. Proponents envisioned Title IX as promoting equal pay for teachers and removing sex bias from curricula; neither the law nor its advocates made explicit mention of sports. But Title IX would have its most tangible and dramatic consequences in American athletics, which had long been hostile to females. Olympian skier Suzy Chaffee (later the "Suzy Chapstick" of advertising fame) was urged to quit the sport by her own college coach, who warned that it was "bad for the ovaries"; the first woman to run the Boston Marathon, Katherine Switzer, was likewise told that female racers "would never have babies or attract men." Switzer entered the marathon in 1967 by using her initials on the application; when race officials realized she was running, they tried to push her off course and to tear the numbers off her jersey. Switzer eventually finished the race, shielded by a cordon of her male college teammates running alongside her. For most American female athletes, however, Title IX would provide the real protection. In 1971, a year before it passed, just 295,000 girls—or 7 percent of American high school athletes—participated in high school sports; by 2001, 2.8 million girls had joined their ranks, making up 41.5 percent of the total. A similar revolution seized college sports, where 43 percent of athletes were female in 2001. Like bilingual and special education, sports were no longer seen as a privilege; thanks to the federal government, they had become a right.[16]

Indeed, going back to the original ESEA, all of these measures were designed to assist a particular group that had been *denied* a right. So they were tailored—however narrowly or loosely—to that specific population. Even more, as rights measures, they emphasized equality of opportunity rather than of outcome. Disadvantaged groups earned the chance to enter the race and also received special services to help them compete. But nobody would judge them—or the services they received— based on their performance in the race itself: win or lose, the services would continue. Robert F. Kennedy captured the spirit of this dilemma in a revealing exchange with federal education commissioner Francis Keppel, during congressional hearings on ESEA in 1965. "Look, I want to change this bill because it doesn't have any way of measuring those damned educators like you, Frank, and we really ought to have some evaluation in there," Kennedy complained. The final bill did include allocations for research about the effects of ESEA, but nothing in the measure tied future allocations to the results of that research. "In 1965 everyone had a naïve view of education," one former federal staffer recalled, in 2002. "Educators were all good people and all you needed to do was give them some tools and some dollars and good things would happen."[17]

By the time Ronald Reagan entered the White House, in 1980, Americans had lost much of the optimism that marked this earlier vision. Reviving a long-standing conservative critique, Reagan insisted that the federal government should stay out of education; he even pledged to eliminate the Department of Education, formed just a year earlier. But Reagan undercut his own position by selecting Terrel Bell as secretary of the department. A moderate Republican, Bell helped stave off attacks from elsewhere in the Reagan White House on Title I and other antipoverty programs. More important, he focused the nation's attention on the substandard quality of public schools as a whole. In 1983, a blue-ribbon panel commissioned by Bell released a damning portrait of American education. Its name told the whole story: *A Nation at Risk*. "The educational foundations of our society are presently being eroded by a rising tide of mediocrity that threatens our very future as a Nation and a people," the report declared, citing stagnating test scores and graduation rates. "If an unfriendly foreign power had attempted to impose on America the mediocre educational performance that exists today, we might well have viewed it as an act of war." Invoking the *Sputnik* launch of a quarter-century before, *A Nation at Risk* called for a new commitment to improving education—not just for the poor, but for everyone. The report made such a splash that Reagan—who had planned to bury the report—made it a centerpiece of his 1984 reelection campaign. The federal role in education was here to stay.[18]

But the role itself was changing. Unlike *Sputnik*-era reforms, which focused on the best and the brightest, federal education policy now aimed to upgrade schools across the board. And unlike ESEA, which gave cash carte blanche to school districts, the federal government would soon demand results in exchange for its dollars. The new watchword was "accountability," and it was deeply bipartisan. The next two presidents, George H. W. Bush and Bill Clinton, both won legislation encouraging states to develop standards and to reward (or punish) schools for their performance in meeting the targets. By the time Clinton stepped down, in 2001, all but two states had developed standards and tests for their K–12 schools. But only thirteen of the states evaluated students annually in reading and math, and even fewer of them tied sanctions to the tests that they did give. How would schools succeed, critics asked, unless they faced tangible consequences for failing? And why should the federal government keep pleading for such accountability systems, instead of simply establishing its own? In yet another illustration of cross-party consensus, both candidates for president in 2000—Al Gore Jr. and George W. Bush—called for a federal law to hold all schools accountable for student achievement.[19]

That set the stage for No Child Left Behind (NCLB, in 2002), easily the most expansive federal educational measure in American history. It, too, was eminently bipartisan, passing the House of Representatives by a vote of 384 to 45 and the Senate by 91 to 8. Although critics of the law often talk of NCLB as if it were imposed in a military-style coup by George W. Bush, its sponsors included the liberal lion Senator Edward Kennedy and Representative George Miller of the Bay Area, one of Congress's most left-leaning members. The law requires every district to test all students in grades 3–8 in reading and math, and to penalize schools that fail to show progress. It also requires districts to certify that all of their teachers are "highly qualified," which has set off predictable debates about what that term means. Most of all, the measure symbolizes the massive transformation of the federal role in American education since the 1960s. As its name indicates, NCLB is a universal act: it affects every child, not just specific populations. Most prior federal laws identified a needy group and set about trying to assist it. No Child Left Behind begins from the assumption that all schools need to get better, and it creates concrete incentives to make them do so.

Does it work? We don't really know. As in the past, though, we have scant indication that it has made any difference for America's poorest communities. Defenders of the law point to improvements in test scores and graduation rates. But with every state creating its own tests—one of the many anomalies of NCLB—we can't tell whether these results actually signify more learning. Even more, some school districts have gamed the system by giving kids answers beforehand or by erasing incorrect answers; some offenders have been caught, but untold others probably get away with it. Finally, there is considerable evidence that NCLB encourages rigid and formulaic instruction, or "teaching to the test." Wealthier schools have always provided better instruction than poorer ones, of course. But NCLB has probably increased this discrepancy, because disadvantaged schools are under more danger of failing to show progress and thereby incurring sanctions under the law. So they tailor their curricula as precisely as possible to the annual tests, even providing minute-by-minute scripts for teachers.[20]

Seen another way, however, NLCB also embodies the federal government's historic commitment to the goal—however elusive—of educational equality. Consider that the law requires school districts to report their test scores according to race; districts that show an "achievement gap" between races must devise plans to close it, and they can face sanctions if they fail. Even if NCLB has inadvertently widened this gap, as some critics insist, its explicit attention to the issue echoes a long-standing tradition of federal action on behalf of the least fortunate among us. Whether this aid has "worked" or not is in some sense beside the point: it has underscored the problem, which is always the first step toward solving it. Over the past half century, the federal government has been our central symbol and engine of social justice and equality in American education. You need not agree with everything it has done—and I certainly don't—to acknowledge that fact; and it's hard to imagine how much *more* unequal our schools would be, if the federal government had *not* intervened in them.

Consider the history of state-enforced school segregation, certainly one of the ugliest chapters in the American past. As every child now learns, federal courts started dismantling that system with *Brown v. Board of Education* (1954). But it was federal aid—or, more precisely, the threat of its withdrawal—that provided the key impetus for change. When the Civil Rights Act of 1964 barred discrimination by agencies receiving federal funds, almost no one imagined schools as part of the mix: their share of federal dollars was still negligible. The 1965 ESEA law—and its countless amendments and reauthorizations—changed all that. By 1967, many school districts in the South were already receiving 20 percent of their revenue from federal sources; in some districts, the federal share topped 30 percent. So they also had to stop segregating kids by race, lest they lose millions of new dollars in federal aid. In 1964, on the eve of the Civil Rights Act, only 2.2 percent of African American children attended a formerly all-white school. By 1966, a year after ESEA, the percentage shot up to 16.9 percent; two years after that, in 1968, it was 32 percent. The movement for school integration would stall in the 1970s and 1980s, amid controversies over busing and shifting court doctrines. But surely our overall society has become more racially integrated—and more tolerant of racial difference—over the past fifty years. And, just as surely, the federal government—and its efforts in education—deserves a big part of the credit.[21]

Likewise, our changing attitudes toward disability, language, and gender owe a good deal to federal intervention in our schools. When I was growing up, in the 1960s and early 1970s, I never knew a disabled child: those kids were warehoused in other institutions, so the rest of us couldn't see them. Today, my own daughters interact with disabled kids on a daily basis; as one of them recently put it, in her ubiquitous teen-speak, it's NBD ("No Big Deal"). Second-language English speakers are sprinkled throughout their school district, too, receiving a variety of different services under federal law. Bilingual education has meant many different things since the 1960s, ranging from classes conducted entirely in native languages to "transitional" courses designed to wean children off these tongues. But the simple idea that they *do* require special attention—whatever form it takes—is a relatively new idea; in prior generations, kids who spoke languages other than English were punished, teased, or ignored. Finally, the same years have witnessed a stunning revolution in the education of women, who now match or outpace men in almost every academic category. And they even play sports! The revolution has many causes, of course. But we owe it in part to federal educational initiatives, including revisions of our textbooks (to eliminate sexist images and stereotypes) and regulations barring gender discrimination in the schools.

Indeed, when it comes to education, we *all* owe something to the federal government. My own student loan and fellowship were just the tip of the iceberg, which extends backward into my family history and forward into its future. My father was a member of the Reserve Officer Training Corps, which sent him to college and law school in exchange for several years of military service afterward. He then joined the Peace Corps, which helped pay for my own education as a child; I would join the Peace Corps myself, as a young adult, where I received my first training as a teacher. My wife, a pediatrician, works at a hospital that has been showered with millions of federal dollars; over the years, some of these funds have paid for her own research and salary. Our two daughters have benefited from a huge array of federally subsidized services in our local public schools, ranging from gifted and talented programs to new educational technologies. And now that the elder daughter has started college, we get an annual tuition tax credit from—you guessed it—the federal government.

But the future is anyone's guess. As I completed this essay, I learned that Congress had declined to fund the Jacob K. Javits Fellowship that paid for the great bulk of my graduate education. So the Department of Education is not accepting new Javits applications for 2012–2013, and it's unclear if the program will continue after that. Despite an infusion of federal funds from Congress's 2009 stimulus package, meanwhile, over two-thirds of American states have made cuts to K–12 education since 2008. Arizona eliminated preschool for over 4,000 children; Hawaii shortened the 2009–2010 school year by seventeen days; New Jersey cut funding for after-school programs serving over 11,000 students; and budget deficits in North Carolina left twenty schools without a nurse or social workers. But these cuts would have been much more severe without the stimulus bill, which included nearly $50 billion in assistance to state education budgets. Stimulus funds in 2009 filled a 9 percent shortfall in California, a 12 percent gap in Florida, and a whopping 23 percent deficit in Illinois. Again, it's unclear whether the federal government will provide yet more money to assist struggling schools, as it did throughout the New Deal. Already, however, federal stimulus-related projects have either created or saved almost 400,000 jobs for teachers, principals, school nurses, and other educational workers. If you're employed in a public school—or if you patronize one—you've almost certainly benefited from federal educational aid. And so did your parents and grandparents, if they lived on these shores.[22]

Whether we realize or not, in short, we're all in Uncle Sam's debt. Let's thank him, then, for everything he has done to further our own schooling. And let's resolve yet again to assist the poorest among us, perhaps by looking beyond education to issues of health, housing, labor, and more. In asking the federal government to remedy poverty via our public schools, we may be asking more of the government—and of our schools—than they can possibly bear.

CHAPTER 4

Banking on Government

Elizabeth Tandy Shermer

In 2003, just before moving to California, I abandoned my Virginia-based bank for the giant Bank of America. The accounts manager assured me that I could do business at any branch in any state without a hassle or a burdensome transaction fee. I was sold, confident that graduate school would make me a jetsetter who would need ready access to ATMs across the country.

But then I noticed an all-too-familiar logo in the corner of my paperwork. An emboldened "FDIC" stood out, less so the smaller print: "Backed by the full faith and credit of the United States government." I'd never paid this symbol any mind before, but I asked the banker what it meant. Was there a charge? Was this some kind of overdraft protection? Why did this major bank have the same kind of program as the local firm that had been handling my paltry undergraduate earnings? After all, I was supposed to be upgrading. She of course smiled at me, the naïve twenty-one-year-old, and explained that FDIC stood for Federal Deposit Insurance Corporation, a government institution and program designed to insure every investor's deposits. Up to a whopping $100,000!

I never made that much in graduate school, but I learned much more about the FDIC, not as a consumer but as a student of American politics, policy, and capitalism. The FDIC's establishment had been part of a landmark piece of New Deal legislation, the Banking Act of 1933 (commonly called Glass-Steagall). Congress passed this bill in the wake of unprecedented bank failures, 4,000 in 1933 alone. These collapses wiped out personal savings but also left bankers wary of making new investments or easing credit, both vital to recovery. Policy makers had more than a quick rebound on their minds when they drafted Glass-Steagall. FDIC not only insured individual deposits in institutions belonging to the Federal Reserve (guaranteeing a maximum of $2,500 at that point) but had oversight over all commercial banks as well. The law also included new rules, which, for example, prohibited banks from paying interest on checking accounts. Major firms were required to divorce their commercial dealings from their investment programs, effectively separating ordinary Americans' savings and small-scale loans from high-level securities trading, the wheeler-dealer transactions vital to corporate mergers and acquisitions.

That year, 1933, thus proved a watershed moment for Americans, their banks, and their nation's financial health. The federal government provided the kind of regulatory and fiscal infrastructure that had been missing from banking, much to the detriment of ordinary Americans who depended on commercial banks to provide them with credit, enable them to save, help them invest, and let them pay for goods and services. Such personal, now routine dealings had previously been difficult. A jumbled system of national institutions, state-chartered banks, private companies, and ad hoc arrangements had forestalled both long-term individual security and general economic stability. Reform had proven difficult, almost always stopped or limited by those who considered centralized regulation an affront to personal liberty, local authority, or a free market. But financial chaos and catastrophe convinced increasingly more Americans that an unrestrained market actually imprisoned the citizenry in a perilous cycle of booms and busts. They then promptly forgot this lesson during the three decades of postwar prosperity that Glass-Steagall heralded. Critics in fact dismantled oversight rules and agencies with the same arguments that had previously stymied reform. Who paid the price? Twenty-first-century savers, consumers, and homeowners desperate for the assurances that New Deal regulation had once provided.

Creating, let alone regulating, a banking system has never come easily. Financial policies have, in fact, largely been born out of war. Paying for the American Revolution, for example, had convinced members of the Second Continental Congress that they needed some sort of fiscal infrastructure. The colonial economy, largely structured around harvesting, bartering, and exporting North America's natural resources, had put relatively little gold or silver into circulation. The British government had also chartered few banks and restricted the use of their bank notes or bills of credit to pay taxes and settle debts. Rebels subsequently struggled to fill their war chest. Delegates borrowed money, sold bonds, and confiscated Loyalist property, but they mostly relied on printing money (Congress had issued more than 160 million paper "Continentals" by September 1779). Funds also came from the "Pennsylvania Bank," an institution Philadelphia merchants organized to finance the fight. They raised £300,000, which bought 500 barrels of flour for starving troops. Yet wealthy trader Robert Morris did not think it was enough. Growing popular unrest over the widening disparity between wealthy privateers and barefoot soldiers, the rebellion's escalating cost, and the steadily depreciating Continental dollar spurred the Philadelphian to donate £10,000 from his own sizable fortune and also persuade his friends to donate to the cause.

Congress rewarded Morris, naming him the Superintendent of Finance in February 1781. He was innovative, issuing promissories, "Morris Notes," backed by his personal reputation. They functioned like paper money and served as a fiscal stopgap while he reorganized the Pennsylvania Bank to cajole the wealthy into depositing and lending. Rather than have reluctant congressmen tax or beg for revenue, he embraced variable interest rates to guarantee a return on investing in the war effort. But his next experiment worried congressmen. Morris chartered a commercial bank, the Bank of North America, through the state of Pennsylvania in early 1782. The Articles of Confederation made no allowances for such financial arrangements, which did not dissuade Morris from enshrining the policy of providing returns in exchange for risk and expanding into short-term loans to generate additional revenue.[1]

Morris's fiscal ingenuity kept the rebellion going but also established a cornerstone of early US banking: state-chartered banks. By 1800, more than thirty existed. These financial houses were private enterprises, which did far more than accept deposits and make loans. They printed money, bank notes that operated as the legal tender to pay taxes and settle debts. Incorporation worked in favor of clients, financiers, and commerce. It allowed the state a measure of influence in exchange for the kind of accreditation that often boosted investor confidence in a bank. Specific legislative acts established charters, licenses that generally dictated a firm's life span, initial capitalization, reserve requirements, responsibility to state governments and programs, and the right to issue notes. Among the most important rules for residents was whether a firm would be permitted to open branches to serve clients outside its immediate vicinity.

These regulations guarded the general welfare of individual states and the new nation's fiscal health. Reserve requirements, for example, did not prohibit banks from lending money for new enterprises; they just guaranteed a stockpile so that firms could offer credit while ensuring that a reasonable number of depositors could make withdrawals. Compulsory loans and contributions to state treasuries and programs also funded universities and public infrastructure projects. But branching clauses reflected an issue at the heart of America's financial history: Were citizens better served by a few big banks with offices in many places or by a plethora of small, local firms, which freely competed for clients? States that discouraged branching tended to have large firms in urban areas but an array of smaller institutions in rural districts, whereas permitting this practice encouraged financiers to open additional offices outside major cities, the early home to these financial houses.[2]

Still, many people did not consider a state-based fiscal infra-structure adequate for colonies at war or a growing republic. "A national bank," Robert Morris warned Thomas Jefferson in 1781, "is absolutely necessary." Jefferson's faith in local control and allegiance to states' rights, however, left him wary of pow-erful centralized institutions. Federalist Alexander Hamilton, in contrast, shared Morris's convictions, even confiding that he regarded a national repository, modeled on the Bank of England no less, "as an expedient essential to our safety and suc-cess.... There is no other that can give to government... exten-sive and systematic credit."[3]

Hamilton remained steadfast in his convictions when he was asked to head the Department of the Treasury under George Washington. The first secretary of the Treasury not only pre-sided over the young republic's finances but also had the leeway to shape what the agency did then and in the future. Hamilton certainly thought so. The department of course collected taxes, paid the nation's bills, and advised the president on fiscal pol-icy, but Hamilton also considered it well within the "necessary and proper" function of the federal government to provide the financial stability necessary for economic and territorial expan-sion through a national bank. In 1791, he was politically unable to make the Bank of the United States (BUS) a permanent insti-tution. He settled for a twenty-year charter but did manage to ensure that his department would manage BUS to, in theory at least, insulate the institution from any volatile congressional bickering over the annual budget.

Such control enabled Hamilton to build a powerful, essentially private bank. The national government held but 20 percent of its shares, even though BUS accepted federal deposits, made loans to the central government, had branches in multiple states, and established a sound circulating currency easily convertible into gold or silver, which greatly eased interstate trade and international commerce. This national bank left chartering, regulating, and auditing banks up to the individual states but effectively had the power to police how much money firms printed and held in reserve. BUS held onto state bank notes and had the authority to force banks to buy back their notes with gold, silver, or BUS banknotes, essentially forcing these enterprises to remain solvent. BUS managers could also decide that citizens could not pay their taxes with a state bank's notes, a tool to dissuade investors from doing business with institutions that had shaky finances and inadequate reserves. Capital stock worth $10 million complemented this regulatory power, which enabled the BUS, though far less powerful than modern central banks, to discipline state banks as well as provide loans to individuals and businesses and meet new and existing federal loan obligations.[4]

Ideological disagreements, which would forever plague American banking to the detriment of its customers, led both to BUS's demise and its successors' creation. In 1811, a razor-thin congressional majority, inheritors of Jefferson's Anti-Federalist sensibilities, declined to recharter BUS, an institution that embodied Federalist faith in a strong central government. Yet the system of state banks, now numbering eighty-eight, could not finance the War of 1812, which tripled the nation's debt, largely through the issuance of short-term, interest-bearing federal Treasury notes that essentially functioned like paper money (holders could even pay their taxes with them). State banks nonetheless carried the war's financial burden. Their numbers almost tripled during the conflict. An unprecedented $68 million in assorted bank notes circulated, which, after individual bank managers stopped exchanging them for gold or silver to protect reserves, all depreciated at varying rates. The subsequent inflation and general uncertainty increased demand for a new federal bank, which Congress chartered in April 1816, more than a year after hostilities had ended. Policy makers looked back a generation to draft another twenty-year charter. The Second Bank of the United States (SBUS), like its predecessor, was a big, powerful, and essentially private institution. The federal government still owned but one fifth of its official depository's shares, appointed just five of its twenty-five directors, and accepted SBUS banknotes as a form of tax payment.[5]

The Treasury Department retained control of the national bank but once again could not insulate it or the nation's financial security from partisanship. Long-standing unease with centralized financial power only increased when bank president Nicholas Biddle spent the mid-1820s broadening his powers and the institution's activities. He bolstered gold and silver reserves, regularized inspections, and increased the loans made, much to the relief of credit-starved merchants, farmers, shippers, and manufacturers across the country.

Democrat Andrew Jackson had little use for these supposed privileged classes, but this champion of the common man and states' rights did not oppose *the idea* of a national bank. True, the recently inaugurated president's 1829 State of the Union address included an assertion that SBUS had "failed in the great end of establishing a uniform and sound currency," but subsequent congressional messages asked only for significant charter modifications or a new, truly federal institution. Biddle ignored these overtures, instead attempting a policy maneuver to forestall Jackson's reelection. The infuriated popular president subsequently vetoed the early renewal of SBUS's charter. The banker printed and distributed thousands of copies of Jackson's populist veto message to enrage voters, who did not respond to Biddle's technocratic justifications but to Jackson's "stand against all new grants of monopolies and exclusive privileges, against any prostitution of our Government to the advancement of the few at the expense of the many, and in favor of compromise and gradual reform in our code of laws and system of political economy."[6]

The bank wars' conclusion once again left the citizenry financially adrift. Biddle did recharter SBUS branches with individual states, but state-chartered banks were the only entity in charge of American finances. A host of institutions had actually long done business outside the network of chartered state banks. Philadelphians, for example, had established the first mutual savings bank in 1816; roughly 500 such repositories existed by century's end. These establishments were owned by depositors, usually people of modest means with little to save and thus a lot to lose. Small-scale loans were available through cooperative banks (called thrifts or savings and loans). Generally, a group started such an establishment with an initial contribution, regularly contributed funds until a predetermined total was reached, and then disbursed money to each member to construct a house, culminating in the cooperative's dissolution when all depositors had their new homes. Both arrangements increasingly took on the duties of full-service state-chartered banks in this so-called free banking period.

More worrisome was the netherworld of unincorporated institutions, confusingly called private banks. They had also been lending money and accepting deposits outside the system of state-chartered private banks, which was not advantageous either for their clients or for the country's fiscal health. American discomfort with state interference and compulsory obligations was at least partially to blame: nineteenth-century legislatures often did not require, nor in fairness did they have the capability to compel, such businesses to establish a charter. Such firms increased in number after the SBUS's demise and did ready business on the American frontier, far from the established laws and customs that regulated banking in the East. These operations, like antebellum insurance companies, railroad outfits, towns, and private merchants, often issued their own notes, the same practice that had produced the volatile mix of currencies during the War of 1812 and now left customers in the free banking era unable to ensure their deposits' security and availability, easily buy and sell goods, or even pay their taxes. Worse still, these operations often proved insolvent or fly-by-night, and state governments had difficulty policing the firms. Antebellum legislators thus increasingly turned to general incorporation laws, which allowed any one person or group to start a bank once they met the general requirements for incorporation but did not provide the same measure of oversight as an individual charter.[7]

A patchwork system of private banks operating within or outside the purview of state bureaucracies proved once more of little use to a nation at war, this time against itself. The Civil War forced the central government first to print money, the federally issued greenback, and then to construct a federal financial system—but not through one national bank controlled by the secretary of the Treasury. Congress instead created a division within the Treasury, the Office of the Comptroller of the Currency, to manage a system of national banks. The 1863 and 1864 National Banking Acts facilitated the sale of government bonds to finance the war; established a uniform, stable currency in the form of banknotes backed by federal bonds; and empowered the comptroller of the Currency to charter, regulate, and supervise national banks to issue these bills. The firms within this national system had specified capitalization requirements, set reserve levels, and restricted branching.

Yet Congress followed the dangerous precedent that the states had set: membership in this system was not required, either for new or existing banks. Indeed, stiffer regulations, branch banking restrictions, and oversight policies did more to deter banks from abandoning their state charters than to force or entice them to incorporate. As a result, few became federally chartered financial houses until after 1865, when Congress imposed a 10 percent tax on all state bank notes, a measure designed to cajole, rather than stridently compel, financiers to submit to the kind of oversight needed for war and its aftermath.[8]

Thus American discomfort with centralized control continued to limit the country's ability to regulate banks and facilitate commerce. The National Banking System (NBS), for example, could not police banking or end the confusing network of state and private banks. The latter actually flourished during Reconstruction, particularly in poor rural communities that could not sustain a federally chartered firm. Incorporation became increasingly lucrative, not restrictive, in this industrializing period because the acts had not created another Bank of the United States with the power to monitor the capitalization, reserves, or note circulation of state-chartered banks. Indeed, federal officials had enough trouble assuring compliance from firms within the NBS.

But at least they tried. Enforcement of state regulations was notoriously lax, an important trade-off when financiers weighed whether to apply for a national charter. Legislatures increasingly eased banking regulations by matching or lowering capitalization requirements, setting low reserve rates, allowing banks to make loans backed by real estate, permitting banks to branch, and establishing incorporation standards, which freed banks from applying for a charter or meeting general incorporation law dictates. These and other policies effectively offset the cost of not belonging to the NBS. The result: the number of banks again nearly tripled between 1900 and 1914, but the federal government chartered fewer than 15 percent of them.[9]

This surge coincided with explosive economic growth. Yet periodic booms and busts defined this Gilded Age, an apt descriptor for an era characterized by the rising inequality and unprecedented wealth generated from new enterprises, daring investments, technological innovations, lax production standards, and continually depressed wages. Radicals, social reformers, muckraking journalists, union organizers, and Progressive politicians famously questioned this new status quo, variously offering socialism, charity, education, solidarity, and regulation as solutions.[10]

Big businessmen, often those at the helm of this period's largest corporations, were also appalled. Alarmed captains of industry increasingly considered stability and cooperation good for business and were disdainful of the eager entrepreneurs who advocated an unrestrained market while they cut labor costs, lowered product standards, and depressed prices through over-production. Critics saw a direct link between this unbridled competition and the periodic fiscal crises, or "panics," that accompanied economic downturns. Rapid withdrawals during the 1893 downturn led to the collapse of 141 national banks and the suspension of operations in more than 500 private firms. In the wake of this disaster, journalists, lawyers, academics, and politicians publicly asserted that an increasingly corporate America needed a sounder currency and a central bank.[11]

The Panic of 1907 only intensified demands for fiscal over-haul. The mix of private, state, and national banks had the effect of concentrating reserves in the largest firms. Rural and small-time bankers, especially prevalent in those states that discour-aged branch banking, had nonetheless tended to invest their reserves in large urban firms with the expectation that they would receive a good return and could demand immediate withdrawals. Top financiers put this money to good use: their loans funded enterprising industrialists. Problems arose when America's large banking trusts recklessly used the deposits of wealthy clients and lesser banking outfits to make risky loans. When the speculative bubble burst, bankers in large urban and small rural outfits alike suspended payments. Hoarding money further eroded public faith in American finance. In dramatic fashion, industrialist J. P. Morgan used his fortune and power to end this crisis by forcing top New York financiers to create a $25 million pool to save other floundering trusts.[12]

"We may not always have Pierpont Morgan," Senator Nelson Aldrich (R-RI) warned when he convened the National Monetary Commission in 1908. Policy makers spent the next five years crafting a new system that relied on a modern central bank that promoted stability, guaranteed fiscal solvency, and made the Fed, not Morgan, the lender of last resort. The legislation still did not resolve the ideological tensions that had hamstrung banking regulation and frustrated the country's economic health for more than a century. The 1913 Federal Reserve Act, unlike the 1864 law, did reward affiliation with discounted loans and annual dividends on Reserve stockpiles. Yet the 1913 bill continued the tradition of divvying up responsibility to guard against centralized control. The Federal Reserve Note, familiar to us as the dollar, became the nation's currency, but regional reserve banks would be liable for this Treasury Department obligation. The president, with Senate approval, appointed the Federal Reserve Board's seven members, who had more power than the ex officio officers (the comptroller of the Currency and secretary of the Treasury). The Fed's public servants still had less influence than the local bankers and businessmen whose peers selected them to direct the twelve regional reserve banks and their boards. Congress also did not compel state-chartered banks to join the Federal Reserve System, whose members had to purchase nontransferable stock from and deposit non-interest-bearing reserves into their regional bank. Yet the Board could lessen or increase the amount of cash regional banks had on hand to lend.[13]

States could not control the money supply in the same manner, which left legislators to experiment concurrently with policies, like deposit insurance, to stop bank runs. In this period, Congress also entertained proposals for federal insurance, but only states created such programs. Few legislatures mandated such guarantees before the 1907 Panic, which reinforced the need to protect individual savers, keep the public confident, and forestall bank runs. The various early twentieth-century methods tried in Oklahoma, Kansas, Nebraska, South Dakota, Texas, Mississippi, North Dakota, and Washington State all failed because they had not done enough to assure financiers' compliance and oversee their business practices. The earliest plans, for example, had not included regulations to guard against risky lending. Programs also had not forced firms to buy into insurance schemes. Small, less-solvent banks volunteered, happy that insurance calmed their clientele, whereas large banks tended to pursue national charters rather than be compelled to join a state's system. As a result, officials struggled to keep deposit insurance funds available, especially as the number of bank failures increased during the 1920s.[14]

Herbert Hoover consequentially inherited a federal system unable to deal with a crisis as profound as the Great Depression. Only entrepreneurs, industrialists, and top financiers had a federal life preserver because the federal system privileged large firms, which could afford to join and to speculate wildly. Weaker outfits and smaller banks, in contrast, did not have the capital to put into reserve. They also held the savings of ordinary Americans, few of whom had deposit insurance. The 1920s' steady stream of collapsing banks thus turned into a tidal wave after the 1929 stock market crash. Runs shuttered more than 1,300 banks in 1930, 2,000 in 1931, and 5,700 in 1932. Business loans declined by more than half in these years because the surviving financiers clamped down on credit. Hoover soon learned that he needed far more federal authority to revive the economy. Too many institutions operated outside the Reserve System, and not enough Board members and regional bankers even entertained his recommendations to ease credit in the name of increasing economic activity and public confidence. Hoover, in frustration, increased the executive branch's power through the Reconstruction Finance Corporation (RFC), a federal agency Congress created in 1932 to make loans to state and local governments and a range of financial intermediaries, including commercial banks, trusts, savings and loans (S&Ls), and insurance companies.[15]

Hoover's successor, Franklin Delano Roosevelt, mercifully embraced federal power, claiming the central state a champion of, not an enemy of, recovery and commerce. Dams, roads, and public murals were the most high-profile products of New Deal statecraft, but the less visible overhaul of American finance and banking was more important. FDR's appointee to head the RFC, Texas banker Jesse Jones, funded scores of factories and thousands of infrastructure projects. The "economic emperor of America," as one journalist dubbed Jones, did so with a commitment to conservative banking principles. He rejected projects that he considered risky, no matter who in Congress or in the federal bureaucracy backed or proposed the ventures. He also condemned those executives who still did not understand, as one historian summarized, that "government regulation stabilized banking, protected bankers from themselves and gave depositors confidence in banks."[16]

These principles guided the congressmen who crafted Glass-Steagall. The hearings were quick but spirited. Bankers, particularly those whose profits depended on their dealings in securities, opposed separating commercial and investment banking. Some financiers also feared, as did a few Reserve Board members, that purely commercial firms could not produce the capital to make enough consumer and banking loans to serve customers and facilitate recovery. The American Bankers Association simply considered the bill draconian and unwise. Journalists were also not convinced. A *Los Angeles Times* columnist predicted "a measure of governmental supervision and control of the banking system hitherto unknown in the United States." This recalcitrance faded after March 1933 Senate investigations publicized the most unseemly securities practices, revelations that forced some of the nation's preeminent financiers, the heads of Chase National and National City Banks, to reconsider their arguments.[17]

Yet deposit insurance remained controversial. Jones had championed Texas's earlier deposit insurance experiment. The program's collapse and other states' failed attempts had then left him convinced that only the federal government could make such a guarantee. Critics insisted that such failures meant insurance should not be included. No preceding statute, the Merchants Association of New York proclaimed, had "eliminate[d] moral hazards and bad judgment," but all had caused "a relaxation of vigilance as to who enters the banking business and a relaxation of caution on the part of some of those already in it." A leading Georgia financier declared it "wrong for the Government to begin guaranteeing a man's investment and thousands and thousands of deposits in the savings departments of the banks by people who look upon their savings as an investment and who draw the interest twice a year and live on it for 12 months."[18] Businessmen were not the only skeptics. Even FDR initially opposed the scheme: "For a number of reasons of sound government finance, such a plan would be quite dangerous." Nonetheless, the president recognized that the public needed some kind of guarantee to keep their money in banks. In the end, deposit insurance would be temporary, if only, as FDR proclaimed in his first fireside chat, to protect "the confidence of the people," unquestionably "more important than currency, more important than gold."[19]

Only such a strong commitment to the citizenry and commerce was able to restore faith in the banking system. Glass-Steagall continued the tradition of balancing local sovereignty against central control. States retained limited chartering and supervisory responsibilities, and the federal government exercised its new regulatory powers through gentle coercion and popular will. For example, the act made deposit insurance voluntary, but consumer demand for security forced state banks to obtain federal deposit insurance and thus open their books to FDIC regulators. By June 1934, 14,000 of the nation's 15,000 commercial banks were insured. Congress then strengthened the FDIC's regulatory power and made deposit insurance permanent in 1935, a year after bank runs and failures plummeted from 4,000 in 1933 to 61 in 1934. This banking act also reorganized and empowered the Federal Reserve Board, which further centralized control of American banking. By this time, financiers had almost completely rearranged their partnerships to divorce commercial and investment banking. The latter was to be policed by the Securities and Exchange Commission, an agency empowered under the 1934 Securities Exchange Act to promote confidence in the stock market by stopping fraud and ensuring full disclosure.[20]

Regulation heralded a genuinely prosperous era, not a tarnished Gilded Age. Decades of prosperity followed. The fiscal regulatory framework in place by the end of World War II eased the transition between mobilizing for war and providing consumer goods in peacetime. Corporations had the financial structure in place to expand their product lines, build state-of-the-art factories across the country, and create the conglomerates that would serve military and civilian needs. Their employees and customers could also save, invest, and borrow with confidence. Commercial banking was blessedly predictable; "3-6-3," the joke went, "bankers paid 3 percent on deposits, charged 6 percent on loans, and hit the golf course by 3:00 P.M." Annual bank failure rates would not exceed twenty-five until the 1980s.[21]

This regulated prosperity had its critics, many of whom sounded as strident and uncompromising as Jackson and Biddle had been more than a century earlier. Preeminent western financier Walter Bimson, a Commerce Department consultant during the Truman administration, considered many federal restrictions an affront to the American "system of democratic capitalism and individual freedom." His bold postwar statements won the admiration of bankers who thanked him "for going ahead in the face of criticism." They then found a champion in University of Chicago economist Milton Friedman, who made a name for himself in the pages of *Newsweek*. His 1960s columns attacked the New Deal broadly, particularly its regulatory impulse. His 1963 *Monetary History of the United States* also offered no praise for Glass-Steagall or deposit insurance. "The reduction in failures," he asserted, "is not of course attributable to any corresponding drastic improvement in the quality of bank officials or in the effectiveness of supervisory authorities; nor is it attributable to the addition of still another examination agency."

Economists even began to recycle Depression-era warnings in the 1970s and 1980s. "Federal deposit insurance assessments are effectively subsidies from sound to reckless banks," two professors declared in the *Cato Journal*. They dismissed the dramatically reduced failure rate because earlier state experiments proved that "deposit insurance is found to increase—rather than reduce—bank failures." An Office of Management and Budget appointee even rejected security's desirability. Deposit insurance "is failing," he asserted. "Insurers invite further risk taking... by reducing the market discipline that unprotected depositors and other creditors would impose."[22]

Many financiers, federal appointees, and politicians also came to embrace deregulation in the 1970s and 1980s, but not for the common man. They wanted to help out the common banker, who worked under far more restrictions than their securities counterparts. Their regularized dealings had been "boring" but profitable until the 1970s, when mutual funds and securities firms began courting depositors with high-interest money market accounts and loans from commercial paper and junk bonds. "Banks are fenced in," an executive complained. "Others can come inside the fence, but we can't get out." Indeed, many types of financial institutions, including investment houses, increasingly operated as if they could do any type of business not expressly prohibited by federal law. Commercial banks were thus at a disadvantage to both domestic outfits and foreign businesses that used telecommunication improvements to do business in America. Of particular concern were the smaller banks and financial outfits, like savings and loans, which were just not big enough to compete, unlike their large commercial counterparts. "You got to remember that each community has a savings and loan; some have two; some have four, and each of them has seven or eight board members. They own the Chevy dealership and the shoe store," a senator explained. "And when we saw these people, we said, gosh, these are the people who are building the homes for people, these are the people who represent a dream that has worked in this country."[23]

Congressional representatives and federal appointees thus gradually disemboweled Glass–Steagall in the name of the free market and the public. The Carter administration did much to help savings and loans vie for customers: S&Ls were allowed to pursue investment opportunities far outside their local communities, compete for customers with higher interest rates and promises that the federal government would ensure up to $100,000 in deposits through the Federal Savings and Loan Insurance Corporation, an FDIC derivative. Regulators ensured that other firms had a broad market soon after. The comptroller of the Currency allowed national banks to sell insurance nationwide in 1986, just before a major crisis sank the S&L industry. A record number of S&Ls folded, victims of questionable investments, risky loans (it was common to provide full financing for an array of ventures with no down payment), and a softening real estate market. But regulation's critics were largely undeterred. In the 1990s, the Reserve Board gradually increased the profits that banks could earn from trading securities. Congress also removed restrictions on intrastate and interstate mergers and acquisitions, which enabled Bank of America to build a national clientele. Banking became even more interesting in 1997, when a large commercial bank was allowed to buy a major securities firm.[24]

Hence, the 1999 Financial Services Modernization Act, described by the media and President Bill Clinton as a repeal of Glass–Steagall, really put into law what had already begun to be done in practice. Financiers were now legally allowed to offer commercial, investment, and insurance services, which gave rise to the "universal bank." But policy makers had not created a regulatory apparatus to supervise these diversified financial firms, instead foolishly following the tradition of dividing oversight. A firm's various operations were in fact monitored piecemeal by the Federal Reserve, Treasury Department, FDIC, Securities and Exchange Commission, Department of Labor, and state legislatures. Thus, no individual agency had any sense of a business's overall portfolio.

Regulation would admittedly have been a challenge. Financial whiz kids hatched incomprehensible schemes to slice and dice mortgages for resale, speculate on their firms' securities, and insure commercial bank holdings through credit-default swaps. Few knew how these arrangements worked. "I didn't understand the retail market; I just wasn't close to it," former Treasury secretary and Goldman Sachs executive Henry Paulson admitted when asked about the marketing of toxic mortgage assets.[25]

This most recent crisis, like the wars and panics before it, tested what remained of America's once formidable regulatory apparatus. Bank failures had steadily increased since the 1980s but escalated dramatically during the Recession. The FDIC was unprepared. The deregulatory impulse had not only loosened restrictions but also inspired lawmakers to slash the agency's budget and workforce, the only line of defense left after 1999. Morale was hence already low when the mortgage crisis unfolded. Regulators were forced to raise the insurance guarantee to $250,000, more than double the amount promised to me when I opened my Bank of America account in 2003. These funds were a lifeline to depositors in the hundreds of banks that failed between 2007 and 2011. Yet the FDIC could not keep up with the tidal wave of collapsing firms. By November 2009, the deposit insurance fund was $8.2 billion in the red, which forced insurers to spend two years rebuilding reserves by demanding that banks prepay their insurance premiums.[26]

Most policy makers and congressional representatives proved themselves most concerned with using the federal government to facilitate profit making. Gone was concern for the common man or even the common banker. Universal banks, not the public, were considered "too big to fail." Consequently, the 2008 Troubled Asset Relief Program spent billions to purchase or insure junk holdings to prevent these companies' collapse. Executives used this bailout to improve profitability and to quickly buy back government shares because policy makers had not forced banks to lend this money to small businesses or consumers.

Two years later, Congress passed the expansive Dodd-Frank Wall Street Reform and Consumer Protection Act. This law consolidated oversight agencies, regulated financial markets, outlined plans to extend credit and manage bankruptcies during downturns, and established added protections for consumers and investors. The populist spirit of reform was best summed up in the new Consumer Financial Protection Bureau's mission statement: "make markets for consumer financial products and services work for Americans."[27]

Financiers balked. They especially detested moratoriums on fees for using debit cards and overdrafting accounts. Banks immediately began charging customers for routine transactions such as making deposits, wiring money, mailing paper statements, and maintaining checking accounts—Bank of America included.[28]

But I, like every other saver, had little recourse. Few Americans have learned all the lessons from 200 years of financing America. True, the nation no longer trades in a confusing hodgepodge of banknotes, the FDIC continues to compensate depositors for losses when a bank fails, and the Federal Reserve Board continually evaluates the money supply. But partisanship, right on par with the grandstanding that destroyed SBUS and left the citizenry and their savings at the mercy of state-chartered and independent banks, stymied the Obama administration's ability to even staff the new consumer protection agency. Faith that the market could police itself also remained. Prominent politicians even openly supported the dissolution of the Federal Reserve during the Recession, even though the crisis proved deregulation's postwar champions had been wrong. The federal government does not restrain growth. It was regulation that created and policed the banking system responsible for America's remarkable mid-twentieth-century economic growth.[29]

CHAPTER 5

Twenty-Nine Helmets

Government Power and the Promise of Security

Kevin Boyle

On the day the president came to town they lined the stage with helmets. Not the sort of helmets that miners actually wear—chipped and dented and streaked with sweat—but gleaming new ones, sparkling white to match the white of the crosses they were placed upon, one for each of the men killed on Easter Monday 2010, when a massive explosion ripped through the Upper Big Branch mine deep in the coal country of southern West Virginia. Twenty-nine helmets, twenty-nine crosses, twenty-nine families, twenty-nine lives.

There was fierce disagreement about why the tragedy occurred. The mine's owner, the company formerly known as Massey Energy Corporation, insisted that the explosion was triggered by a dramatic inundation of natural gas along the rock face, a gruesome act of God. Miners blamed the company's refusal to follow even elementary safety procedures. "Man, they got us up there mining and we ain't got no air," one of the victims told a friend the day before he died. "I'm just scared to death to go to work because...something bad is going to happen." A special committee appointed by the governor of West Virginia went further. Yes, the Big Branch mine was a terribly dangerous place, it said. But Massey Energy was able to run it that way because the regulatory system put in place to protect miners had broken down, eviscerated by endless litigation, chronic under-funding of mine inspections, and Big Coal's undue influence over the political process. "The story of Upper Big Branch," the committee concluded, "is a cautionary tale of hubris."[1]

And of history. It's the story of a Dickensian America soft-ened by a patchwork of government programs stitched together over half a century; of the security and stability those programs provided, the creation of a country where ordinary people didn't have to fear that they were one illness, one layoff, one accident away from catastrophe; of the gradual dismantling of those pro-grams in the past thirty years as state and federal governments lurched to the right; and of the burdens that dynamic has placed on millions of Americans, with the most vulnerable bearing the heaviest weight.

Twenty-nine helmets, twenty-nine lives.

Twenty-year old Bartolomeo Vanzetti arrived in New York City in the summer of 1908 carrying two of the most valuable things an immigrant could have: a skill and a connection. He was a candy maker by trade, trained in the confectionaries of Piedmont and Torino. And he had a cousin working as a chef in an exclusive club uptown, the sort of place that might appreci-ate having a man of his particular talents on staff. Nothing was guaranteed. But there was every chance that Vanzetti was going to do just fine in America.[2]

It didn't work out that way. His cousin's club took him on, but as a dishwasher rather than a pastry chef, and then only for the summer season. When that job petered out, he moved to a fine French restaurant in midtown, a favorite haunt of writ-ers, artists, and suburban slummers. Again his bosses set him to washing dishes. Fourteen hours a day, seven days a week standing over a sink of boiling water, the steam rising to the ceiling above him, where it mixed with the grease and dirt that accumulated there and fell, drop by blackened drop, back on his head. After eight months he quit, fearing that he was about to contract tuberculosis.

But no one else was interested in hiring him. By May 1909, his second month without work, he'd eaten through almost all his savings; a week or two more and he'd tumble into destitution. Rather than trying to live on the streets of Manhattan, with its attendant horrors, Vanzetti decided to spend his final few dollars on a ticket for the ferry that ran up to Hartford. From there he went on the tramp, a fine Italian artisan reduced to wandering the Connecticut countryside, begging Yankee farmers for something to eat, somewhere to sleep, some scrap of work to do. "Don't believe that America is civilized," he wrote his sister after he'd finally found steady work in a Meriden stone quarry. "Remove its elegant dress and you find semi-barbarism."[3]

He had a point. In the latter half of the nineteenth century the United States had become the workshop of the world. At its center lay a sprawling complex of mines, mills, and factories stretching from Baltimore to Boston, across the Alleghenies, through Pittsburgh, Cleveland, Detroit, and Chicago, all the way to St. Louis. Into that complex flowed the natural bounty of the south and west: cotton from Alabama and Mississippi, lumber from Arkansas, copper from Montana, wheat from Kansas and Nebraska, iron ore from the Mesabi Range. Out of it flowed more goods than from any other nation on earth, from cigarettes and pinafores to tons of steel.

For all its creative power, though, industrialization was also a tremendously destructive force. Wherever it spread, it shattered traditional ways of life, pulling apart long-standing systems of mutuality—however uneven and exploitative—and putting in their place the less-than-tender mercies of the marketplace.[4]

Nowhere was the transformation greater than in the country-side. In the late 1800s steamship lines and railroad tracks reached into parts of the world that not long before had been considered impenetrable. In the process they created a genuinely global economy, linking what had been largely local markets into a single system of trade. In rural areas, not only American but European as well, the consequences were catastrophic. Suddenly small-town craftsmen found themselves competing against mass-produced goods flooding into village stores, while landowners and tenants watched their incomes collapse beneath waves of imported crops: in the 1880s an influx of cheap American grain shattered the economies of Italy's wheat-growing regions; ten years later a surge in Egyptian cotton pushed the price of the American version to its lowest point in forty years. Millions of people struggled through as best they could, sometimes in extraordinarily dire circumstances: at the turn of the century a sharecropper in the Mississippi delta was fortunate to earn $300 a year, less than half of what he needed to cross the poverty line. Millions more gave up, abandoning the countryside for the mining camps, factory towns, and cities where they might find steady work.[5]

Migration took people across the industrial world, filling Liverpool with Irishmen, Budapest with Slovaks, Buenos Aires with Italians, the Ruhr with Poles. It hit the United States with tremendous force. More than 5 million Americans moved from farms to cities in the half century after 1860. Immigration added another 22 million, a movement so mammoth it transformed the nation's great industrial centers into bastions of the foreign-born: by 1910, 32 percent of Detroiters, 34 percent of Chicagoans, and 40 percent of New Yorkers had come to the United States from abroad.[6]

There they found higher wages than they ever would have earned at home, a consequence of the economy's fabulous growth and chronic labor shortage. But many employers didn't run their businesses year-round: in 1900, a prosperous year, 22 percent of

American workers were unemployed for some period of time, half of them for four months or more. For those who employers thought would make poor workers—the blind, the deaf, the physically impaired, the aged most of all—there was almost no chance of finding steady jobs. So those fine American wages didn't translate into fine American incomes. While firm figures are impossible to come by, the best estimates suggest that at the turn of the century about 40 percent of Americans lived below the poverty line.[7]

That was a very grim place to be. Industrial America was a charnel house. The worst accidents were horrific events: 362 men killed in a West Virginia mine collapse three weeks before Christmas 1907; sixty killed while building a tunnel beneath the Chicago River in January 1909, half them incinerated, the other half drowned; 146 people burned to death in Manhattan's infamous Triangle Shirtwaist Factory fire in March 1910. But the problem was endemic. Between 1888 and 1908, approximately 35,000 people were killed on the job, half a million injured. "It is difficult to believe that such slaughter is permitted to go on year after year," wrote a middle-class reformer in 1904, "but, strange as it is to say, [businessmen] resist powerfully every attempt made to have them adopt safety standards."[8]

Outside the workplace the dangers only increased. To ease the strain on their budgets, the poor often packed as many people as they could into already overcrowded rentals in the cities' least desirable neighborhoods. The worst section of Chicago's Back of the Yards housed 250 people per acre, Detroit's African American ghetto, jammed with southern migrants, 300. New York outdid them both. Vanzetti was lucky to find a bed in a decrepit brownstone on the edge of the Tenderloin; had he settled across town, on the Lower East Side, he'd have been living in the most densely populated place on the face of the earth. Poor sanitation made matters worse. At the turn of the century indoor plumbing was still a luxury in the poorer sections of urban America; Back of the Yards didn't even have sewer lines. Any number of city streets weren't paved. And garbage removal was sporadic at best. Little wonder that disease ran rampant. Pittsburgh's working people were eight times more likely than most Americans to die from typhoid, in large part because they were drinking unfiltered water from the poisonous Monongahela.[9]

Everyone understood what would happen if disaster struck. An accident at the mill or mine might produce a small payment from the company, a fatality a little more. After that a family would have to fend for itself. A bout of unemployment or, worse yet, an extended illness would produce nothing except a yawning gap where a paycheck used to be. The poor did whatever possible to protect themselves against such a turn. Families scrounged for any extra income they could—taking in boarders, playing the numbers, putting their children out to work—so that they might have some savings set aside when a crisis hit, though no one was going to save enough to offset a truly catastrophic event. They flocked to fraternal organizations and mutual aid societies that paid out benefits in case of accident or illness. And they had an absolute mania for insurance. By 1910, companies that catered to the working class had written almost 25 million policies. They wouldn't cover some of the most common calamities; there was no way for the poor to insure themselves against unemployment or the risk of childbirth or the ravages of old age. So they insured what they could. Of all the policies written at the turn of the century, the most common covered the cost of a funeral.[10]

Still every year a portion of poor—precisely how many isn't clear—tumbled downward, plummeting through the threadbare safety net beneath them into destitution. In small towns, those who had no other option could turn to public relief: "outside work" if they were lucky, a place in the poorhouse if they weren't. But by 1900, most major cities no longer offered those alternatives. Instead, the destitute filled flophouses, foundling hospitals, charity wards, orphanages, prisons, and potters' fields. Moralists dismissed them as vagrants, drunks, and hopheads steeped in "habits of dependence," as one put it, that stripped them "of manliness and self-respect." Undoubtedly some of them were. Far more were victims of an economic system as callous as it was powerful. Vanzetti remembering seeing them during the two months he spent looking for a job in the spring of 1909, perfectly employable men sleeping in doorways or rummaging through garbage barrels "to find a cabbage leaf or a rotten potato." That was probably the reason he left Manhattan in the end. Because he didn't want to end up one of them, and he knew that if he stayed much longer he would.[11]

It isn't clear why policy makers decided that government ought to do something about the enormous burdens industrialization imposed. In part they were driven by the desire to control the immigrant masses, which seemed a bit too alien for some Anglo-Saxon tastes. Altruism also played a role, most obviously in the settlement house movement, as did changing ideas about the state's relationship to the economy. Then there was politics, pure and simple. A stirring defense of laissez-faire didn't win many votes in working-class wards. But the possibility of reform did.[12]

The transformation of public policy came in three stages, each building on the previous. The first stage, which ran from the turn of the century to about 1920, had the most modest results. Then again, it had the most to overcome. Most troubling were legal precedents. It took ten years for reformers to convince a Supreme Court fiercely dedicated to the defense of business rights that it was constitutional for states to limit the number of hours women could work in factories each week. At least that was a victory. Over the same period progressives waged a titanic struggle to pass a federal law banning child labor. Congress finally gave them what they wanted in 1916. Two years later the Court struck it down.[13]

The decentralization of American politics didn't help. Progressives fought most of their battles on the state and local levels, the center points of public life in the early twentieth century. As a result, reform lurched, rather than spread, across the industrial landscape. New York passed an imposing tenement reform law; Detroit didn't. Illinois set up a powerful factory inspection system; North Carolina, with its expanding industrial base, did not. Even when progressives managed to knit together something close to a national policy, the results were uneven. Between 1911 and 1920, reformers convinced forty-two states to create workmen's compensation programs, a stunning achievement. But the specifics differed dramatically from state to state. So a worker was much better off getting injured in Ohio, where the program was generously funded, than he was in New York, where the insurance lobby set the rules.[14]

The reformers' other sweeping success was limited in a different way. In the 1910s, progressives discussed a whole range of welfare programs, from sick pay to old age insurance. But the only one they put into place—in a remarkable thirty-nine states this time—was the narrowly defined "mother's pension," a government grant to support impoverished widows and their dependent children. There was clearly some calculation in their decision to promote that particular policy: even the cruelest state legislator was going to have a hard time turning his back on women and children plainly in need, especially when the program was means-tested and its promised payments miserly. But progressives also didn't push for a more comprehensive welfare state because they believed that some poor people were deserving of aid and others—able-bodied men, for instance, or women who bore children out of wedlock—were not.[15]

To stress the limits of the progressive moment, though, is to miss the more important point. In twenty years of agitation, reformers gave millions of ordinary people a chance to live in slightly better housing, work in safer factories, or pick up pensions that, however small, would keep their fatherless children fed. Through that jumble of programs they shaped a vision of governmental responsibility fundamentally different from the one they'd confronted. The progressives may not have remade

America. But they remade the possibility of America for millions of ordinary people.

It took the greatest economic crisis of the twentieth century to give reformers the chance to build on what the progressives had done. By the time Franklin Roosevelt became president in March 1933 the industrial system was in complete collapse, its financial underpinnings stripped away, its warehouses full of unsold goods, 11 million of its workers dismissed since the Crash of '29. Fraternal organizations, charities, and local governments tried to help, as always, but were quickly overwhelmed, many driven to insolvency.

So the poor, now nearly 50 percent of the population, were left to fend for themselves. Reporter Lorena Hickok described an old woman she met while visiting the Kentucky coal fields. "Half dead from pellagra," Hickok wrote, "she stumbled along on her bare, gnarled old feet, clutching under her arm a paper bag containing a few scraggly string beans she'd begged off somebody.... She reached out and laid her hand on my arm and said in a voice that was barely more than a whisper: 'Don't forget me, honey! Don't forget me!'"[16]

Misery created opportunity, politically at least. "This nation asks for action," FDR said in his inaugural address. That's what he delivered, pulling long-standing progressive proposals off the shelf, mixing in new ideas, and giving the combination a catchy title that made it sound much more coherent than it actually was. The administration's policies, complained an old progressive, were nothing more than an amalgam of "confused and contradictory nostrums." Its programs were also often twisted, and occasionally warped, by the political process. And until 1938, the Supreme Court loomed over the entire enterprise just as it had the progressives, a conservative specter in a liberal age. Yet the New Dealers managed to do more in FDR's first two terms than the progressives had done in two decades. Two months after he was elected a third time, Roosevelt said that he envisioned a world where people could live free of want and fear. That was the vision that guided the administration throughout the 1930s—and to a remarkable degree it made the vision real.[17]

The New Dealers' most pressing goal was to get people back to work. For much of FDR's first two terms they focused on direct relief, putting millions of people on the federal payroll, mostly doing construction and conservation projects. In the late 1930s, the administration began to move in a radically different direction. The government could best help the unemployed not by giving them jobs, policy makers decided, but by promoting economic growth. That was best done by using vigorous public investment to stimulate demand, thus spurring the private sector to hire more workers. In short, the New Dealers discovered Keynesianism.[18]

The Keynesian turn was laid upon reforms the New Dealers had put in place to counter the cruelties of the marketplace. One set of policies reached into the countryside, which the Depression had savaged; in 1933, cotton was selling at 6 cents a pound, down from 18 three years before; wheat at 32 cents a bushel, down from $1.12. In response, the New Deal created a complex system of price supports designed to restore and stabilize farmers' incomes. Another set of programs promised to help those the market had shunted aside. There were a number of such initiatives: electric power for farm families, labor camps for the rural poor, public housing for the urban poor.

But the key piece of legislation was the Social Security Act of 1935, which pushed to new levels the progressive idea of helping the deserving poor. One piece of the act provided a federal supplement to the old state system of mothers' pensions, now renamed Aid for Dependent Children (ADC). Another provided newly unemployed workers three or four months of government benefits, long enough, it was hoped, to get them back on their feet. And the most popular provision gave the aged a monthly stipend, a transfer payment that almost everyone came to believe was a pension plan.

Then there were those reforms aimed at the factory floor. In 1933 and again in 1935, federal law guaranteed working people the right to form unions of their own choosing. It took them a few years to grab hold of the opportunity. But when they did, in the late 1930s, unionization rolled across the industrial heartland, bringing with it seniority systems, safety standards, and grievance procedures that workers embraced as fervently as they did their new union wages. The first few years after the United Automobile Workers organized the sprawling Chrysler Assembly Plant in Detroit, workers flooded their new grievance process with demands for improved working conditions. And of all the changes they might have asked for, none was more important than having Chrysler provide them with heavy-duty gloves.[19]

Of course, the New Deal did not end the Depression, as its critics continually point out. It didn't spend enough. Its relief payments were too low. It excluded too many people from coverage altogether: to cite the most egregious case, Social Security's retirement provisions excluded both farm laborers and domestic workers, a blatantly racist move intended to prevent many southern blacks from receiving the same benefits as whites. And some of the poorest Americans it hurt more than it helped, none worse than the sharecroppers and tenant farmers, black and white, who were forced off the land by the administration's agricultural policies.[20]

What the New Dealers didn't accomplish in the 1930s, though, they did during the Second World War. Wartime spending pumped an astounding 130 billion federal dollars into the economy, almost three times the amount the New Dealers spent during the entire Depression decade. Spectacular spending triggered spectacular economic growth, as Keynes had said it would: unemployment, still at 14.6 percent in 1940, fell to less than 2 percent by 1943. And because much of the money went to unionized companies—General Motors, General Electric, U.S. Steel—a fair share was pumped into workers' paychecks; between 1940 and 1945, industrial workers' real income went up by 27 percent, even as farm prices shot up by 50 percent. "Going to work in the navy yard, I felt like something had come down from heaven," one man told an interviewer years later. "I went from forty cents an hour to . . . two seventy-five an hour. . . . After all the hardships of the Depression, the war completely turned my life around."[21]

That was only the beginning. After the war, the economy entered into a dizzying upward spiral, as Americans made up for almost two decades of deprivation in an orgy of consumer spending. To meet the demand, factories hired even more workers: in the 1950s, the United States added 2 million manufacturing jobs, a substantial portion of which were unionized. So wages continued to rise even as profits soared—between 1950 and 1960 the median family income increased by 30 percent— while the number of Americans living in poverty tumbled. At the end of World War II, about a third of the population fell below the poverty line, an extraordinary improvement since the depths of the Depression. By 1960, that figure had been cut to 21 percent.[22]

Three years later came the century's third great burst of reform. It was sparked by the civil rights revolution then surging across the South, which thrust into public life fundamental questions of justice and equality. It was shaped by the promise of prosperity. "We have the opportunity to move not only toward the rich society," said President Lyndon Johnson at the height of his power, "but toward the Great Society." Already Social Security had expanded its reach by eliminating the unconscionable exclusions of the 1930s. Now its benefits could be made more generous so beneficiaries could live a little better. The ADC rolls had likewise grown since the 1930s; now eligibility rules could be loosened so more families could be served. For the first time, the elderly and the poor could be given health care along with their checks, through the marvels of Medicare and Medicaid. The government could spend more money on education, too, creating reading programs for preschoolers, improving grade schools and high schools, offering free lunches to poor kids, giving young people training in the trades, and providing those who needed them with college loans. And it might even remake the inner cities, tearing down the slums and putting in their place new communities.[23]

If all that sounded like the New Deal, well—it was. LBJ wanted nothing more, said Doris Kearns Goodwin, than "to out-Roosevelt Roosevelt." But the new reform movement moved in other ways as well, stretching past the New Deal to the progressive tradition, from social welfare to regulation. For the good of the whole, some liberals argued, the federal government had to prevent corporations from polluting the atmosphere, making harmful products, or maintaining dangerous facilities, just as the progressives had tried to regulate tenements and factory floors. Obviously the new rules cut into corporate profits. But the country could afford to trim back business just a bit. In the 1960s, it seemed, the United States could afford anything it wanted.[24]

It's important not to exaggerate prosperity's reach; to imagine, as some observers did, that in the twenty-five years after World War II America had become a middle-class nation. In 1967, a typical auto worker, one of the best paid industrial workers in the country, earned barely enough to meet the government standard for a "modest" standard of living. To live modestly in the mid-1960s, though, was to own your own home, albeit a small one; to own your own car, albeit an older one; to have enough money to feed and clothe your family and even to take them out to dinner and a movie once in a while; and to imagine that you might send your kids to college instead of the factory, maybe just a community college or a state school, but a college nonetheless. It meant that you didn't have to live in dread of being injured on the job, because if you did there'd be compensation; or being laid off, because there'd be a couple of months of benefits; or growing old, because you had a Social Security card tucked away in your wallet, a union pension plan sitting in a drawer, and health care coverage waiting for you when your working days were done.[25] It meant that you were safe, something your parents and grandparents couldn't have said, couldn't have really imagined when they were your age. And there was nothing modest about that.

Bit by bit the fear returned. First came the great economic crisis of the 1970s, an upheaval so profound it toppled the industrial system reformers had spent seven decades trying to tame. Battered by inflation and surging international competition, manufacturing firms began to shed jobs, while investors flocked to the service sector, where profit margins were much more attractive. The old industrial core went into free fall: by 1982 Detroit had an unemployment rate of 16 percent, while neighboring Flint, once the blue-collar heart of the General Motors empire, hit 21 percent.

As the system fell, so did the promise of postwar liberalism. Late in the decade, conservatives took control of the national agenda, led by an intellectual phalanx preaching the virtues of the free market and a political class promising to get government off the backs of its people. For the past three decades that's what they've done, slowly stripping away the policies liberals had put in place, making government over in their own image. In the process they shattered the sense of security that defined mid-century America and put in its place the callousness of a new Gilded Age.[26]

The change hit the poor with particular force. Attacking welfare cheats had long been a stock part of conservative politics. In the 1970s and 1980s, the right turned against the very idea of welfare, which they insisted had created a permanent underclass utterly dependent on federal largesse. "We fought a war on poverty," Ronald Reagan liked to say, "and poverty won." That was patently untrue, as even a glance at the statistics would have shown: in 1974 only 11.2 percent of Americans lived in poverty, by far its lowest rate in the twentieth century, down from 19 percent ten years before, thanks to the social and economic policies Reagan derided. But the rhetoric proved to be incredibly powerful.

Throughout the 1980s, policy makers slashed the funding for poverty programs. In the 1990s, they ended ADC altogether, replacing it with a "welfare to work" program designed to move the poor into the job market. But that assumed there were jobs to be found. When the Great Recession hit in 2007 and the unemployment rate skyrocketed, the poor had a dangerously shredded safety net to catch them: a family relying solely on the federal government's temporary assistance program, ostensibly the poor's last line of defense, would have an income 80 percent below the poverty line. Little wonder that almost 50 million Americans struggled to feed themselves or their families at some point in 2010.[27]

The conservative ascendancy transformed working-class life as well. Together, deindustrialization and government hostility all but destroyed the labor movement; today, less that 12 percent of workers belong to unions. As unions withered, so did the protections they offered. An average factory worker makes less now, in real terms, than he or she would have in 1960. The number of firms offering employees health care and pension plans has declined precipitously. And in workplaces everywhere—not just in factories but in stores and offices, even classrooms—power rests almost completely at management's hands.

Abuses inevitably follow, especially at the lower end of the job market. Researchers recently surveyed New Jersey day laborers, many of them immigrants drawn to the United States by the latest upheavals in the global economy, about their experiences on the job. Two-thirds reported that at least once last year they were paid less than they'd been promised, while some of them weren't paid at all; 40 percent said they weren't given even rudimentary safety equipment; and 26 percent said that a boss had physically assaulted them. But in New Jersey, as in much of the country, the state isn't willing to demand that employers do the right thing, and to turn the force of law against them when they don't. So the violations go unnoticed, except by those who have to endure them.[28]

Now the assault on big government is spreading. At the moment, 55 million people get Social Security checks each month. More than 90 million rely on Medicare or Medicaid to cover their health care costs. And 7.5 million are receiving unemployment benefits, up from 2.6 million a few years ago. But all of those programs, once considered sacrosanct, are under threat, some in small ways—policy makers are talking about adjusting Social Security's cost-of-living mechanism, for instance—and some large: by the end of this year, the federal government will have scaled back the maximum time the unemployed can receive benefits by six months in those states hardest hit by the recession, more in states where the economic downturn hasn't been as severe. As that happens, the insecurity that haunts poorer neighborhoods has started to seep into the once safe streets of the middle class. For many Americans, that's the legacy of the last thirty years: the terrifying realization that the future isn't necessarily going to be better, that with one unlucky turn everything could go terribly wrong. An echo of the nineteenth century reverberating through the twenty-first, a Dickensian America reborn.[29]

As the memorial service began, they turned on the helmets' lamps, pinpricks of light for the president to pass as he made his way to the podium. When he spoke he seemed to understand. "All the hard work; all the hardship; all the time spent underground; it was all for their families," he said. "For a car in the driveway. For a roof overhead. For a chance to give their kids opportunities they never knew; and enjoy retirement with their wives. It was all in the hopes of something better. These miners lived—as they died—in pursuit of the American dream.... How can we fail them?... How can we let anyone in this country put their lives at risk by simply showing up to work; by simply pursuing the American dream?"[30]

He hugged them—fathers and mothers, brothers and sisters, sons and daughters, and far too many widows—and said a few words to each. Then his handlers swept him away. The lights went off. And they drifted back to their too-quiet houses and their half-empty beds and the thought of what might have been.

Twenty-nine helmets, twenty-nine lives.

CHAPTER 6

The Right to a Decent Home

Thomas J. Sugrue

"A man is not a whole and complete man," wrote poet Walt Whitman, "unless he owns a house and the ground it stands on." America's lesser bards sang of "my old Kentucky home" and "Home Sweet Home," leading no less than that great critic Herbert Hoover to declaim that their ballads "were not written about tenements or apartments...they never sing about a pile of rent receipts." To own a home is to be American. To rent is to be something less.[1]

Every generation has offered its own version of the claim that owner-occupied homes are the nation's saving grace. During the Cold War, homeownership was moral armor, protecting America from dangerous outside influences. "No man who owns his own house and lot can be a Communist," proclaimed builder William Levitt, most famous for his massive Levittown communities in New York, Pennsylvania, and New Jersey.[2]

With no more Reds hiding under the beds, President Bill Clinton launched National Homeownership Day in 1995, offering a new rationale about personal responsibility. "You want to reinforce family values in America, encourage two-parent households, get people to stay home?" Clinton answered his own question, "Make it easy for people to own their own homes and enjoy the rewards of family life and see their work rewarded. This is a big deal."[3] And in a rare pause in the partisan warfare of the early 2000s, George W. Bush similarly pledged his commitment to creating "an ownership society in this country, where more Americans than ever will be able to open up their door where they live and say, welcome to my house, welcome to my piece of property."[4]

Surveys show that Americans buy into such gauzy platitudes about the character-building qualities of homeownership. A February 2009 Pew survey reported that nine out of ten homeowners viewed their homes as a "comfort." And even those who did not own their own homes planned to do so in the future and believed that homeownership is not only a lifestyle choice but also a sound investment.[5]

Americans have come to see their homes as both a comfort and as an investment; the source of both their identity and their wealth. For most Americans, their home is their single most important (and often only) asset—a more essential part of a family's financial portfolio than stocks and bonds, pensions, and savings accounts.

This is the most distinctive feature of homeownership in the United States. Some countries—such as Spain and Italy—have higher rates of homeownership than the United States, but in those countries homes are often purchased with the support of extended families and are places to settle for the long term, not to flip to eager buyers or trade up for a McMansion. In France, Germany, and Switzerland, renting is more common than purchasing. There, most people invest their earnings in the stock market or pension funds or squirrel it away in savings accounts. In those countries, whether you are a renter or an owner, houses have greater use value than exchange value.

But in modern America, it has become axiomatic that a home can be both a dwelling and an investment vehicle, even if studies have shown that—with the exception of boom years—real estate has not appreciated more rapidly than stocks for most of the last century.

America's homeowning exceptionalism is a relatively new development. For most Americans, until recently, homeownership was a dream, and a pile of rent receipts was the reality. From 1900, when the US Census Bureau first started gathering data on homeownership, through 1940, fewer than half of all Americans owned their own homes. Homeownership rates in the United States actually fell in three of the first four decades of the twentieth century. But from that point forward (with the exception of the 1980s, when interest rates were staggeringly high, and the post-2006 years, after the collapse of the mortgage market), the percentage of Americans living in owner-occupied homes marched steadily upward.

Today more than two-thirds of Americans own their own homes. Among whites, more than 75 percent are homeowners today. Homeownership is enshrouded in myth—the stuff of some of the hoariest clichés of American history, the supposed consequence of the work ethic. But the story of how the dream became a reality is not one of independence, self-sufficiency, and entrepreneurial pluck. It is not the story of the triumphant march of the free market. Instead it is a different kind of American story, of government, financial regulation, and tax policy.[6]

We are a nation of homeowners and home speculators because of the close collaboration of the federal government and the home construction, banking, and real estate industries. It was not until government stepped into the housing market, during the extraordinary crisis of the Great Depression, that renting began its long downward spiral and rates of homeownership skyrocketed. Before the Crash, government played a minuscule role in housing Americans, other than building barracks and constructing temporary housing during wartime. And in a little-noticed provision in the 1913 federal tax code, allowing for the deduction of home mortgage interest payments.

Until the early twentieth century, holding a mortgage came with a stigma. You were a debtor, and chronic indebtedness was a problem to be avoided, like too much drinking or gambling. The four words "keep out of debt" or "pay as you go" appeared in countless advice books. "Thriftlessness—debt—mars and stains the soul," proclaimed a 1920s sermon. Fearful of the sin or stigma of indebtedness, many middle-class Americans—even those with a taste for single-family houses—rented or spent years saving money so they would not have to take on large amounts of debt to buy a home. Home Sweet Home did not lose its sweetness because someone else held the title.[7]

In any case, mortgages were hard to come by. Lenders typically required 50 percent or more of the purchase price as a down payment. Interest rates were high and terms were short, usually just three to five years.[8] In 1920, John Taylor Boyd Jr., an expert on real estate finance, lamented that with the high cost of home loans, "increasing numbers of our people are finding homeownership too burdensome to attempt."[9]

As a result, there were two kinds of homeowners in the United States: working-class folks who built their own houses because they were not eligible for mortgages or could not afford high-interest home loans, and the wealthy, who usually paid for their places outright. (During the last decades of the nineteenth century and the first three decades of the twentieth, wealthy suburbanites moved into homes built to resemble large-scale colonial homes or plantation houses or British country estates or manors in Normandy.) Still, even many of the richest rented— because they had better places to invest than in the volatile housing market. During the 1920s, nearly every big city saw the development of grand apartment houses, with huge rooms and such luxuries as libraries, fireplaces, and servants' quarters.[10]

The Depression turned everything on its head. Between 1928, the last year of the boom, and 1933, new housing starts fell by 95 percent. Half of all mortgages were in default. To shore up the market, Herbert Hoover signed the Federal Home Loan

Bank Act in 1932, laying the groundwork for massive federal intervention in the housing market. (Though Hoover would become a staunch critic of government programs during most of his post-presidential career, during the period from World War I, when he directed government-run war relief efforts, through the early 1930s, he was not averse to strengthening government's role in the economy, nor was he an economic libertarian).[11]

Hoover's program was but a first step in expanding the federal role in the housing market. The New Deal went much further. In 1933, as one of the signature programs of his first hundred days, President Franklin Roosevelt (FDR) created the Home Owners' Loan Corporation to provide low-interest loans to help out foreclosed homeowners. In 1934, he created the Federal Housing Administration (FHA), which set standards for home construction, instituted twenty-five- and thirty-year mortgages, and cut interest rates. And in 1938, his administration created the Federal National Mortgage Association (Fannie Mae), which created the secondary market in mortgages. In 1944, the federal government extended generous mortgage assistance through the Veterans Administration to returning soldiers, most of whom could not have otherwise afforded a house. Together, these innovations had epochal consequences.[12]

President Roosevelt and the New Dealers had many reasons for stepping up their intervention in the housing market. They responded to pressure from farmers and homeowners who were thrown out of their houses and took to the streets in protest. The federal government also hoped to bolster the flagging construction industry and spur the purchase of building materials—from wood beams to cement mix to copper wire and steel for furnaces—thus jump-starting consumption and creating jobs for hundreds of thousands of Americans as carpenters, electricians, plumbers and pipefitters, plasterers, tile-layers, masons, and roofers. And Roosevelt wanted to stabilize the banks and savings and loan associations involved in home finance. Above all, Roosevelt couched his pro-homeownership policies in moral terms, perhaps best summed up in his 1944 Inaugural Address, in which he spoke of "the right of every family to a decent home."[13]

Easy credit, underwritten by federal housing programs, boosted the rates of homeownership quickly. By 1950, 55 percent of Americans had a place they could call their own. By 1970, the figure had risen to 63 percent. For many Americans, it was now cheaper to buy than to rent. Federal intervention also unleashed vast amounts of capital that turned home construction and real estate into critical economic sectors. The banking, financial, and insurance industries expanded exponentially as they bought, bundled, and sold mortgages, insured titles and houses, and invested in real estate. Federally backed mortgages reduced the risk in the housing market and allowed developers to assemble the capital necessary for large-scale housing developments. (Mass-produced suburban communities like Lakewood, California; Forest Park, Illinois; and the Levittowns in New York, New Jersey, Pennsylvania, and elsewhere would have been impossible without government-backed financing.) In 1959, for the first time, the US Census Bureau began collecting monthly data on new housing starts—which quickly became a leading indicator of the nation's economic vitality.[14]

The story of government involvement in the housing market is riddled with irony—for at the same time that Uncle Sam brought the dream of homeownership to fruition, he kept his role mostly hidden, except to the army of banking, real estate, and construction lobbyists who arose to protect their industry's newfound gains.

Tens of millions of Americans owned their own homes because of government programs, but they had no reason to doubt that their homeownership was a result of their own virtue and hard work, their own grit and determination—not because they were the beneficiaries of one of the grandest government programs ever. Federal housing officials did not post billboards that read "Park Forest made possible by government largesse" or

"Big government is housing YOU!" The only housing programs prominently associated with Washington's policy makers were underfunded, unpopular public housing projects built in urban centers, mostly between the late 1930s and the early 1970s. (Under America's two-tiered system of housing policy, subsidies for private housing dwarfed expenditures on public housing developments.) Chicago's bleak, soulless Robert Taylor and State Street Homes and their ilk, which provided apartments for working and low-income families—not New York's vast Levittown or California's sprawling Lakewood—became the symbol of big government. Urban renewal projects and their impoverished, segregated minority residents became the face of federal housing policy.[15]

The main reason for the invisibility of the federal role in suburban sprawl was that the Federal Housing Administration and the Home Loan Bank Board, working closely with the real estate and home construction industry, engaged in an extensive advertising and public relations campaign, casting federal mortgage programs as little more than incentives to unlock the potential of the private sector. The FHA was, in the words of its promotional literature, "a helper only," a "do-it-yourself program" that succeeded because of "the builders, lenders, realtors, and other members of industry with whom it has worked and the American families whose enterprise and integrity have made the program succeed." The centrality of public policy was obscured in the mists of celebratory rhetoric about the market and self-help. But the modern housing market was in no sense private: it was the creature of federal policy, created and transformed by the government.[16]

Behind the scenes in the post–New Deal years, the real estate, home finance, and construction industries built a close relationship with the government agencies that funded them—and spent considerable sums on lawyers and lobbyists who ensured that the interests of the housing industry were well represented on Capitol Hill. In addition, federal housing agencies collaborated closely with the private sector—many housing officials came to government with experience as bankers, brokers, and builders, and vice versa, many housing officials used their experience to open doors for future careers working for mortgage and real estate firms.

Together, federal housing agencies and real estate professionals laid the groundwork for the rise of large-scale housing development firms that could build mass-produced housing on a vast scale; they enshrined the ideal of detached, single-family homes surrounded by large lawns as the norm for all Americans; and they created and perpetuated patterns of residential segregation by race, all of which proved deeply resistant to change.

Federal housing policies remade the whole landscape of America. Most important, they made possible the rapid expansion of suburbia. For most of the nineteenth and early twentieth centuries, suburbs housed well-off households and the servants, groundskeepers, and maintenance workers who depended on them. The prosperity of the 1920s led to a growth in suburbs—but nothing of the scope and scale of the postwar years. The sprawl of postwar housing developments would have been impossible without federal programs that minimized risk and thus allowed developers to accumulate the capital necessary to build on a large scale.

Likewise, federal home loan guidelines favored the construction of a certain type of housing in a very distinctive landscape—namely, the single-family detached home on a relatively large lot. As early as 1938, in a pamphlet entitled *Planning Profitable Neighborhoods*, the Federal Housing Administration encouraged developers to lay out houses in a pattern that would become commonplace after World War II—along curvilinear streets and cul-de-sacs, distant from business districts, cut off from thoroughfares. It was not solely or primarily Americans' desire for green open space that led to suburban sprawl; it was the guidance of federal housing agencies in collaboration with real estate brokers, developers, and planners.[17]

The invisible hand of federal policy democratized homeownership—but with a very important exception.

Between the 1930s and the 1960s, the dream of homeownership was branded "whites only." The Home Owners' Loan Corporation, Federal Housing Administration, and Veterans Administration played a decisive role in creating and maintaining racial segregation in America's housing market. Under guidelines for lenders and builders, federally underwritten mortgages and home loans were unavailable to residents of racially mixed or "transitional" neighborhoods. The presence of even a single black family—unless they were live-in servants or household staff—rendered a whole neighborhood "actuarially unsound."

To provide lenders with guidance, the Home Owners' Loan Corporation prepared "neighborhood security maps" that were elaborately drawn and backed up with detailed descriptions of a neighborhood's housing stock and racial, ethnic, and class composition. The best neighborhoods were denoted "A" and "B" and colored green and blue on maps; the riskiest neighborhoods were labeled "C" and "D" and colored yellow and red. If any "inharmonious racial and ethnic groups" lived in the same neighborhood, "stability" would be at risk. Residents in neighborhoods with old housing stock (at risk of "transition to lower class occupancy," as federal guidelines specified) or with even a handful of black residents were marked "D" and were usually ineligible for government-backed loans. To preserve "stability," FHA officials supported the use of restrictive covenants—clauses in home titles that forbade the use or occupancy of a property by any group other than "whites" or "Caucasians"—until such restrictions were ruled unenforceable by the Supreme Court in 1948.[18]

The racial guidelines that federal housing agencies used were similar to those devised by bankers, actuaries, and planners—here, too, there was a feedback loop between practices in the real estate industry and federal guidelines. Neither party—federal housing officials nor mortgage lenders—had incentive to change the racial categories. Real estate brokers and builders did not want to jeopardize a development's eligibility for federally backed loans; federal housing officials did not want to undermine racial practices that were condoned by actuaries and real estate professionals.

Racial discrimination was built into the very code of ethics in the real estate industry. From the 1930s through the 1960s, the National Association of Real Estate Boards (which trademarked the name Realtor) issued guidelines that specified that a Realtor "should never be instrumental in introducing to a neighborhood a character of property or occupancy, members of any race or nationality, or any individual whose presence will be clearly detrimental to property values in a neighborhood." Lest there be any confusion, an industry brochure offered guidance. "The prospective buyer might be a bootlegger who would cause considerable annoyance to his neighbors, a madam who had a number of call girls on her string, a gangster who wants a screen for his activities by living in a better neighborhood, a colored man of means who was giving his children a college education and thought they were entitled to live among whites.... No matter what the motive or character of the would-be purchaser, if the deal would institute a form of blight, then certainly the well-meaning broker must work against its consummation."[19]

Neighborhood ratings became a self-fulfilling prophecy. Minorities were confined to neighborhoods with older housing stock, but were usually unable to get subsidized mortgages and home improvement loans to better their properties. As a result, housing conditions in older, urban neighborhoods often deteriorated rapidly. Without federal subsidy, developers were usually unwilling to build new houses that would be open on a nondiscriminatory basis. Between 1920 and 1990, nearly every major American metropolitan area grew more segregated by black and white. Many observers then, as now, attributed racial divisions to the sum of individual choices—"birds of a feather flock together," "like lives with like."[20]

But racially separate neighborhoods were not the norm in the United States before the early twentieth century. In most big cities in the North before the first decades of the twentieth century, blacks shared the same neighborhoods as many European immigrants; in much of the South, they lived on or adjoining the properties of whites who employed them as domestics or household laborers. Racial segregation in housing gained real traction only with the advent of federal housing programs. And it remained in place because Congress was unwilling to tinker with racial restrictions on mortgages. Even as the black freedom struggle escalated in the 1950s, the Eisenhower administration resisted efforts to abolish discrimination in housing. The issue was so controversial that it took civil rights activists two years to persuade President John F. Kennedy to issue a mild executive order forbidding discrimination on all federally backed mortgages, and even then, he limited it to houses built after 1962 and signed the order on the Saturday before Thanksgiving, after the midterm elections, when it would attract little attention.[21]

In 1964, President Johnson and Congress did not seriously consider adding an antidiscrimination measure to the landmark Civil Rights Act. Not until 1968 did Congress forbid discrimination in the real estate market, but even then it left weak enforcement mechanisms in place, making it costly and time-consuming to document and challenge racial bias in housing. It proved to be too little, too late—housing segregation had become so deeply entrenched, so much a part of people's expectations, that it proved very difficult to uproot.[22]

By the 1960s and 1970s, however, those who had been excluded from the postwar housing boom demanded their own piece of the action—and slowly got it. The newly created Department of Housing and Urban Development (HUD) expanded homeownership programs for excluded minorities; the 1976 Community Reinvestment Act required banks to channel resources to underserved neighborhoods; and activists successfully pushed Fannie Mae to underwrite loans to homebuyers once considered too risky for conventional loans. Minority homeownership rates crept upward—though they still remained far behind those of whites and it was still difficult for minorities to buy houses in all-white communities. Even at the peak of the early twenty-first-century real estate bubble, just under 50 percent of blacks and Latinos owned their own homes. It is unlikely that minority homeownership rates will rise again for a while. In the last boom year, 2006, almost 54 percent of blacks and 47 percent of Hispanics assumed subprime mortgages, compared to only 18 percent of non-Hispanic whites. One in ten black homeowners is likely to face foreclosure proceedings, compared to only one in twenty-five whites.[23]

Roosevelt had invoked the right of every American to a decent home and to the security that came with low interest rates and affordable mortgages, and the federal government delivered on that promise for tens of millions of Americans—most of them white. Homeownership offered real benefits—perhaps most significant was the creation of wealth.

For most Americans, housing is the most important asset in a portfolio that might also include stocks and bonds, art and jewelry, and items of rapidly depreciating value like cars. Homeowners could use the equity in their real estate to get access to home improvement loans, to pay for college tuition, and to pass on inheritances to their children. Here, too, however, the long history of racial discrimination had devastating effects. In 2003, the average household wealth of African Americans was just one-tenth that of whites, in large part because of differential holdings of real estate.[24]

During the late 1990s and the first years of the new century, the dream of homeownership turned hallucinogenic. The home-financing industry—with the impetus of the administrations of both Bill Clinton and George W. Bush—engaged in the biggest promotion of homeownership in decades. Both presidents pushed for public-private partnerships, with HUD and the government-supported financiers like Fannie Mae serving as the mostly silent partners in a rapidly metastasizing mortgage market.[25]

At the same time, government regulators loosened their control of the mortgage market and allowed bankers and financiers to develop new tools, including the securitization of mortgages and the expansion of subprime lending. Rates of homeownership rose during this period to record highs—but lenders also pushed high-interest and risky mortgages on people desperate to own their own homes. Predatory lenders fanned out over poor and working-class neighborhoods, playing on people's deep-rooted desires to own their own homes. They engaged in reckless profit seeking at the expense of would-be homeowners. Frequently, lenders did perfunctory background checks on mortgagors, disregarded individuals' problematic credit histories, appraised properties for more than they were worth, and issued loans that were often greater than a home's value at interest rates well above the standard. Another common practice—which expanded because of lax regulation—was to issue flexible mortgages, at interest rates that were initially low but would quickly rise, making it more difficult for homeowners to make monthly payments.

Because they had long been excluded from the conventional mortgage market, minorities were especially eager to be homeowners—and especially vulnerable to predatory lending. In 2006, more than half of subprime loans went to African Americans, who comprised only 13 percent of the population. And a recent study of data from the Home Mortgage Disclosure Act found that 32.1 percent of blacks, but only 10.5 percent of whites, got higher priced mortgages—that is, mortgages with an annual percentage rate three or more points higher than the rate of a Treasury security of the same length. The result has been growing economic insecurity among African Americans, even those of middle-class status.[26]

At the same time, mortgage lenders encouraged speculation. As housing values rose astronomically in the first decade of the twenty-first century (fueled, in part, by easy credit), would-be investors looked to real estate as an easy get-rich scheme. Housing developers—eager to meet the seemingly insatiable demand for new housing—overbuilt. Places like the Central Valley of California, metropolitan Las Vegas, and Miami were particularly hard hit by speculative overbuilding. The notion of home-as-haven, already weak, was replaced with the notion of home-as-jackpot.

The housing crisis in the early twenty-first century also shed light on the limitations of a century's worth of federal housing policy—and how far the country had moved from Roosevelt's vision of a decent home for all. For one, federal programs seldom benefited renters (except those very low-income people who competed for a dwindling number of places in subsidized public housing projects or for scarce vouchers that they could use to rent apartments). In addition, the benefits of federal homeownership programs disproportionately went to the richest Americans. Those making between $40,000 and $70,000 (the middle class) were less likely to use the home mortgage tax deduction; those making over $250,000 annually (the richest 2 percent) got the lion's share of pro-homeownership tax benefits and could even deduct interest payments on their second homes from their taxes. Poor and working-class Americans were also much more likely to suffer foreclosures—or to be stuck owing more on their overleveraged homes than the properties were worth in the collapsing housing market.

For millions of Americans at risk of foreclosure, the home has become something else altogether: a source of panic and despair. Those emotions were on full display in August 2009, when an estimated 53,000 people packed the Save the Dream fair at Atlanta's World Congress Center. The fair's planners, with the support of the US Department of Housing and Urban Development, brought together struggling homeowners, housing counselors, and lenders, including industry giants Bank of America and Citigroup, to renegotiate at-risk mortgages. Even though Georgia's housing market has been devastated by the current economic crisis, the rush of desperate homeowners surprised everyone. Fear and panic have turned the dream of homeownership into a nightmare.[27]

Atlanta represents the current housing crisis in microcosm—similar stories could be told of Detroit or Charlotte, or smaller cities like Stockton, California, or Euclid, Ohio. Since the second quarter of 2006, housing values across the United States have fallen by one-third. Over a million homes were lost to foreclosure nationwide in 2008, as homeowners struggled to meet payments. Foreclosure rates continued to rise in 2009, when during the summer, owners of one in every 355 houses in the country received default or auction notices or had their homes seized by creditors.[28]

The collapse in confidence in securitized, high-risk mortgages also devastated some of the nation's largest banks and lenders. The home financing giant Fannie Mae alone held an estimated $230 billion in toxic assets. Even if there are signs of hope on the horizon (the collapse in home prices seems to have leveled off in some parts of the country), analysts like Yale's Robert Shiller expect that housing prices will remain level for the next five years. Many economists, like the Wharton School's Joseph Gyourko, are beginning to make the case that public policies should encourage renting, or at least put it on a level playing field with homeownership. A June 2009 survey commissioned by the National Foundation for Credit Counseling found a deep-seated pessimism about homeownership, suggesting that even if renting does not yet have cachet, it is the only choice left for those who have been burned by the housing market. One-third of respondents did not believe they would ever be able to own a home. Of those who had once purchased a home but did not own one at the time of the survey, 42 percent believed that they would never own one again.[29]

Those desperate homeowners who gathered at Atlanta's convention center—and their counterparts nationwide—having lost their investments, abruptly woke up from the dream of trouble-free homeownership and endless returns on their few percent down. They spent hours lined up in the hot sun, some sobbing, others nervously reading the fine print on their adjustable rate mortgage forms for the first time, wondering if their house would be the next to go on the auction block, their dream, going going gone.

History, however, does not usually repeat itself. The current housing crisis—the most severe since the Great Depression—has not prompted a new round of policy innovation. After the 2008 bailouts of lending institutions, policy makers and politicians talked about creating programs to bail out struggling homeowners. In 2009, the Obama administration did create a program to help struggling homeowners—through a partnership with major mortgage lending firms. But the program has had little effect in stabilizing the market. In addition, efforts to step up the regulation of the housing finance sector have met with fierce political resistance. It would be bad history to romanticize the New Deal efforts to protect homeownership: like most public policies, their results were mixed at best.

What is clear is that the federal government—whether it stands back and leaves mortgagors loosely regulated or whether it redirects housing policies to improve housing for ordinary, working Americans—has been a major player in real estate for decades, and whether by default or neglect or action, will remain so for a long time to come. At the beginning of the second decade of the twenty-first century, however, it does not appear that the housing crisis will lead to the policy innovation of the New Deal.

CHAPTER 7

Solving the Nation's Number One Health Problem(s)

Karen Kruse Thomas

Consider these two data points from opposite ends of the twentieth century:

> In 1900, a newborn American citizen had an average life expectancy of 47 years. A heartbreaking 10 percent of all infants died before their first birthday, and infant mortality was far higher among the rural and urban poor, whether on southern farms or in northern tenements.

> A century later, an American born in 2000 could expect to live 75 years, and infant deaths had been cut by 93 percent.[1]

These striking reductions in morbidity and mortality rates resulted from not only a rising standard of living but also the advent of effective methods for detecting, preventing, and treating disease; new breakthroughs in medical research; and markedly improved access to health facilities and services.

In all these areas of medical and public health progress, the federal government has played a fundamental role as both sponsor and coordinator of a remarkably concerted effort involving communities, states, organizations, and institutions across

American society. The federal government therefore deserves a great deal of credit for doubling life expectancy for Americans, as well as for tackling a long and ever-changing list of problems regarded as the worst enemies of the nation's health.

In the early 1900s, for example, tuberculosis, pneumonia, diphtheria, and typhoid fever thrived in the densely crowded, foul-smelling cities that mushroomed in the era of rapid industrialization and immigration. By the 1920s, the major killers were heart disease, cancer, and stroke, but millions still suffered chronic disability caused by syphilis, tuberculosis, and polio. By 1950, over half a million Americans were institutionalized in state mental hospitals. In the 1960s and 1970s, drug addiction and alcoholism reached epidemic proportions. Rates of lung cancer rose steadily throughout what has been called "the cigarette century," increasing fivefold in males from 1930 to 1990 and continuing to rise in women. Acquired immunodeficiency syndrome (AIDS), caused by the human immunodeficiency virus (HIV), emerged as one of the most feared diseases in the 1980s and 1990s.[2]

Not only did the federal government respond to every major public health problem with legislation and the expertise of agencies such as the Food and Drug Administration, the Public Health Service (PHS), the National Institutes of Health, and the Centers for Disease Control but it also helped democratize advances in public health so that they reached areas of the country with the greatest need. And, as we shall see, no place has benefited more from federal health initiatives than the American South.

Indeed, the public health infrastructure of the nation—from research labs to hospitals to communication networks and immunization campaigns—stands as one of the triumphs of federal policy over the last century, and one that most of us simply take for granted. Oscar R. Ewing, who from 1947 to 1953 headed the Federal Security Agency (the predecessor of Health, Education, and Welfare and later Health and Human Services), was right when he said, "Our public health programs protect the health of the people in a thousand ways, often so silently and efficiently that most people do not realize that without them they would hardly last out the week."[3]

Public Health in a Progressive Age

We think of medicine and health as issues of individuals. Clinical medicine has been oriented toward curing acute disease in the individual patient, and the whole structure of the private health system, including medical education and research, centered on the seriously ill hospital patient.[4]

Public health, on the other hand, emphasizes preventing disease and controlling its transmission in large populations. The basic public health disciplines of epidemiology and biostatistics allowed health officers to survey the forest of disease among whole populations. Those scientists also used bacteriology and immunology to confirm the identity of disease-causing organisms in the laboratory.

In the post–Civil War era, perhaps the most influential public health research site was the Hygienic Laboratory, established in 1887. In 1902, Congress authorized it to regulate laboratories that produced "biologicals" for use in diagnostic tests and therapeutic compounds. The Hygienic Laboratory's four divisions (Bacteriology and Pathology, Chemistry, Pharmacology, and Zoology) conducted pathbreaking early studies on hookworm, plague, tularemia, Rocky Mountain spotted fever, poliomyelitis, pellagra, brucellosis, typhus, and influenza, which proved the value of careful epidemiological fieldwork teamed with top-notch laboratory investigation. The Hygienic Laboratory developed some of the most important diagnostic tests as well as the vaccines and antitoxins to prevent communicable diseases. Public health departments and private physicians cooperated to apply these discoveries in mass screening and immunization programs that became standard for American children.[5]

During the Progressive Era, the federal role in public health grew through measures such as the US Death Registry (begun in 1900 to track the causes and locations of deaths, which provided critical information for fighting epidemic disease), the 1906 Pure Food and Drug Act (which created the US Food and Drug Administration), the medical examination of arriving immigrants by PHS officers, and the reorganization and expansion of the PHS in 1912.

By 1920, public health departments in large northern cities provided services including sanitation, communicable disease control, maternal and child health, health education, laboratory tests, and collection of vital statistics. But these services were absent in much of the rural South and West, and what public health departments did exist were typically grossly understaffed by personnel with little or no public health training, often on a part-time basis.[6]

Working with Charles Wardell Stiles of the PHS, the Rockefeller Foundation committed $1 million to establish the Rockefeller Sanitary Commission to Eradicate Hookworm in 1909. The hookworm was known as "the germ of laziness" among southerners because it drained its host of energy by causing rapid weight loss, malnutrition, and often severe anemia. The Sanitary Commission's field agents tested rural citizens for hookworm, provided thymol to cure those who were infected, and built sanitary privies to prevent further spread of the disease. By 1915, over half a million southern children in 600 counties had been examined, over one-third of whom were infected. In Alabama, hookworm was present in every county, with infection rates as high as 62 percent.

Although hookworm was not entirely eradicated from the South, the campaign was extremely successful. It dispensed roughly 700,000 thymol and salts treatments and, more important, raised awareness among the public and medical profession of the disease's causes and clinical symptoms as well as how it could be prevented and cured. The campaign became a model for subsequent attacks on rural health problems both here and internationally.

The campaign against hookworm also helped to professional-ize public health and to build a national network of full-time local public health departments led by trained, state-appointed health officers. Armed with knowledge gained from the campaign, the PHS spearheaded the rural sanitation movement and initiated health education and disease prevention programs with the assistance of such organizations as the National Tuberculosis Association, the American Red Cross, and the federal Children's Bureau.[7]

During the 1930s and 1940s, however, the federal govern-ment assumed the lead in all public health efforts as national and international crises exhausted private sector resources and fos-tered public-private cooperation to address a new wave of health problems besieging the nation.

A New Deal for American Health

The Great Depression had a catastrophic impact on the health of Americans who could not afford medical care or even adequate diets. Rising levels of unemployment and poverty began to erase the recent gains in health status, particularly among those hit hardest and earliest in the agricultural sector. Between 1925 and 1935, death rates rose from pellagra, pneumonia/influenza, malaria, meningitis, and measles.[8]

The first aspect of public health to be targeted under the New Deal was sanitation. Public works programs constructed thousands of miles of water and sewer lines and built new treatment plants at a time when labor was available but local governments could not afford to make improvements. By 1942, federal programs had constructed nearly 3 million sanitary priv-ies in thirty-eight states and Puerto Rico.

Significantly, nearly two-thirds of these were in the under-improved South. Works Progress Administration (WPA) sani-tation projects drastically reduced the incidence of typhoid and dysentery in rural southern communities, which were also the primary beneficiaries of PHS and WPA malaria control programs.

To curtail mosquito breeding, the WPA drained several million acres of swamp and PHS officers sprayed mosquito-ridden areas with larvacides from airplanes and on foot. The incidence of waterborne illnesses dropped steadily, and the national typhoid mortality rate decreased by 90 percent from 1920 to 1945.[9]

The passage of the Social Security Act in 1935 marked a major health policy milestone and tipped the balance of federal-state cooperation decidedly toward Washington. Known primarily as a retirement program, the act also included Titles V and VI, which aided maternal and child health, and helped support health departments by providing matching grants to stimulate state and local spending. Social Security offered nearly $15 million to states annually for public health services, representing the first large-scale resources for many previously unserved areas.

Within two years, the number of full-time health units had doubled, and federal Social Security funds accounted for more than a third of public health spending in some states. The South's low per capita income and greater health needs resulted in larger allotments, and the PHS focused on the primarily southern problems of hookworm control, typhus, trachoma, and psittacosis as well as on the nationwide issues of syphilis, cancer, mental health, and rodent control.

Social Security grants helped train over 4,000 public health workers during the program's first four years, including large numbers of African American health professionals. The state universities of North Carolina, Michigan, California, and Minnesota established schools of public health, and most students received PHS Social Security fellowships. Despite overt resistance from conservatives suspicious of creeping federalism, the extreme conditions of the Great Depression fostered PHS-led efforts to equalize community access to public health and sanitation services across the nation.[10]

Public health was not only a preventive branch of medical science but also a government function designed to protect the common welfare. During the Franklin Roosevelt administration, policy makers increasingly relied on public health programs as a versatile tool to solve a wide range of problems—from reducing rates of loan defaults among farm families (commonly caused by health crises that left farmers unable to work) to ensuring the maximum productivity of defense industry workers and rehabilitating men who had been rejected for military service.[11]

By the late 1930s, New Deal reformers were eager to enact legislation to create a national system of financing health care for all who needed it. The framers of the Social Security Act had considered including health insurance as a benefit, but President Roosevelt had opposed the idea as too controversial.

Many reform groups, however, including organized labor, farmers, civic organizations, and philanthropies, grew more vocal in their calls for federal action to promote broader access to medical and hospital care. Senator Robert Wagner of New York introduced the first comprehensive national health legislation in 1939, and the Wagner-Murray-Dingell National Health Bill, introduced in 1943, was the first proposal for universal health insurance coverage underwritten by the federal government. But the American Medical Association (AMA) attacked national health insurance as "socialized medicine." Most physicians staunchly opposed any perceived government encroachment into the private health system, which they feared would interfere with the sacred relationship between doctor and patient and result in lower standards of care.[12]

Still, the success of New Deal public health efforts prompted many doctors to acknowledge, along with North Carolina's state health officer, Carl V. Reynolds, that "the government has a definite responsibility in the prevention and cure of disease and the preservation of health."[13]

World War II and the Health Front

The appeal of national health legislation surged after the attack on Pearl Harbor on December 7, 1941. Rising employment as well as wartime shortages of health professionals increased public demand for health care, the aspect of social policy (along with labor) most critical to national defense. When newspaper headlines announced that a high percentage of draftees had been rejected for various health reasons, national leaders recognized serious health deficiencies as threatening America's fighting effectiveness. Draft rejection statistics also revealed that illness and disability disproportionately affected southerners, rural residents, and African Americans, which further fueled the drive for health reform targeted at these groups.

The numbers were sobering: at least 40 percent of the 22 million men of military age were unfit for general military duty, and 4.5 million of these were classified as "IV-F"; this number included half of southern recruits versus only one third of nonsoutherners. In North Carolina, which posted the highest rejection rate, 71 percent of black and 49 percent of white recruits were deemed unfit for service.[14]

The wartime drive to pass federal health legislation also fueled civil rights activism. During an era of hostility to any civil rights measures, congressional hearings on the national health legislation of the 1940s gave representatives of every major national black organization an alternative forum to promote equality and the full inclusion of blacks in federally sponsored health programs.

Although segregation remained in effect in the South, this medical civil rights movement succeeded in enacting federally enforced nondiscrimination provisions to ensure that black patients could receive equal care in public health clinics and modern new hospitals that accepted federal grants. Federal support for training programs such as the Army Cadet Nurse Corps and medical residencies in Veterans Administration hospitals increased the ranks of health professionals while also offering equal opportunity to Americans of all races and religions.[15] As Surgeon General Thomas Parran put it, "every citizen, North and South, colored and white, rich and poor, has an inalienable right to his citizen's share of health protection."[16]

To develop solutions to high-priority health problems of military importance, the PHS and the Armed Forces Epidemiological Board took responsibility for protecting the health of American troops through measures such as venereal disease (VD) and malaria control, tropical disease research, and mental hygiene programs to prevent and treat combat-related disorders. Parran's mobilization of the PHS for the war effort was a master stroke that framed health reform as an urgent matter of national defense and garnered unprecedented federal funding for broad-based programs to support public health and sanitation services, medical research, and hospital construction. Wartime federal spending rose to ten times that for peacetime New Deal programs, and health was among the top beneficiaries.[17]

Dollar for dollar, two of the most valuable investments of federal funding for medical research were the wartime trials of antimalarial drugs and the determination of effective regimens for treating syphilis with penicillin.

The development of synthetic antimalarial drugs was a top priority for the US military, particularly after the supply of quinine was cut off in 1942 by the Japanese offensive in Southeast Asia. The malaria research program proved to be the largest biomedical undertaking to date, and it became a model for postwar scientific medical research. After surveying over 14,000 drugs between 1942 to 1946, the Office for the Survey of Antimalarial Drugs decisively identified cloroquine as the drug of choice against malaria.[18]

Along with malaria, syphilis was the disease that posed the greatest threat to the fighting effectiveness of American soldiers. As surgeon general, Thomas Parran waged an all-out campaign to wipe out syphilis, which could not even be mentioned on the radio when he assumed his post in 1936. Parran strove to bring syphilis, which struck one in ten Americans, out of the shadows and to address it as a national problem. By emphasizing the ravages of syphilis on infant health and labor productivity, Parran sought to redefine syphilis as not a venereal but a communicable disease that, like tuberculosis and typhoid, would readily respond to the scientific application of modern medicine and epidemiology.

Before methods to mass-produce penicillin were perfected in 1943, the standard treatment regimen for syphilis was long and complicated, and relied on potentially toxic arsenic and mercury compounds to kill the spirochetes. The PHS Venereal Disease Clinic at Hot Springs, Arkansas, developed a new, more efficient method of administering intravenous drug therapy for syphilis and gonorrhea to large numbers of inpatients with a minimum number of personnel.

With federal funds from the Social Security Act and the 1938 National Venereal Disease Control Act, the number of venereal disease rapid treatment centers had tripled to more than 2,400 by the end of 1939, with 9 million treatments given annually to over 100,000 patients. New syphilis cases declined by over half from 1936 to 1939, and infant deaths from congenital syphilis were halved.[19]

(It should be acknowledged that during this period, the PHS was conducting the longest nontherapeutic medical study in US history, the Tuskegee Study of Untreated Syphilis in the Negro Male, which was grounded in assumptions that reflected the pervasive "scientific" racism among white medical professionals of the era.)[20]

During the war, the federal Office of Scientific Research and Development's cooperative clinical trials of penicillin to treat early stage syphilis demonstrated that penicillin could drastically shorten the length of treatment to only ten days for syphilis patients and three days for gonorrhea cases, with some requiring only a single injection. Using the penicillin studies as a guide, the PHS also used randomized controls to evaluate streptomycin in treating tuberculosis.

The PHS energetically promoted VD screening, prevention, and education programs for military and civilian populations, with special attention to military bases and defense production areas. After the war, as the country celebrated victory and prepared for demobilization, the PHS announced that rates of venereal disease among civilians had not markedly increased during wartime, as they had in every previous conflict.[21]

At the end of the war, Congress authorized the highest funding levels yet to continue treating VD patients in rapid treatment centers and hospitals, a measure that reduced venereal disease rates to such low figures in the civilian and military populations that most rapid treatment centers had closed by the early 1950s.[22]

But venereal disease became a cautionary tale that demonstrated the danger of declaring victory too soon: after the reduction of federal venereal disease control expenditures during the 1950s, rates of syphilis and gonorrhea surged to epidemic proportions during the 1960s and 1970s, and by 1980, an estimated 20 million Americans had contracted genital herpes. There seems little doubt that this resurgence resulted from reduced spending on the problem rather than from changing sexual behavior.[23]

Federally funded and orchestrated wartime research yielded therapeutic compounds to prevent and cure three of the top killers of all time: malaria, syphilis, and tuberculosis. More than just fighting specific diseases, these efforts made fundamental contributions to the development of basic medical research methodology.

For the modern pharmacopeia from which nearly every American has benefited, we can thank the federally sponsored model of research and development provided by the intensive laboratory evaluations of antimalarial drugs. Likewise, the government-coordinated experiments to test the effectiveness of penicillin set the scientific standard for the modern clinical trial that forms the basis for another essential federal role in health, the regulation of the drug industry to ensure the safety and effectiveness of thousands of new pharmaceutical compounds before they reach the market.[24]

Mothers, Babies, and Hospitals

Total domestic federal public health spending (excluding facilities construction, medical research, and medical care programs) increased from $7 million in 1935 to $88 million in 1950 and had reached $283 million by 1964. Federal aid also stimulated total state and local spending for public health to rise substantially, from $119 million in 1935 to $332 million in 1950 and $706 million by 1964, but the ratio of federal to nonfederal funds steadily mounted throughout the period.[25]

As the US birth rate topped 4 million in 1954, the largest category of PHS public health grants to states was for maternal and child health programs. Amendments to the Social Security Act between 1950 and 1963 continuously increased the annual appropriations for maternal and child health and crippled children's services, which rose from a combined $1.9 million the first year of Social Security in 1936–37 to $87.3 million by 1966–67. Congress recognized the importance of maternal and child health research by authorizing the National Institute of Child Health and Human Development in 1962 and by including a research component in new Social Security initiatives passed in 1963 and 1965 to improve the health of low-income pregnant women and young children who lived in substandard housing and lacked access to primary care.[26]

Closely related to the problems of maternal and infant health was access to hospital care. In the South in 1941, only one-third of all births took place in hospitals versus three-quarters of nonsouthern births, and 23 percent of southern babies were delivered by midwives versus only 1.5 percent of nonsouthern births. In 1938, toxemia killed women in southern states at rates from 50 to 150 percent higher than in the rest of the United States, largely due to lack of medical care. Since most southern hospitals did not admit blacks and many rural counties had no hospital at all, rural black mothers and infants benefited least from the medical advances available from trained professionals in modern hospitals.[27]

From 1947 to 1971 the Hill–Burton Hospital Survey and Construction Act built a modern health care infrastructure with $3.7 billion in federal funds, matched by $9.1 billion from state and local governments, to create space for nearly a half million beds in 10,748 projects, including nursing homes and other specialized facilities. Hill–Burton was among the first and most successful examples of a new postwar brand of federal reform that garnered bipartisan support by blending centralized planning, economic development, and a rationale for domestic spending based on national defense.[28]

In the absence of a national health insurance program, Hill–Burton substantially increased access to charity care by expanding the number of government-owned hospitals and the overall proportion of beds in public hospitals, particularly teaching institutions affiliated with medical schools. This act had major implications for the racial desegregation of hospitals, since participation in the Hill–Burton program constituted "state action" that placed private as well as public hospitals under the equal protection clause of the Fourteenth Amendment and obligated them to admit patients without regard to race.[29]

Hill–Burton's provisions benefited the South most of all. The program's need-based allocation formula paved the way for federal sponsorship of southern health, education, and welfare, as well as costly new infrastructure that made Sun Belt prosperity possible while allowing southern states to maintain low taxes. By 1955, southern states drew 20 percent of their revenues from federal sources, well above the national average of 14 percent.

Ironically, Mississippi, the epicenter of antifederal sentiment and the backlash against federally mandated desegregation, tied for fourth with Arkansas among states with the highest percentage of their budgets from federal funds. Today, despite the marked improvement of the southern economy since the Great Depression, many southern states receive more in federal aid than they pay in federal taxes. As the culmination of the post-1938 New Deal that targeted federal resources to the South,

Hill-Burton was the last and most progressive expression of redistributive midcentury liberalism.[30]

Civil Defense, the Cold War, and the CDC

The Malaria Control in War Areas program gave birth in 1946 to the Communicable Disease Center (CDC), now known as the Centers for Disease Control and Prevention. To fulfill its charge to prevent and control a wide range of diseases, the CDC teamed with state and local health agencies to staff programs that ranged from mobile health units in Alaska to community mental health clinics and new federally funded immunization campaigns. Since the mid-1950s, the CDC has also been a major source of continuing education for thousands of public health workers across the country.[31]

The head of the CDC Epidemiology Unit during the 1950s and 1960s, Alexander Langmuir, defined and instituted modern methods of disease surveillance that proved invaluable for guiding national health policy and allocating public health resources. By emphasizing the Cold War threat of biological warfare and the strategic need to maintain close relationships with state and local health authorities in the event of a national emergency, Langmuir secured additional funding to train a new force of CDC epidemiologists.

This comprehensive system of surveillance, which Langmuir named the Epidemiological Intelligence Service, proved to be crucial to mounting a prompt and effective response to national health crises, and it has been continually refined to protect Americans from emergent threats. As the extension of international travel and transportation networks brought more and more Americans into contact with individuals and organisms from foreign countries, the CDC has acted as a watchdog to prevent the introduction and spread of diseases ranging from bubonic plague to severe acute respiratory syndrome (SARS) to avian flu.[32]

The CDC's health emergency management function originated during the Cold War. As hostility grew between the United States and the Soviet bloc, public officials issued strident warnings of the potential dangers of nuclear, biological, and chemical warfare on US soil. While communicable disease epidemics were fading in frequency and severity, these new threats seemed even more terrible than the ravages of polio or diphtheria. In July 1954, the Department of Health, Education and Welfare assigned to the PHS responsibility for the public health aspects of civil defense, which included planning a national program to protect essential community health facilities and to restore them in the event of a national emergency or attack. Civil defense necessitated close cooperation between the PHS and other national agencies, including the Federal Civil Defense Administration, Atomic Energy Commission, Walter Reed Army Institute of Research, and Army Chemical Corps.

To minimize the effects of a biological or chemical attack, civil defense personnel needed to provide an early warning and to implement control measures promptly. The PHS worked with public health departments to develop procedures to more rapidly and accurately detect, identify, and control disease-producing and poisonous agents used in biological weapons. Such research had important applications for environmental health goals such as monitoring the effects of air and water pollution or protecting workers and consumers from the hazards of toxic chemicals and radiation.[33]

Although the Cold War emphasis on the public health aspects of civil defense faded over time as international tensions subsided, the September 11, 2001, attacks on the United States and the creation of the Department of Homeland Security brought the threat of bioterrorism back to the forefront of national consciousness. The CDC is a crucial national resource for coordinating all health-related aspects of emergency preparedness, whether from natural disasters, contagious disease epidemics, or environmental accidents such as the 2010 oil spill in the Gulf of Mexico.

On the Cutting Edge of Research: The NIH

In 1930, the PHS Hygienic Laboratory was renamed the National Institute of Health (NIH), which signaled an increased federal investment in medical research, particularly on chronic diseases, which had replaced infectious diseases as the most common killers. Since the end of World War II, the NIH and the CDC have been the main channels through which the federal government has invested in protecting and promoting the health of Americans by means of research, training, and disease tracking programs.

After World War II, the NIH (with "Institutes" now plural) grew rapidly to become the single largest funder of biomedical research in the world. By 1950, the NIH included seven institutes to support the study of cancer, heart disease, microbiology, dentistry, mental health, neurological diseases and blindness, and arthritis and metabolic diseases. From the 1950s on, the agency emphasized basic science research, particularly the cellular and molecular biology of disease, which in turn underwrote the establishment and expansion of a nationwide network of academic medical centers whose primary mission was research.

Of all the arms of federal health policy, the NIH has enjoyed the largest and most consistent appropriations and the greatest bipartisan support. Unlike other areas of federal research and development funding, which have fluctuated on the basis of external events, the NIH budget has grown steadily decade after decade. Its annual appropriation increased from $81 million in 1954 to $1.6 billion by 1968. By 2004, it had reached nearly $28 billion.

No other federal agency enjoys quite the same combination of lobbying support from disease-specific constituencies, unwavering faith in its core mission of biomedical research, and public demand for government protection from health threats. One key reason for the ongoing expansion of the NIH has been that politicians of all stripes can vote for medical research as a demonstration of commitment to improving the country's health while avoiding the much costlier and more divisive issue of reforming the system of financing health care services.

Perhaps the best known branch of the NIH is the National Cancer Institute (NCI), created in 1937, which inaugurated the first national cancer chemotherapy program in 1955. The NCI became the best funded NIH unit, especially after the National Cancer Act of 1971 gave the NCI special status, including more direct presidential influence over its budget and administration, and elevated its research appropriations to an all-time high of $400 million.[34]

Yet if there was a special interest in Congress that could rival biomedical research, it was Big Tobacco. The majority of credit for reducing rates of cancer (as opposed to treating it) goes to the 1964 Surgeon General's Report on Smoking and Health, which definitively linked cigarette smoking with significantly higher risks of lung cancer as well as heart disease, emphysema, and bronchitis. Annual per capita cigarette consumption increased from 54 cigarettes in 1900 to an astounding 4,345 cigarettes in 1963, but then slowly decreased to 2,261 in 1998.[35]

Despite the tobacco industry's best efforts to stop it, the report was widely distributed and reported in the media, creating the necessary atmosphere for public health officials to pursue regulations. These included placing the now ubiquitous surgeon general's warnings on packaging, and federal bans on cigarette advertising on radio, television, or billboards. The 1964 Surgeon General's Report set a precedent for establishing and publicizing all types of health risks, as well as for the scientific resolution of controversial issues via the collective, objective review of evidence. Finally, the report accorded the surgeon general and the federal government a powerful new level of authority in protecting national health.[36]

Health as Foreign Policy

One of the most important long-term effects of the Cold War was to stimulate the growth of international health as a tool of US foreign policy. Not only did federally funded military research produce peacetime health benefits for American civilians but it also developed critical tools for global health that ultimately prevented millions of deaths worldwide.

After World War II, intensifying fears of communism provided a new and powerful political justification for increased US support for public health services at home and abroad. Under the auspices of the United Nations, the US government was the largest contributor to the World Health Organization (WHO) and the United Nations International Children's Emergency Fund (UNICEF).[37] In 1955, WHO initiated its global antimalaria campaign using two compounds developed in the United States: chloroquine to treat the disease and DDT to kill the mosquitoes that carried it. The US government provided the majority of funding and many of the trained public health personnel for the campaign. In India, where malaria had caused an estimated 1 million deaths annually, the number of recorded cases fell from 75 million in 1951 to 50,000 in 1961.[38] UNICEF assisted maternal and child health projects in seventy-one countries and territories, including the vaccination of nearly 120 million children against tuberculosis as well as smaller programs to combat yaws, leprosy, and trachoma.[39]

The US State Department provided the largest support for international health through the International Cooperation Administration (ICA). By the end of the 1950s, the ICA Office of Public Health oversaw cooperative health programs in thirty-six countries with a budget of $80 million and a staff of more than 300 public health workers from the United States.[40]

In the decades since the ICA was reorganized as the US Agency for International Development (USAID), its international health programs have been at the heart of accomplishing the goals that President John F. Kennedy set for the agency in 1961. He predicted that without a strong foreign aid program, "widespread poverty and chaos [would] lead to a collapse of existing political and social structures which would inevitably invite the advance of totalitarianism into every weak and unstable area. Thus our own security would be endangered and our prosperity imperiled. A program of assistance to the underdeveloped nations must continue because the Nation's interest and the cause of political freedom require it."[41]

With only one-half of 1 percent of the current federal budget devoted to economic and humanitarian assistance, USAID estimates that its immunization programs save 3 million lives each year and its oral rehydration programs, originally developed to fight cholera epidemics in Bangladesh, have prevented tens of millions of deaths from diarrheal diseases. USAID has sponsored family planning programs that have enabled twenty-eight developing countries to reduce the average number of children per family from 6.1 in the mid-1960s to 4.2 today, which has contributed to greatly improved levels of maternal and child health, nutrition, and education.

One of the most important areas of federal international health assistance in recent years has been targeted at fighting the devastation of HIV/AIDS. Since 1987, USAID's HIV/AIDS prevention programs in thirty-two countries have reached over 850,000 people with HIV prevention education, and USAID has trained 40,000 people to support HIV/AIDS programs in their own countries.[42] The US President's Emergency Plan for AIDS Relief (PEPFAR) is the largest effort by any nation to combat a single disease worldwide. Initiated by President George W. Bush in 2003, PEPFAR committed $15 billion over five years to assist countries with limited resources in providing antiretroviral treatment (ART) to 2 million HIV-infected people, preventing 7 million new infections, and supporting care for 10 million people. By 2008, at least 1.2 million Africans were receiving ART as a result of PEPFAR. The program was renewed in

2008 and expanded to include tuberculosis and malaria, with authorization for up to $48 billion through 2013.[43]

In the past half century, life expectancy in the developing world has increased by about one-third, infant and child death rates have been reduced by 50 percent, and smallpox has been eradicated worldwide. In the past twenty years, chronic malnutrition has been reduced by half. In the last ten years, the USAID played a major role in the United Nations Drinking Water Supply and Sanitation Decade program, which provided safe drinking water sources to 1.3 billion people and sanitation to 750 million people for the first time. It is no exaggeration to say that health conditions around the world have improved more during the last fifty years than in all of human history to that point, and that US government aid to global health has largely underwritten these achievements.

National Health Insurance: A Dream Deferred?

During the 1960s and 1970s, a highly favorable social and political climate fostered innovation and expansion in federal health programs. As a keystone of President Lyndon B. Johnson's Great Society, the 1965 Medicare-Medicaid amendments to Social Security together helped to extend medical and hospital care to millions of Americans who had been excluded from the private health system on the basis of both race and income. By the mid-1960s, more than 40 million of America's 193 million people remained uninsured. Not only did Medicare-Medicaid remove financial barriers for the elderly and many (but not all) of those under sixty-five who could not afford care but it also brought about the racial desegregation of health care by requiring compliance with the 1964 Civil Rights Act for all participating hospitals.[44]

Medicare and Medicaid, originally intended to include the two largest groups of uninsured who lacked employer-based coverage, now function as much to preserve the financial status of middle-class Americans as to enable the poor to purchase health care. Many middle-class individuals become beneficiaries of both Medicare and Medicaid, which pays at least part of the costs for 70 percent of nursing home residents, thereby sparing them from having to rely as heavily on their families' resources. Medicare foots the bill for health care at the age when it is typically most expensive, while Medicaid subsidizes the long-term care needs of the nation's elderly and chronically disabled. Medical and nursing home care rank alongside postsecondary education and home mortgages as the most expensive items that most Americans will buy in their lifetimes. All three are federally subsidized, but college loans and mortgage interest are less universal, and the federal government pays a much lower share of the total than for long-term care and medical costs for those over age sixty-five.[45]

With the passage of the 2010 Affordable Care Act, President Barack Obama signed into law a major milestone in federal health reform. While it still fell short of the long-pursued goal of universal comprehensive health coverage, the act won important concessions from the insurance industry, such as ending the practice of denying coverage to children under nineteen on the basis of a preexisting health condition, enabling parents to keep their children as beneficiaries on their health insurance up to age twenty-six, ending lifetime and most annual limits on care, and providing free access to recommended preventive services such as colonoscopies and mammograms. The law also offered tax credits to encourage small businesses to insure more workers and grants to enable states to establish affordable insurance exchanges designed to increase competition among health insurance providers.[46]

Passage of the Affordable Care Act marked a historical first: the AMA solidly endorsed federal health insurance legislation, although it opposed the president's public option plan to compete with private insurers. The AMA had supported the goal of universal health care in 1921, but the association's policy stance had been to oppose vigorously every national health insurance bill since 1939.[47] The AMA's leaders (notwithstanding considerable dissent among the membership) held fast to the private insurance system as the only acceptable method of financing health care, which pitted them against any proposed government-sponsored health plan.

With the passage of Medicare, however, physicians became dependent on reimbursements from the program and lobbied hard to preserve rates they deemed acceptable. AMA support for the Obama administration's bill can be interpreted in part as a strategic move to retain the allegiance of key Democrats for the AMA's Medicare and other policy positions. Yet it was also a striking departure from past practice for the AMA's executive vice president, Michael D. Maves, to admit, "We do not believe that maintaining the status quo is an acceptable option for physicians or the patients we serve."

It remains to be seen how the law will be implemented, but the AMA committed its support for "achieving enactment of comprehensive health system reform legislation that improves access to affordable, high-quality care and reduces unnecessary costs."[48] As long ago as 1969 the AMA called adequate health care "a basic right of every citizen," yet we still have not achieved that goal.

CHAPTER 8

Culture for the People

How Government Has Fostered the Arts and Culture

Steven Conn

Sydney Smith was generally regarded as an affable, sunny sort of man. He had a successful career as an English cleric, and he achieved a measure of fame as a writer, critic, and preacher. But what he wrote about the United States was not kind.

In an 1820 essay published in the *Edinburgh Review*, the Reverend Smith asked: "In the four quarters of the globe, who reads an American book? Or goes to an American play? or looks at an American picture or statue?"

The question was purely rhetorical, and the implicit answer was as obvious as it was designed to insult: No one.

Americans in 1820 might have felt a justifiable pride in their political system, and they might have reveled in the possibilities of freedom in a land unburdened by the baggage of the European past (though Smith also went on to burst that balloon when he asked caustically, "Finally, under which of the old tyrannical governments of Europe is every sixth man a slave, whom his fellow-creatures may buy and sell and torture?").

But it seemed undeniable that Americans in 1820 had not yet produced much in the way of "culture." Smith's quip stung because it was true.

Plenty of Americans in the founding generation acknowledged that art, literature, music, and the other fine arts represented the very best products of a society. In a famous letter to his wife, Abigail, John Adams put this in almost evolutionary terms: "I must study politics and war, that my sons may have the liberty to study mathematics, philosophy, geography, natural history and naval architecture, navigation, commerce and agriculture in order to give their children the right to study painting, poetry, music and architecture." But as the nineteenth century wore on, many felt the nagging sense that we were a nation devoted to "commerce and agriculture" and not much else.

The reasons for this seemed obvious: Adams's own New England had been founded by Puritans whose ideas of fun excluded painting, music, and architecture, among many other things. Likewise, Pennsylvania Quakers had no interest in art or adornment of any kind, though they were quieter about their objections than many New England preachers. Not for nothing were they called "the plain people." Besides, art was elitist, and the very idea of it offended the democratic sensibilities of many Americans.

Who Pays? The Problem of Patronage in a Democratic Society

More important, however, was the question of patronage. Art to express the ideals and vision of the nation didn't simply require talented artists. It required someone to pay for it, too, and here the comparison with Europe seemed most invidious. European artists for centuries enjoyed the support of royal families, aristocrats, and the church. And as those institutions began to wane in the eighteenth and nineteenth centuries, secular governments often stepped in to promote the arts.

America had none of that. Indeed, in the nineteenth century, American painters and architects had to travel to Europe if they wanted a proper training.

The one area government did promote in the nineteenth century was the last item on John Adams's list: architecture. President George Washington oversaw the plans for the new capital city, and he wanted it to be a physical embodiment of the ideals of the nation. Ironically, or perhaps unavoidably, he hired a French engineer, Pierre L'Enfant, to design the new District of Columbia.

In 1792, even before the capital moved to the new city, Thomas Jefferson organized a design competition for a new home for Congress, though the ten submissions to the competition were all regarded as amateurish. Without a tradition of architectural patronage, America really had no architects worthy of the task.

Architecture, many people believed, had a power to communicate ideas and values because of its public nature. Abraham Lincoln understood that when he insisted that construction on the Capitol dome continue even after the Civil War broke out. The Capitol became the very symbol of the enduring Union during those years.

What the federal government did with the Capitol, states did as well. From Pennsylvania to Washington, states used the building of their capitols to make grand statements about their civic aspirations. These capitols served as a source of state pride and as expressions of civic boosterism, and of a broader sense that the institutions of our government deserved to be housed in impressive and imposing buildings. And in some cases, even these buildings were sponsored indirectly by the federal government. When Washington state entered the union, for example, President Benjamin Harrison donated 132,000 acres of federal land to the new state with the stipulation that the income generated by it be used solely to build a new capitol.

Still, it is fair to say that beyond the sponsorship of government buildings, government did little to promote the arts directly in the United States—until the Great Depression.

A New Deal for Arts and Culture

By the time Franklin Roosevelt took the oath of office in March 1933, the nation was at its lowest ebb.[1] The free-market, laissez-faire economy of the 1920s had collapsed in October 1929, and after three and a half years, President Herbert Hoover had failed to get it moving again. In fact, the Great Depression was considerably worse in 1933 than it had been in 1930, and Hoover was viewed by many Americans as dithering and incompetent at best, callous and indifferent to human suffering at worst.

By March 1933, the unemployment rate in the United States stood at approximately 25 percent. Subtract the agricultural sector of the economy, and the figure rose to roughly 40 percent. But it is worth remembering that the Great Depression hit the nation's artists just as hard as it affected its farmers and factory workers. Of the nation's professional musicians, 70 percent were out of work, and book sales had fallen 50 percent nationally. The private market had failed for artists just as it had for so many others.

Artists and writers were certainly not at the top of Franklin Roosevelt's agenda as he initiated his New Deal. Even so, he wanted to stimulate the economy and put people back to work, and artists were workers, too. "Hell," said his aide Harry Hopkins, "they've got to eat just like other people."[2]

Artists found work in a wide range of federally sponsored public works projects. The Civil Works Administration often employed painters to decorate its projects with murals, like the wonderful frescoes that adorn San Francisco's Coit Tower. If you have an image in your mind's eye of what the Great Depression looked like, it is probably because you've seen some of the 66,000 black-and-white photographs produced by the Resettlement Administration and the Farm Security Administration, taken by artists like Ben Shahn and Dorothea Lange.

In 1935, however, with unemployment still stubbornly high, Roosevelt created the Works Progress Administration (WPA) in order to put even more people to work, and with it he turned the federal government into a major patron of the arts—all kinds of art.

The WPA generated a particular anger among conservatives in the 1930s and continues to do so today. Derided as nothing but a wasteful make-work program—We Putter Around, as one joke at the time put it—it became a symbol of everything conservatives hated about the New Deal.[3]

Under the WPA's Federal Project Number One, the federal government began employing painters, writers, actors, and musicians directly. Before they could get a WPA job, they had to qualify for relief, and they were paid an hourly wage, just like every other relief worker. The program, like the rest of the WPA, lasted only seven years, but it had a remarkable run.

There are two ways we can measure the success of the WPA's Federal One program. First, we can tally the artists whose careers were nurtured because of the support they received from the WPA. These include painters like Raphael Soyer, Jacob Lawrence, and Arshile Gorky; writers like Richard Wright, Ralph Ellison, Studs Terkel, and John Cheever; actors and playwrights, including Burt Lancaster, Orson Welles, and Arthur Miller. It is a hall of fame of midcentury American artistic talent.

Even this partial list is extraordinary, and it is almost impossible to imagine how impoverished the American cultural landscape might have been without these artists. Looking back on his own career, actor E. G. Marshall believed he "might not have made it if it hadn't been for the Federal Theater."[4] Saul Bellow might still have won the Nobel Prize in Literature in 1976, but then again, without the support he received from the WPA he might not have become a writer at all.

Perhaps more significantly, however, the WPA democratized the world of art and culture through the sheer size and range of its projects. Opera productions in the Ozarks; Shakespeare's *Macbeth* produced with an all-black cast in Harlem. By 1939, the Federal Music Project employed 7,000 musicians and had sponsored 225,000 concerts around the country in places big and small. Approximately 150 million people heard those performances, many of whom had never seen professional theater or heard professional music before.

Writers working for the WPA produced travel guides for each of the forty-eight states, and many of these remain wonderful records of the local history and culture of those places. Much of what we know about the institution of slavery comes from the interviews WPA writers conducted with ex-slaves, most in their eighties and nineties at the time. The 5,000 or so artists employed by the WPA produced over 100,000 canvases, nearly 18,000 sculptures, and 2,500 murals, and not just in the traditional art centers of New York, Chicago, Boston, and Philadelphia but in Omaha and Spokane and Yellow Springs, Ohio.

By employing thousands of painters, writers, photographers, and other artists, the federal government may have taken those people off the streets and kept them out of the soup lines. But more important, it created an invaluable archive of the nation at that pivotal moment in our history. The art made possible by the federal government enabled the nation to hold a mirror up to itself, to understand itself more broadly and more deeply, and to celebrate the vast variety that is the United States. As Russell Lee, a Farm Security Administration photographer, put it in 1941, "I am a photographer hired by a democratic government to take pictures of its land and its people. The idea is to show New York to Texans and Texas to New York."[5]

The WPA made that possible.

Cold War on the Cultural Front

Among those artists who survived the 1930s by working for the WPA was the painter Jackson Pollock. He isn't remembered for his WPA work, of course, but for being at the vanguard of the postwar art movement called abstract expressionism. Pollock dripped, splashed, and threw paint on and at his canvases, producing paintings often greeted by viewers with a bemused "My four-year-old could do that."

Modern art after the Second World War might have confused some audiences, but it also attracted the attention of influential people who saw the potential of culture as a tool in the Cold War against the Soviets.

In February 1949, *Time* ran a story about Pollock designed to make fun of this "darling of the highbrow cult." After it appeared, the director of New York's Museum of Modern Art, Albert Barr, wrote to *Time's* publisher, Henry Luce, reminding him that attacking modern art was something totalitarian regimes did. By contrast, Pollock and the other abstract expressionists represented "artistic free enterprise." Luce, a vigorous Cold Warrior, was apparently convinced, and shortly thereafter his *Life* magazine ran a laudatory feature on Pollock with photos of him in action.

The federal government saw art and culture as a way of demonstrating the values of freedom during the Cold War. During the 1950s and 1960s, the State Department (overtly) and the CIA (covertly) sponsored a wide range of cultural productions around the world. (A great deal has been written recently about the role of the State Department and the CIA in promoting and sponsoring American art. Some, like Frances Stonor Saunders, have argued that this relationship was entirely corrupting and turned American art into little more than propaganda.)[6] They did not necessarily employ artists directly, but they did promote American art and culture internationally. American culture, so the State Department and the CIA believed, would demonstrate to a world choosing between the American way and the Soviet system that we were the land of artistic and intellectual freedom.

Much of what the State Department and the CIA showed to the world was decidedly middlebrow, like the State Department-sponsored world tour of the musical *Oklahoma*.

Some was more provocative, like their tour of the opera *Porgy and Bess* in the mid-1950s. The production toured Latin America (a major Cold War battleground), the Middle East, and Europe in the fall of 1954.

In February 1955, the company was invited to perform at La Scala, the renowned opera house in Milan, the first time an American company had ever received such a prestigious invitation. Maya Angelou, who played the role of Ruby in the production, remembered it this way:

> This was something unique: famous white American performers had appeared at La Scala, but never blacks, especially not a huge cast of blacks such as *Porgy* provided. Both audience and company were tense. Every member of the cast was coiled tight like a spring, wound taut for a shattering release. The moment the curtain opened, the singers pulled the elegant first-night audience into the harshness of black Southern life. The love story unfolded with such tenderness that the singers wept visible tears. Time and again, the audience came to their feet, yelling and applauding. We had performed *Porgy and Bess* as never before, and if the La Scala patrons loved us, it was only fitting because we certainly performed as if we were in love with one another.[7]

It was a perfect American moment: an opera written by a New York Jew about African American life in the South performed by a black cast to an adoring Italian crowd in one of the sacred spaces of European high art in the very year that the civil rights movement would explode onto the international scene—brought to the world by the US State Department.

Not all of this federal sponsorship of American culture ended in triumph, nor did it escape controversy. In fact, the State Department's first postwar foray into the world of cultural promotion came with an art show it organized in 1946 titled "Advancing American Art." The show was put together to demonstrate that Americans were not simply bourgeois philistines but were on the cutting edge of artistic expression because such expression was possible in the United States.

The State Department purchased seventy-nine paintings by contemporary American painters for the show, half of which were sent on tour to Latin America, the other half to Paris and then to

Prague. The exhibit included works by Ben Shahn, John Marin, Jacob Lawrence, and Georgia O'Keeffe. The European part of the exhibit was supposed to travel around Eastern Europe at the very moment when the Soviet Union was exerting dominion over those nations, but the paintings never got beyond Czechoslovakia. Back in Washington, the show was being denounced as a waste of taxpayer money and an affront to the sensibilities of real Americans.

Michigan congressman George Dondero made himself (briefly) famous for his attacks on modern art and on the State Department's work promoting such art overseas. In a 1949 speech he gave a wonderfully buffoonish art history lesson to his listeners:

> Cubism aims to destroy by designed disorder.
> Futurism aims to destroy by the machine myth....
> Dadaism aims to destroy by ridicule.
> Expressionism aims to destroy by aping the primitive and insane....
> Abstractionism aims to destroy by the creation of brainstorms.
> Surrealism aims to destroy by the denial of reason.

Today, of course, we have given a name to the kinds of cultural projects begun during the Cold War. We call it "cultural diplomacy," and it is increasingly central to the nation's foreign affairs. More than a half century after these initial forays into the world of cultural diplomacy, we all recognize the power and beauty of Georgia O'Keeffe's work.

No one cares any more about George Dondero.

Culture as Part of a Great Society

As he inherited the presidency from his assassinated predecessor, Lyndon Johnson moved skillfully and carefully to soothe a grieving nation, and to cast his own agenda as the continuation of John F. Kennedy's.

Kennedy, and his first lady, Jacqueline, had turned the White House into a major cultural venue. The president invited

American Nobel Prize-winners to dine there; he invited celebrated cellist Pablo Casals to perform there. The arts and culture were a central part of Camelot's chic.

Receiving an honorary degree from Amherst College in 1963, Kennedy told the assembled crowd, "I look forward to an America which commands respect throughout the world not only for its strength but for its civilization as well."[8] But Kennedy was dead a month after that speech, and it remained for Johnson to pick up the challenge of promoting the arts and culture.

Johnson began his long career in Washington as a New Deal congressman from east Texas, and he became a trusted advisor to Franklin Roosevelt. Now as president himself he envisioned expanding the New Deal to create a Great Society. In a message to Congress in 1965, Johnson told legislators that "the pursuit of artistic achievement, and making the fruits of that achievement available to all its people, is among the hallmarks of a Great Society."

That message accompanied a bill to create a National Foundation on the Arts and Humanities. It was passed by Congress in September 1965 and signed by the president on September 29. Thus the National Endowment for the Arts (NEA) and the National Endowment for the Humanities (NEH) came into being, and with their creation the federal government officially became a patron of the arts and culture.

Neither the NEA nor the NEH are true endowments. They are not funded through the interest generated by an investment fund, like a university endowment, for example, but rather through an annual appropriation from Congress. This, in turn, means that both are subject to congressional scrutiny and all the debate and controversy that can come with that.

Interestingly, however, for the first fifteen years of their existence, the NEA and the NEH generated little of either. Richard Nixon, whose own cultural tastes ran more to football than to fine arts, saw the importance of the federal role in arts and culture, especially in the context of his Cold War foreign policy. In a speech he gave to Congress on arts policy late in 1969, Nixon called for Congress to double the amount of money it appropriated to the NEA and the NEH. "Few investments we could make," he told members, "would give us so great a return." Amid the tumult of the era, Nixon stated, "The arts have a rare capacity to help heal divisions among our own people and to vault some of the barriers that divide the world."[9]

Through the 1970s, the national endowments went about their work in relative quiet. And then Ronald Reagan came to town.

The Arts and Culture in the Age of Reagan

Certain conservatives had never been happy about federal funding for the arts and culture, and with Reagan's election they expected the NEA and the NEH to be shut down. Some simply believed that the government had no business spending money this way; others were convinced that the NEA and NEH funded "elitism"—that is, eggheads, perverts, and subversives.

Early in his first term, Reagan created a task force for the arts and humanities that included Reagan campaign financier Joseph Coors, with future National Rifle Association president Charlton Heston as its chair. The report they issued outlined an arts policy that echoed back to the president everything he had already said about the role of government more broadly: federal funding should be slashed; the burden of funding should be shifted to the states; the private sector ought to "fulfill and extend its traditional role as the principal benefactor of America's cultural heritage."[10]

(Coors later made good on this promise to be a benefactor of America's culture "heritage" by founding the Heritage Foundation, and his philanthropic vision extended beyond our own borders. For example, he generously bought a light cargo plane for the contras in Nicaragua with money he funneled illegally through Oliver North. One kind of cultural diplomacy, I suppose.)

Funding was indeed cut, and the costs of the arts were indeed shifted to the states. By 1985, the states were spending as much as the NEA to support the arts; by 1990 the states were spending far more.[11] And Reagan curtailed the semi-autonomous way the NEA had run by appointing Frank Hodsall as its chair. Hodsall had no background in the arts and culture, as his predecessors did, but he had worked on Reagan's campaign and had been a deputy to Reagan's chief of staff James Baker. Art was apparently too important to be left to arts professionals.

Diminished though they might be, however, the national endowments survived the Reagan years, much to the disbelief of many conservative activists. A decade later, conservatives made their next attempt to kill the national endowments.

Under the first George Bush, the NEA provided funding for a handful of controversial art exhibits—including the work of Andres Serrano, which offended conservative Christians, and the naughty photographs of Robert Mapplethorpe—which helped ignite the "culture wars" of the 1990s.

Newt Gingrich, as he became Speaker of the House in 1995, vowed to eliminate the national endowments. Their budgets were certainly slashed, but they survived, albeit with far fewer programs and a damaged reputation.[12]

The reason, perhaps, that the endowments have hung on despite the anger and vitriol directed at them is because they have been quite successful. Fittingly, the fights that have taken place over the NEA and NEH make terrific theater, but behind all the hyperventilation and fulminating, the national endowments have made it possible for a wide public to enjoy the arts and culture: from regional symphony orchestras to local historical museums to art education programs in out-of-the-way places.

And it is worth putting this spending in some context.

Forty years after its creation, the NEA had made grants totaling just over $4 billion—on average $100 million each year, give or take—which is no small sum. Compared to the real big-ticket items in Washington, however, this is chump change. One nuclear-powered Trident submarine, to take one example, costs roughly $2 billion, and that's before it is armed with missiles and warheads. The navy currently deploys twenty such subs, though their Cold War rationale vanished more than two decades ago. It costs almost as much as the NEA gets each year just to operate one of these underwater behemoths.

The annual budgets of the national endowments, in other words, don't even amount to a rounding error at the Pentagon.

Over the course of their history, the national endowments have undoubtedly funded bad art and trivial scholarship. But like their predecessors in the 1930s, both the NEA and the NEH can be proud of their record of cultural accomplishment. Fifteen Pulitzer Prize–winning books have been nurtured by NEH grants to their authors. Ken Burns brought the Civil War to life for millions of Americans with his pathbreaking documentary funded in part with money from the NEH.

Mostly, the NEA has not funded exhibits like the Mapplethorpe photographs, despite the headlines that show grabbed. Instead it has supported the Alabama Dance Council, and the Dallas Chamber Music Society, and a touring exhibition of artist Leon Polk, put together by East Central University in Oklahoma[13]— small grants made to small organizations that cumulatively have made possible a remarkable variety of cultural activity all across the country.

The American Model: Indirect Subsidies to the Arts and Culture

Charlton Heston's call that the private sector "fulfill and extend its traditional role as the principal benefactor of America's cultural heritage" and replace public funding for the arts and culture fit squarely within Ronald Reagan's larger agenda.

But it also served as a reminder that for roughly a century the United States has developed another mechanism to fund our cultural life: the nonprofit sector.

Americans have always been energetic joiners and throughout our history have come together in any number of groups, clubs, and associations to undertake civic projects that neither the government nor the private sector wanted to pursue.

But in the twentieth century, those organizations became formalized through the tax code. They became "tax-exempt" (501c-3 organizations in IRS-speak), and contributions to them became tax deductible. That "spirit of voluntarism" so frequently called on by conservatives comes with a public subsidy, albeit an indirect one.

In 1940, there were 12,500 secular, charitable tax-exempt organizations. By the end of the twentieth century, there were well over 700,000.[14] Add churches to this list and it grows even larger.

Consider this: in 2009 Americans donated roughly $300 billion to nonprofit organizations, almost $2,000 for each household in the country. That figure represents about 2 percent of the nation's total GDP.[15]

Of that figure, far and away the largest amount—33 percent or $100 billion—was donated to churches. These tax-exempt donations are one of the ways religion is subsidized in the United States, the separation of church and state notwithstanding. Another 13 percent went to educational organizations, which helps explain why the endowments of some American universities have grown larger than the entire economies of some small countries.

A scant 4 percent of those tax deductions were taken for contributions to arts, culture, and humanities organizations. But 4 percent of $300 billion still amounted to $12.3 billion, which means that in 2009 alone Americans donated to the arts and culture three times the amount of money that the NEA has spent over the course of forty years.

This indirect subsidy for arts and culture (and for the rest of the nonprofit sector as well) is perhaps the biggest difference between how the United States funds its cultural enterprises and the way countries in Europe and Asia do it. Many Americans remain suspicious of direct funding for the arts and culture, but most have embraced this way of funding them indirectly— perhaps because they haven't thought about how tax deductions and credits are a form of public subsidy. We ought to acknowledge this fact.

And we ought to acknowledge how successful these subsidies have been. Through the tax code, the United States has created a vibrant nonprofit sector that in turn has funded pathbreaking medical research, created colleges and universities without equal, and built a set of cultural organizations and institutions that are among the finest in the world.

Successful as this model has been, we ought to acknowledge its downsides as well.

When Charlton Heston identified the private sector as the "traditional" source of arts funding, he really called for a return to an older kind of patronage. In effect he was saying that the arts and culture are for the elite, and those elites should pay for them as well. Using the tax code to provide indirect subsidies to the arts and culture reinforces elitism at two levels.

First, it benefits wealthy donors who are best in a position to take advantage of these tax breaks. Museums are enriched by collections donated by individuals, and performance venues are named after their biggest benefactors. Institutions hail these donations as selfless and altruistic. And they may very well be. But those donors also benefit substantially from tax write-offs. Tax breaks matter much less to ordinary Americans, whose charitable gifts are necessarily more modest.

Second, I suspect that these indirect subsidies reinforce an elitism of location. The wealthy individuals who support museums and opera companies and symphony orchestras live disproportionately in the major metropolitan centers, and they donate to the institutions in those places.

Boston, New York, Chicago, and Los Angeles have become international cultural centers in large part because of the private philanthropic support they receive from their wealthy residents, made possible in part because of the federal tax code. Whether our system of indirect subsidies also benefits the arts and cultural life in less wealthy places isn't clear.

In other words, our system of indirectly subsidizing the arts and culture, successful though it has been, not only makes rich individuals richer but makes rich places richer as well.

The question, then, is not whether we will subsidize our artistic and cultural endeavors. Clearly, as a nation, we have chosen to do so, both directly and indirectly and to great effect. The question is how best to democratize access to art and culture. Indirect subsidies have helped create the Metropolitan Museum of Art and its cousins. Direct subsidies, first from the New Deal and more recently from the national endowments, have brought the arts and culture into the daily lives of all those Americans who don't live in New York or Chicago.

Even Charlton Heston and Joseph Coors, in their report to Ronald Reagan, conceded that the NEA assistance to arts projects around the country had been important, and that abolishing federal support altogether would be a mistake. Reagan abandoned his original plan to shut down the NEA after getting this assessment.[16]

Two hundred years after Sydney Smith made his snarky remark about American culture, millions of people around the world read American books. And listen to American music and admire American paintings. Our dual system of funding the arts and culture through direct and indirect subsidies is in no small way responsible for that.

More to the point, however, it has made it possible for millions of Americans across the entire country to be enriched by the arts and culture.

CHAPTER 9

From Franklin to Facebook

The Civic Mandate for Communications

Richard R. John

It has become a cliché to predict that the most fundamental innovations in information technology in the twenty-first century will originate in the garage of some teenage entrepreneur. While this prediction is intuitively appealing, it is almost certainly wrong. No one can predict the future, and forecasting is notoriously inexact. Yet we will have a better chance of avoiding detours, wrong turns, and traffic jams if we have in front of us a road map of where we have been.

In the past two centuries, the vast aggregations of power and authority known informally as "big government" have exerted a potent and enduring influence on communications networks in the United States. Three governmental institutions have been especially consequential: the postal system; the regulatory agency; and the Internet. The postal system and the Internet are federal institutions; regulatory agencies, in contrast, have derived their authority not only from the federal government but also from the states. Each of these institutions had its greatest influence in a different century: the postal system in the 1800s; the regulatory agency in the 1900s; the Internet today. All had certain features in common. None originated in anyone's garage, and each was a product less of market incentives or technological imperatives than of political fiat.

Communications Networks in a New Republic: The Postal System

The informational environment in which we live today was by no means coeval with the United States. Rather, it is the product of more than two centuries of creative statecraft.

The United States was born during a war of independence against Great Britain that began in 1775. The government was new; the informational environment was not. Few lawmakers envisioned that communications networks in the new republic might assume a form markedly different from those in monarchical Great Britain. All this would change in the years immediately following the adoption of the federal Constitution in 1788. If the people were sovereign, as the new Constitution proclaimed, then it seemed self-evident that they would need to be well informed. In the absence of an informed citizenry, it would be impossible to sustain the bold experiment in representative government that the framers of the federal Constitution had envisioned and lawmakers had sworn to sustain.

How could lawmakers foster the creation of an informed citizenry? One proposal fell by the wayside: nowhere in the Constitution was Congress authorized to establish a national university. Another proposal became the opening clause of the First Amendment to the Constitution: "Congress shall make no law respecting the freedom of the speech and of the press." The ideal of a free press antedated the First Amendment; never before, however, had this ideal been enshrined in a document invested with the authority of fundamental law. In no sense was the First Amendment an expression of big government. It was, after all, a restraint on government power. Even so, it is worth recalling that it was the federal government that had restrained itself.[1]

In the twentieth century, the free press clause of the First Amendment would become a formidable legal weapon. In large part, this is because jurists interpreted the Fourteenth Amendment, which was adopted in 1868, to extend its jurisdiction to the states. This innovation—a triumph of big government—transformed the First Amendment from a constraint on the federal government into a constraint on governmental institutions at all levels: federal, state, and local.

Even schoolchildren know about the First Amendment. This is true even though, for most of the country's history, it had no discernible influence on jurisprudence: the first major constitutional law case to hinge on the free press clause would not be decided until the First World War. Yet only specialists in early American history have heard of the Post Office Act of 1792. This is unfortunate, since the act did more than the First Amendment to create the informational environment in which representative government would flourish in the nineteenth-century United States.

The post office was not new in 1792. The facilities it provided for the circulation of information, however, remained almost entirely confined to an exclusive clientele, just as the colonial post office in British North America had been before the War of Independence. In fact, the post office that Benjamin Franklin had administered in 1775 as the first postmaster general for the rebellious American colonies was largely identical to the post office that Franklin had administered for many years before the war as a placeman for the Crown. And it was much the same post office that the new government had at its disposal during the War of Independence (1775–81), the framing of the federal Constitution in 1787, and the debates over the ratification in the winter of 1787–88. The institution had yet to be transformed into a system invested with a civic mandate to keep the citizenry well informed. All this would change with the enactment of the Post Office Act of 1792.

Prior to 1792, postal administrators had been constrained both in theory and practice. In theory, they lacked an unambiguous mandate to create post routes that lay entirely inside individual states and had no mandate whatsoever to facilitate the circulation of newspapers, then as now a major medium for the broadcasting of information on public affairs. Even had such a mandate existed, they had good reason, in practice, to be wary of new departures. Interior routes and newspaper conveyance were expensive and could not be expected to cover their costs. Postal administrators were judged on their ability to balance the books: if they ran a deficit, they were presumed to have been derelict in their duty.

Only federal legislation could break this impasse. The Post Office Act of 1792 transformed the informational environment in three ways. First, it created a mechanism to expand the route network rapidly into the hinterland; second, it admitted newspapers into the network at highly advantageous rates; and third, it established the privacy of personal communications as a civic ideal.[2]

The mechanism that hastened the rapid expansion of the route network was seemingly prosaic. Instead of leaving control over the designation of new post routes with postal administrators, as had been the norm before 1792, the Post Office Act of 1792 shifted control to Congress. This shift might sound trivial, but it was not. Congressmen were eager to please their constituents, and constituents were eager to obtain access to postal facilities.

The consequences were profound. By 1828, the United States boasted the largest postal route network in the world, a fact that impressed European travelers like Alexis de Tocqueville, and that created the technical preconditions not only for the election of Andrew Jackson, the first president to regard himself as a tribune of the people, but also for the flourishing of voluntary associations, which Tocqueville would hail as a defining feature of the democratic culture that had taken root in the United States.

The communications network that lawmakers created was distinctive both in scale and scope. The post-1792 postal system conveyed not only letters but also newspapers, the primary medium for the circulation of information on public affairs. Here, too, the critical innovation was political, and, here, too, the key shift was embodied in a clause of the Post Office Act of 1792.

Lawmakers agreed that the mail should be open to anyone willing to pay the stiff congressionally mandated fees. For certain favored postal patrons these fees were waived. Lawmakers, for example, granted themselves the right to send an unlimited number of items at no cost through the network, a perquisite known as the "franking privilege."

The expansion in the mandate of the postal system to embrace newspapers as well as letters proved to be more controversial. Small numbers of newspapers had circulated in the mail for decades, primarily through the courtesy of lawmakers who sent them to constituents postage-free. But this practice remained customary and lacked the force of law. The postal system, remarked one postal administrator in 1788, had been established "for the purpose of facilitating commercial correspondence"; and, as a consequence, it had, "properly speaking, no connection with the press."[3]

The Post Office Act of 1792 put the conveyance of newspapers on an entirely different basis. Henceforth, every newspaper in the country, independent of content or place of publication, had the right to circulate in the mail at extremely low rates. To send a two-page letter from Boston to Savannah, Georgia, cost a merchant 50 cents in postage, a considerable sum; if, however, an editor sent a newspaper over the same route, the fee was a mere 1.5 cents. This was true even though newspapers were ordinarily much heavier than letters and, thus, more expensive to convey.

The results were predictable. Newspapers clogged the mail bags. In any given year, newspapers made up as much as 95 percent of the weight of the mail while generating no more than 15 percent of its revenue.[4] While newspaper conveyance posed a challenge for postal administrators, it was a great boon for ordinary Americans. For the first time it became possible for individuals living far from the seat of power to remain well informed about public affairs without having to meet in person with their representative. Within a remarkably short period of time, politicians figured out how to manipulate the new media by staging the artful journalistic spectacles that a later generation would dub "media events."

Among the most resourceful of the many groups to take advantage of the new communications network were the organizers of voluntary associations advocating causes ranging from temperance to women's rights. These voluntary associations, which often had a religious cast, were the first organizations to blanket the country with an identical message, a defining feature of "mass media."[5] One of the most notorious of these media events unfolded in 1835 when, to the horror and consternation of the country's slaveholders, an intrepid group of New York City–based abolitionists mailed thousands of unsolicited tracts to slaveholders advocating the immediate, uncompensated emancipation of slavery.

The Post Office Act of 1792 transformed not only the mandate of the postal system but also its character. European postal administrators routinely opened correspondence to monitor subversive activity. These surveillance techniques were familiar to American lawmakers. John Adams, Thomas Jefferson, and John Jay had each served as diplomats in Europe during the revolutionary era, and, while abroad, had grown accustomed to postal surveillance. Once the United States established its independence, lawmakers vowed that its government would renounce this tool of statecraft as a vestige of the monarchical past. Henceforth, or so the Post Office Act of 1792 decreed, it would be illegal for any government official to open anyone's mail.

The civic mandate of the postal system was broad, dynamic, and open-ended. Beginning in 1792, it embraced information on public affairs; by the 1820s, it had expanded to include information not only on public affairs but also on market trends; and by the 1840s, it had expanded once again to include information not only on public affairs and market trends but also on personal matters. By 1913, with the advent of parcel post, it would expand even further to embrace the conveyance not only of information but also of goods.

Prudent lawmakers had traditionally warned that the circulation of information might threaten established institutions, and the United States in the nineteenth century was no exception. The critical issue was slavery. In much of the United States, slavery enjoyed the protection of a welter of state laws, and in those states where it remained a pillar of the economy, slaveholders feared that the circulation of information might jeopardize their livelihood. The circulation of information on the slavery issue had the potential not only to foment a slave rebellion but also to foster public discussion. And public discussion, or so slaveholders feared, might persuade the non-slaveholding majority to renounce the "peculiar institution."

Thomas Jefferson is often hailed as a libertarian hero. Yet it was Jefferson's anti abolitionist heirs who were the most adamant in blocking the circulation of information on the slavery issue. Had Jefferson lived to witness the abolitionists' mail campaign of 1835—he had, in fact, died nine years earlier, in 1826—he, too, might, as a proponent of states' rights, have applauded the draconian state and local laws banning the circulation of information on the slavery issue. In most states, these laws would remain vigorously enforced until the Civil War. Only big government could lift this cordon sanitaire, and in the pre–Civil War period, federal lawmakers deferred to their colleagues in the states. Anti abolitionists feared not the First Amendment, but the informational environment that had been created by the Post Office Act of 1792.

The First Electrical Communications Networks: The Telegraph versus the Telephone

Most Americans have heard of Samuel F. B. Morse and Alexander Graham Bell. Each invented a technical contrivance that would become an essential component of an electrical communications network: the telegraph for Morse, the telephone for Bell. Few recall that both inventors owed not only their fame but also their fortunes to the regulatory agency that certified their inventions—namely, the US Patent Office.

The protection of intellectual property rights has since 1836 been a key contribution of the federal government's communications policy. Beginning in that year, Congress required patent office administrators to certify that each new invention was, in fact, worthy of federal protection—a mandate that distinguished the American patent office from the British patent office and that helped to facilitate the remarkable spate of information technology innovations in the years to come.[6]

Telegraph inventor Samuel F. B. Morse lobbied strenuously in the 1840s to persuade Congress to purchase his patent rights and authorize the Post Office Department to license promoters to operate the telegraph network. Yet Congress demurred and the licensing of telegraph operating companies devolved on the states.[7]

The mail was regulated by political fiat, the telegraph by market competition. Instead of emulating federal lawmakers and mandating rate caps and performance standards—as Congress had done with the Post Office Department—state lawmakers encouraged new entrants to challenge incumbents, on the assumption that market competition would encourage low rates and high performance standards. Antimonopoly became a rallying cry, with New York state leading the way. The New York Telegraph Act of 1848 made it easy to charter a telegraph company and popularized the presumption that telegraph managers should be free to charge whatever the market would bear. Similar laws were enacted shortly thereafter in many states. Market competition, state lawmakers assumed, was a better regulator than political fiat, and antimonopoly a compelling civic ideal.

The legacy of antimonopoly was far-reaching. Hemmed in by potential new entrants, incumbent telegraph operating companies pursued a business strategy that was narrow and restrictive. The dominant telegraph network provider, Western Union, had no interest in providing a mass service for the entire population, as its president declared in testimony before Congress in 1890. If ordinary Americans wished to communicate over long distances, they could send a letter.[8] The Post Office Department, buttressed by a civic mandate that was broad, dynamic, and open-ended, provided a mass service for the entire population; Western Union, constrained by antimonopoly legislation, remained for many decades the provider of a specialty service for an exclusive clientele of merchants, newspaper editors, and the well-to-do. Western Union would not recast its business strategy until 1910, when, partly in response to federal legislation that put telegraph companies under the jurisdiction of a federal regulatory agency and partly as a result of a change in management, telegraph managers reversed course and expanded their mandate for the first time to provide facilities for the many as well as the few.

The federal government played only a minor role in the early history of the telephone, with the major exception of patent rights. The first telephone exchange, which went into operation in 1878, was operated not by the Post Office Department—as Morse's first telegraph line had been in 1845—but by a state-chartered corporation. The first exchanges were highly localized, and their interconnection into a nationwide network took decades. Telephone inventor Alexander Graham Bell never lobbied Congress to establish a government telephone network, and in the period before 1900 few Americans, other than academic economists and certain frustrated business users, envisioned that the telephone might one day be regulated by a federal agency.

The telephone and telegraph emerged in an age in which the scope of state regulatory agencies remained confined to the publication of financial data. Yet here the similarity ceased. Big-city telephone operating companies were regulated from the outset by city councils, which, in return for providing operating companies with the necessary licenses to string wires over busy city streets, set rate caps and mandated performance standards. Few cities established a designated telephone bureau to regulate telephone service. Yet in all of the country's major cities, as well as in thousands of towns, city councils monitored the performance of telephone operating companies to ensure that they fulfilled their franchise obligations.

Franchise regulation obliged telephone managers to keep rates low and performance standards high. It also encouraged them to institute calling plans tailored to small users and to extend a basic level of service to underserved neighborhoods, innovations that both telephone managers and telephone users had initially resisted on account of their high cost and disruptive potential.

Telegraph service in 1900 remained a specialty service for the few. Telephone service, in contrast, was well on its way to becoming a mass service for the many. Paradoxically, the newer of the two electrical communications media was popularized first. Big government—in the form of city-based regulation—helps explain why. Market incentives and technological incentives cannot explain this surprising outcome; the key, rather, was political fiat.

The popularization of telephone service in the nation's big cities was risky. The construction of the switching equipment necessary to expand access to the network was expensive and the financial return uncertain. In many cities, including New York and Chicago, the financial extortion of telephone operating companies by unscrupulous aldermen posed a recurrent challenge. A further challenge was posed by the possibility that city officials might franchise a new entrant to compete with the incumbent. By transforming telephone service into a mass service, telephone company managers captured the moral high ground and cultivated a political base that insulated them against the vicissitudes of municipal politics.

In 1913, the US attorney general sued the dominant telephone holding company, American Telephone and Telegraph, for illegally monopolizing the business of electrical communications. Bell had recently acquired a major financial stake in telegraph giant Western Union, giving it a dominant position not only in the telephone but also in the telegraph. To prevent the Justice Department lawsuit from going to trial, Bell agreed in the following year to sell its holdings in Western Union and to cooperate with the many rival non-Bell telephone operating companies to create an interconnected nationwide telephone network. This political settlement transformed the telephone business into the legally sanctioned cartel that it would remain until the Justice Department broke it up in 1984.

The civic ideal that informed the Justice Department–Bell settlement was not market competition but market segmentation. Justice Department officials had no interest in atomizing the telephone business to revive market competition; rather, they built a firewall between the telegraph and the telephone business to discourage excessive concentrations of power.

In the seventy-year period between 1914 and 1984, telephone rates and performance standards were determined not by market competition but by political fiat. State regulatory agencies supplanted city councils as the primary regulatory forum beginning around 1907. The telephone business in this period was highly stable, yet in no sense stationary. To foster research and development in wired communications while containing the looming threat posed by disruptive innovations such as radio, Bell plowed millions of dollars into Bell Laboratories, a world leader in research and development that Bell established in 1925. The transistor, the first communications satellite, the UNIX computer operating system (a key component of the Internet), and many other vital components of the digital communications networks of the present-day United States were invented at Bell Labs. The willingness of Bell to invest so heavily in research and development—creating what was, in effect, a national laboratory—would have been inconceivable had lawmakers not transformed the telephone business into a cartel that guaranteed Bell a steady return.

Communicating over the Airwaves: Radio and Television

The cartelization of the telephone business established a precedent that would shape the regulation of a very different communications medium—namely, radio. In the Radio Act of 1927, a cornerstone of communications policy today, Congress extended the principle of government ownership from a city's streets to the airwaves. To minimize the problem of frequency interference, a major technical challenge, lawmakers permitted radio stations to license a portion of the electromagnetic spectrum. The spectrum itself, however, like a city's streets, remained public property. The self-confidence with which Congress claimed ownership over the airwaves was informed by the time-honored presumption that the federal government had an expansive civic mandate in the realm of communications. It also built on the recent public policy debate over municipal franchises in transportation, communications, water, and energy. In this debate, municipal franchise corporations were recast as "public utilities," a new concept dating from the 1890s that would provide a template for the regulation of radio and television in the decades to come.

The regulation of the electromagnetic spectrum devolved first upon the Federal Radio Commission, and, beginning in 1934, upon its successor, the Federal Communications Commission (FCC). The FCC remains the regulatory agency responsible for licensing radio and television stations today. No other governmental institution has done more to encourage broadcasters to promote the public good.[9]

Had Congress established a government-owned and operated broadcast network comparable to the British Broadcasting Corporation, not only radio and television but also the Internet might have been more centrally administered. With the Radio Act of 1927, lawmakers opted instead for planned decentralization, creating the mixed public-private informational environment characteristic of American communications policy ever since.

The cartelization of the telephone business had the further consequence of blocking the establishment of a telephone-radio monopoly. Lawmakers wary of concentrated power repeatedly warned in the 1920s that Bell might use its dominant position in the telephone business to control radio. Radio was a new medium, and Bell feared that the "wireless telegraph" might render valueless Bell's huge investment in a wired telephone network. To parry this threat, Bell made a major investment in radio research and held a valuable portfolio of radio patents. The NBC radio network originated as a Bell subsidiary, and for a time, it appeared likely that Bell might become as well entrenched in the radio business as it had become in the telephone business.

This nightmare scenario for lawmakers was forestalled when, in another section of the Radio Act of 1927, Congress extended to radio the principle of market segmentation. Telephone companies, Congress decreed, could own and operate the wired communications network over which radio signals were transmitted but not the radio stations that created the programming. Had Bell been an ordinary business regulated by market competition rather than political fiat, lawmakers would have found it much more difficult to prohibit it from entering into this promising new market and virtually impossible to enforce the telephone-radio divide.

Market segmentation is a civic ideal that lawmakers have repeatedly invoked to limit concentrations of power. When Congress prevented Bell from owning radio stations, it reaffirmed a principle that was as old as the republic. Had market segmentation not been a civic ideal, the Post Office Department might have retained control of the telegraph in the 1840s; the telegraph might have retained control of the telephone in the 1870s; the telephone might have retained control of the telegraph in the 1910s; and the telephone might have retained control of radio in the 1920s. Lawmakers have repeatedly opposed mergers that permit an entrenched organization to gain control of a new medium, another example of the influence of governmental institutions on American communications.

Communicating in the Digital Age

The computer, like the atomic bomb, was a legacy of federal investment in wartime. It emerged, as did so many of the innovations that we take for granted today, in the hothouse of innovation spawned by the Second World War. The Internet was also a product of military mobilization, though from a slightly later era. It was a product of the Cold War, a four-decade-long smoldering conflict between the United States and the Soviet Union during which policy makers in both countries feared that the world might soon be devastated by a nuclear cataclysm.

Like so many major innovations in communication—including radar, communications satellites, and the computer—the Internet originated not in some teenager's garage but, rather, in a government agency. Commercial considerations played no role in its inception, a fortunate fact, since, had commercial considerations been present, they might have discouraged government engineers from devising protocols to facilitate interconnection, a defining feature of the Internet today.

The Internet was not invented to ensure the survivability of American telephone networks during a nuclear attack. This myth, deeply entrenched in the popular imagination, is an oversimplified and misleading explanation of a complex reality.[10] Yet it does contain a kernel of truth. The Internet was a product of Cold War military planning. And, in particular, it was designed to speed up the calculations necessary to accurately fire intercontinental ballistic missiles, a task that taxed the computational power of the nation's largest computers.

Computational power in the 1960s was so limited that government scientists hit upon the expedient of linking together high-speed mainframe computers at universities located thousands of miles apart. Mainframe computers were originally self-contained; to interconnect them, government scientists had to invent protocols flexible enough to accommodate diversity. The invention of these protocols was a technical triumph. So, too, was the physical linkage of distant computers into a single network. Interconnection was facilitated by the common assumption that the long-distance Bell telephone network had excess capacity, and therefore that utilizing this network to send messages from computer to computer was cost-effective.[11]

None of the Internet-based innovations that we take for granted today—not Facebook, not Twitter, and not Google—could have emerged had the Internet been designed by a private corporation and not a government agency. The Internet was a by-product not of market competition but, rather, of the interdisciplinary, collaborative, knowledge-based research culture of the Cold War military-industrial-academic complex, a culture spawned by political fiat and sustained by federal funding. Unlike even the largest and most powerful of corporations, the military was unconstrained by the financial considerations that would have limited a commercially owned and operated network to a narrow range of applications in a limited domain. In the 1960s, federal administrators seriously considered turning over the administration of the Internet to AT&T, an acronym by which Bell was commonly known. AT&T rejected the proposal, fearful that it might become subject to unwanted regulatory scrutiny. Fortunately, big government prevailed. Paradoxically, and to a degree that free-market fundamentalists may find incomprehensible, it took a huge government bureaucracy to invent a communications network that was flexible, decentralized, and inclusive.[12]

Planned decentralization is a time-honored American civic ideal. It shaped the design of the federal Constitution, the structuring of the Post Office Department following the enactment of the Post Office Act of 1792, and the regulation of the nation's broadcast networks by the Federal Communications Commission. It is also a defining feature of the Internet, a direct result, paradoxically, of the heterogeneity of the nation's mainframe computers.

The commercialization of the Internet in the 1990s coincided with a sea change in conventional assumptions concerning government-business relations. For much of the twentieth century, lawmakers assumed that the FCC would regulate the nation's dominant communications networks—first the telephone and telegraph, then radio and television—in accordance with a civic mandate enshrined in federal law. To the chagrin of media critics, lawmakers never funded public radio or television on the scale that its supporters requested or that exists today in Great Britain, Canada, and Scandinavia. Yet federal regulators did shape the programming that broadcasters created. For almost four decades, for example, the FCC enforced, and the courts largely sustained, a "fairness doctrine" that required radio and television stations to broadcast opposing views on controversial public issues. This doctrine took inspiration from the founders' presumption that the government had a civic mandate to provide the citizenry with access to information on public affairs. This mandate, the FCC ruled in 1949, overrode the broadcaster's right to air whatever opinions it might see fit. All this began to change in the 1970s, with the revival of the nineteenth-century faith in market competition as a civic ideal. In 1987, the FCC abolished the fairness doctrine, hastening the rise of the partisan, vituperative, and more than occasionally irresponsible radio and television broadcasting that is such a ubiquitous feature of the informational environment today.[13]

Lawmakers in the years to come will continue to make basic decisions regarding the structure of the nation's communications networks. If current trends continue, public debate will be dominated by the presumption that the market is a better allocator of resources than the state. Lawmakers have favored market competition over political fiat at certain points in the American past. Market competition, for example, was a cornerstone of communications policy regarding the telegraph, a circumstance that helps explain why the telegraph, unlike the mail, newspapers, radio, television, or the Internet, has ceased to exist. Yet market competition has rarely been the norm. From a historical perspective, the critical issue for the lawmakers of today and tomorrow is not whether the federal government will intervene in the realm of communications. Rather, the critical issue is how it will intervene and on whose behalf.

Historians make poor prophets. Still, if we are to honor the legacy of the founders of the republic, we would do well to recall that for most of our history, lawmakers presumed that they had a civic mandate to coordinate the nation's communications networks. Promotion, regulation, and innovation were the three primary strategies lawmakers relied on; planned decentralization and market segmentation—and not market competition—were the most characteristic tools.

In communications, big government has been not the exception but the rule. The informational environment we enjoy today owes less to the inventive genius of teenage entrepreneurs toiling away in their parents' garage than to the creative statecraft of lawmakers committed to limiting arbitrary power and sustaining the informed citizenry necessary then and now to sustain the founders' bold experiment in representative government.

CHAPTER 10

From Endeavor to Achievement and Back Again

Government's Greatest Hits in Peril

Paul C. Light

Looking back from the edge of a new millennium, it is difficult not to be impressed by what the federal government has tried to achieve in the second half of the twentieth century. Name a significant domestic or foreign problem over the sixty-plus years since the end of World War II, and the federal government has made some effort to solve it, sometimes through massive new programs such as Medicare and Apollo, other times through a string of smaller initiatives to address enduring problems such as disease and poverty. If a nation's greatness is measured in part by the kinds of problems it asks its government to solve, the United States measures up very well indeed.

The proof is in the federal statute books. All told, Congress passed more than 500 major laws between 1944 and 2000 to improve the quality of life in the nation and world. Judged not as individual programs but as part of larger endeavors, these statutes speak to the enormous range of federal engagement since World War II. Having emerged victorious from both the war and the

Great Depression, Congress called upon the federal government to tackle a bold agenda worthy of the world's greatest democracy, and provided the statutory authority to act. Convinced that government could do great things, the nation asked our federal government to do just that.

The question of whether Congress and the president should have asked government to do so much has become central to the contemporary debate surrounding the federal debt. Equally important in the ongoing debate about health care access for low-income Americans are the questions of whether Congress and the president might have achieved more if they had passed greater responsibility to the states or pursued comprehensive action rather than incremental reform. Instead of debating these issues, however, this chapter looks at what the federal government actually sought to accomplish in the last half of the twentieth century, and therefore focuses on what government tried to do, not what it should or should not have done. Simply asked, what was the federal government asked to do, and what did it actually achieve?

The Federal Government's Greatest Endeavors

The footprints of the US government's greatest endeavors can be found in a host of accessible documents, including the *Federal Register,* the *Catalog of Domestic Assistance,* the *Budget of the United States,* the *Public Papers of the Presidents of the United States,* the *United States Code,* the *Code of Federal Regulations,* and the US Constitution.

Because almost all tracks lead back to Congress, what follows is based on an analysis of major laws passed by Congress since the end of World War II. Not only are the major laws easy to identify through public sources such as the *Congressional Quarterly Almanac* but also they authorize much of the activity that occurs elsewhere in government, most notably by setting budget and regulatory priorities.

Let's begin with 538 major statutes as a starting point for building the list of greatest endeavors. Selected on the basis of their significance, visibility, and/or precedent-setting nature, the laws run the gamut of legislative activity, from the creation of new programs and government agencies to the passage of constitutional amendments and ratification of foreign treaties, and cover virtually all areas of federal endeavor, from child health care to economic deregulation, food and water safety to national defense.

We can sort these 538 statutes into sixteen policy areas: agriculture, arts and historic preservation, civil rights, crime, the economy, education, health, housing and urban development, foreign policy and defense, government performance, income security, natural resources and energy, safety, science and technology, trade, and transportation.

Once they are divided by area, we can sort the statutes again based on the specific problem to be solved. Of the twenty-seven statutes dealing with civil rights, for example, three focused on discrimination in public accommodations, seven on discrimination in the workplace, and ten on barriers to voting rights. Of the eighty-one statutes dealing with energy and natural resources, six focused on endangered species, eight on hazardous waste, twelve on wilderness protection, and fourteen on the nation's energy supply.

Taking them all together yields an initial list of the federal government's sixty-seven major endeavors between the end of World War II and the start of the new millennium.

The list has been winnowed further to a final fifty based on the level of effort involved in each of the endeavors. This is not to suggest that the seventeen endeavors cut from the list were unimportant. They included ending discrimination in the armed services, providing help to the victims of natural and manmade disasters, promoting the arts, developing the nation's river valleys, and reforming the federal campaign finance system. Important though these endeavors are, they earned less attention from the federal government than the fifty items that made the final inventory summarized in table 1.

TABLE 1   Government's Greatest Endeavors

(with a few examples of actions taken)

Advance Human Rights and Provide Humanitarian Relief
United Nations Charter, 1945
Comprehensive Anti-Apartheid, 1986
Kosovo Intervention, 1999

Contain Communism
Aid to Greece and Turkey, 1947
NATO, 1949
Korean and Vietnam Wars

Control Immigration
Immigration and Nationality Act, 1952
Immigration Reform and Control Act, 1986
Immigration Act, 1990

Develop and Renew Impoverished Communities
Appalachian Regional Development Act, 1965
Demonstration Cities Act, 1966

Devolve Responsibility to the States
State and Local Fiscal Assistance Act, 1972
Unfunded Mandate Reform Act, 1995
Personal Responsibility and Work Opportunity Act (welfare reform), 1996

Enhance Consumer Protection
Food, Drug and Cosmetics Act, 1962
Fair Packaging and Labeling Act, 1966
Consumer Product Safety Act, 1972

Enhance the Nation's Health Care Infrastructure
Hospital Survey and Construction Act, 1946
Mental Retardation Facilities Construction Act, 1963
Heart Disease, Cancer and Stroke amendments, 1965

Enhance Workplace Safety
Federal Coal Mine Health and Safety Act, 1969
Occupational Safety and Health Act, 1970

Ensure an Adequate Energy Supply
Atomic Energy Act, 1954
Trans-Alaskan Pipeline, 1973
Natural Gas Wellhead Decontrol Act, 1989

TABLE 1 (Continued)

Expand Home Ownership
Housing Act, 1950
Housing Act, 1959
Tax Reform Act, 1986

Ensure Safe Food and Drinking Water
Federal Insecticide, Fungicide and Rodenticide Act, 1947
Wholesome Meat Act, 1967
Safe Drinking Water Act, 1974

Expand Foreign Markets for US Goods
Bretton-Woods Agreement Act, 1945
Organization for Economic Cooperation and Development, 1961
North American Free Trade Agreement, 1993

Expand Job Training and Placement
Employment Act, 1946
Comprehensive Employment and Training Act, 1973
Job Training Partnership Act, 1982

Expand the Right to Vote
24th Amendment, 1964
Voting Rights Act, 1965
26th Amendment, 1971

Improve Air Quality
Clean Air Act, 1963
Motor Vehicle Pollution Control Act, 1965

Improve Elementary and Secondary Education
National Defense Education Act, 1958
Elementary and Secondary Education Act, 1965
Head Start, 1967

Improve Government Performance
Civil Service Reform Act, 1978
Federal Managers' Financial Integrity Act, 1982
Federal Acquisitions Streamlining Act, 1994

Improve Mass Transportation
Urban Mass Transportation Act, 1964
Rail Passenger Service Act, 1970

(Continued)

TABLE 1 (Continued)

Improve Water Quality
Water Pollution Control Act, 1948, 1972
Water Quality Act, 1965, 1987

Increase Access to Postsecondary Education
Higher Education Act, 1965
Higher Education amendments, 1972

Increase Arms Control and Disarmament
Nuclear Test Ban Treaty, 1963
SALT/ABM Treaty, 1972
Intermediate Range Nuclear Force Treaty, 1988

Increase International Economic Development
International Bank for Reconstruction and Development, 1945
Act for International Development, 1950
Peace Corps, 1961

Increase Low-Income Families' Access to Health Care
Medicaid, 1965
Children's Health Insurance Program, 1997

Increase Market Competition
Airline Deregulation Act, 1978
Gramm-Leach-Bliley Act, 1999

Increase Older Americans' Access to Health Care
Medicare, 1965
Catastrophic Health Insurance for the Aged, 1988

Increase the Stability of Financial Institutions and Markets
Insider Trading and Securities Fraud Enforcement Act, 1988
Financial Institutions Reform, Recovery and Enforcement Act, 1989

Increase the Supply of Low-Income Housing
Housing Act, 1949
Housing and Community Development Act, 1965, 1974

Maintain Stability in the Persian Gulf
Gulf War, 1991

Make Government More Transparent to the Public
Administrative Procedures Act, 1946
Freedom of Information Act, 1966, 1974
Inspector General Act, 1978

TABLE 1 (Continued)

Promote Equal Access to Public Accommodations
Civil Rights Act, 1964
Open Housing Act, 1968
Americans with Disabilities Act, 1990

Promote Financial Security in Retirement
Expansions to Social Security
Supplemental Security Income Program, 1972
Employment Retirement Income Security Act, 1974

Promote Scientific and Technological Research
National Science Foundation Act, 1950
Defense Advanced Research Projects Agency, 1958
Communications Satellite Act, 1962

Promote Space Exploration
National Aeronautics and Space Administration, 1958
Apollo Mission Funding, 1962
Manned Space Station Funding, 1984

Protect Endangered Species
Marine Mammal Protection Act, 1972
Endangered Species Act, 1973

Protect the Wilderness
Wilderness Act, 1964
Wild and Scenic Rivers Act, 1968
Alaska National Interest Lands Conservation Act, 1980

Provide Assistance for the Working Poor
Earned Income Tax Credit, 1975
Family Support Act, 1988
Periodic Increases to the Minimum Wage

Rebuild Europe after World War II
Foreign Assistance Act, 1948
NATO treaty, 1949
International Monetary Fund

Reduce Crime
Omnibus Crime Control and Safe Streets Act, 1968, 1994
Brady Handgun Violence Prevention Act, 1993

Reduce Disease
Polio Vaccine Act, 1955
National Cancer Act, 1971

(Continued)

TABLE 1 (Continued)

Reduce Exposure to Hazardous Waste
Resource Conservation and Recovery Act, 1976
"Superfund" Act, 1980

Reduce the Federal Budget Deficit
Balanced Budget and Emergency Deficit Control Act, 1985
Omnibus Budget Reconciliation 1990, 1993
Balanced Budget Acts, 1995, 1997

Reduce Hunger and Improve Nutrition
National School Lunch Act, 1946
Food Stamp Act, 1964
Supplemental Food Program for Women, Infants and Children, 1972

Reduce Workplace Discrimination
Equal Pay Act, 1963
Age Discrimination Act, 1967
Americans with Disabilities Act, 1990

Reform Taxes
Revenue Act, 1964
Economic Recovery Tax Act, 1981

Reform Welfare
Personal Responsibility and Work Opportunity Act, 1996

Stabilize Agricultural Prices
Agricultural Act, 1948, 1961
Agricultural Trade Development and Assistance Act, 1954
Food Security Act, 1985

Strengthen the Nation's Airways System
Federal Airport Act, 1946
Airport and Airways Development Act, 1970

Strengthen the Nation's Highway System
Federal Aid to Highways Act, 1956
Intermodal Surface Transportation Efficiency Act, 1991

Strengthen the National Defense
Authorization of tactical and strategic weapons systems
Department of Defense Reorganization Act, 1958
Department of Defense Reorganization Act, 1986

Support Veterans' Readjustment and Training
Serviceman's Readjustment Act,1944
New GI Bill Continuation Act, 1987

As the table demonstrates, these efforts are extraordinarily wide-ranging—from advancing human rights to helping veterans readjust to civilian life; from protecting consumers to protecting the environment. All but a handful of the fifty endeavors involve closely related sets of laws organized around a consistent strategy for addressing a focused problem such as crime, water quality, or arms control and disarmament.

Hence, the Civil Rights Act of 1964 fits naturally with the Age Discrimination Act of 1967 and Americans with Disabilities Act of 1990 in the effort to end workplace discrimination; the Omnibus Crime Control and Safe Streets Act of 1968 and its 1970, 1984, and 1994 amendments fit tightly with the Organized Crime Control Act of 1970 in the effort to reduce crime; the Bretton Woods Agreement of 1945 fits well with the Trade Expansion Act of 1962, the Trade and Tariff Act of 1984, and the North American Free Trade Agreement of 1993 in the effort to expand foreign markets for US goods.

Some endeavors may seem overly broad, however, whether because they involve eclectic collections of individual statutes or a more diffuse problem. For example, the effort to improve mass transportation includes a mix of statutes covering everything from the creation of Amtrak to urban mass transit and light rail, while the effort to control immigration involves four statutes that share little beyond the word "immigration" in their titles, and the effort to reduce disease combines the Polio Vaccination Assistance Act of 1955 with the National Cancer Act of 1971 and a variety of medical research bills.

This list of the federal government's fifty greatest endeavors is best viewed as the product of a good-faith effort to identify the problems that the government tried hardest to solve over the past half century. As such, the list offers two initial lessons about how the government has sought to achieve results.

First, despite the tendency by both scholars and the general public to focus on grand statutes such as Medicare or welfare reform, most of government's greatest endeavors involved a relatively large number of statutes passed over a relatively long period of time.

Only eight of the fifty endeavors involved fewer than three major statutes:

- promoting equal access to public accommodations
- increasing access to health care for older Americans
- enhancing workplace safety
- devolving responsibilities to the states
- increasing access to health care for low-income families
- reforming welfare, reforming taxes
- maintaining stability in the Persian Gulf

One might speculate that the first Iraq war might well end up in a new endeavor titled the "war on terrorism," which would include the second war in Iraq, the war in Afghanistan, the USAPATRIOT act, and creation of the Department of Homeland Security and Directorship of National Intelligence.

No single piece of legislation could be expected to achieve the results of some of the biggest endeavors that the nation has addressed. Remove these eight tightly focused endeavors from the list, and it has taken an average of nine statutes to move the other major endeavors forward.

For the very biggest challenges, the numbers are correspondingly larger:

- promoting financial security in retirement (21 statutes)
- stabilizing agricultural price supports (19 statutes)
- increasing assistance to the working poor (15 statutes)
- increasing the supply of low-income housing, ensuring an adequate energy supply, and improving mass transportation (14 statutes each)

Almost by definition, great endeavors demand great endurance. That lesson is often forgotten in the headlines about the latest legislative intrigue.

Second, it is difficult to give any single president, party, or Congress the primary credit for launching and maintaining more than a handful of the endeavors. Only nine of the fifty greatest endeavors can be credited primarily to Democratic presidents, and just five can be credited to Republican presidents. The rest span Democratic and Republican administrations. As a result, even though Democrats controlled Congress for the vast majority of the past fifty years, only six can be tied to unified party control of government.

Government's Greatest Achievements

It is one thing to develop a list of government's greatest endeavors by sorting legislative statutes, and quite another to draw conclusions about whether those endeavors involved important and difficult problems and were ultimately successful.

These judgments were ultimately made through a mail survey I sent to historians and political scientists during the summer of 2000. Selected for their interest in twentieth-century American history or American government, these members of the American Historical Association and American Political Science Association were seen as the most likely to have both the training and confidence to rate all fifty endeavors on the three core measures of achievement: (1) the importance of the problem to be solved, (2) the difficulty of the problem to be solved, and (3) the federal government's success in creating significant progress in actually advancing its goals.

As I argued in my book *Government's Greatest Achievements* (2002), the nation did more than aim high in trying to solve great problems. Working through government, business, and nonprofits, the United States produced a long list of achievements. Much as Americans believe that the federal government creates more problems than it solves, my research suggests that government deserves more credit than it receives, especially when it comes time to cut the budget.

On the basis of the survey ratings, I scored government's greatest achievements since World War II by putting the heaviest weight on success, while awarding extra credit for tackling especially important and difficult problems. This approach produced table 1, a list of fifty of the government's most ambitious efforts between World War II and the dawn of the new millennium in 2001, along with representative examples of how the government pursued its goals. Table 2 gives a rank-ordered list of the results, which were tabulated through the final score of success (60 percent of the total), importance to the nation (30 percent), and difficulty (10 percent).

There are four broad lessons from these "greatest hits" for converting endeavor into achievement.

First, achievement requires significant collaboration across the aisles and institutions. Neither Democrats nor Republicans can be credited with any specific achievements. Although one party might have driven the initial achievement, both parties eventually embraced the idea. Even Medicare, which was a signature accomplishment of Lyndon Johnson's Great Society, and the Marshall Plan, which carried Harry S. Truman's imprimatur, had antecedents in earlier Congresses and administrations.

Second, achievement involves persistence and a mix of incremental adjustment punctuated by occasional grand decisions. Although there are great statutes on the list, the United States achieved most of its successes by wearing down the prevailing wisdom, often through incremental adjustments in early gains. The nation did not reduce disease with a single act, for example, but with dozens of statutes over the years; nor did it achieve scientific and technological achievements with one research and development grant.

Third, achievement resides in a lasting commitment to the endeavor at hand. No one knew at the time whether expanding the right to vote, opening public accommodations, or ending workplace discrimination would eventually succeed in their

TABLE 2   Rating Government Achievement

Government Achievements	% Rated Very Successful	% Rated Very Important	% Rated Very Difficult
1. Rebuild Europe after World War II	82	80	38
2. Expand the right to vote	61	89	34
3. Promote equal access to public accommodation	34	78	39
4. Reduce disease	23	65	29
5. Reduce workplace discrimination	13	78	53
6. Ensure safe food and drinking water	14	73	19
7. Strengthen the nation's highway system	40	30	4
8. Increase older Americans' access to health care	24	70	20
9. Reduce the federal budget deficit	33	36	45
10. Promote financial security in retirement	23	60	16
11. Improve water quality	9	72	31
12. Support veterans' readjustment and training	29	40	6
13. Promote scientific and technological research	20	48	7
14. Contain communism	36	32	50
15. Improve air quality	8	72	40
16. Enhance workplace safety	9	56	23
17. Strengthen the national defense	26	28	11

(*Continued*)

TABLE 2 (Continued)

Government Achievements	% Rated Very Successful	% Rated Very Important	% Rated Very Difficult
18. Reduce hunger and improve nutrition	11	72	13
19. Increase access to postsecondary education	15	53	9
20. Enhance consumer protection	11	51	20
21. Expand foreign markets for US goods	15	28	22
22. Increase the stability of financial institutions and markets	11	36	16
23. Increase arms control and disarmament	4	78	65
24. Protect the wilderness	8	49	19
25. Promote space exploration	20	16	34
26. Protect endangered species	8	38	25
27. Reduce exposure to hazardous waste	3	63	34
28. Enhance the nation's health care infrastructure	8	47	19
29. Maintain stability in the Persian Gulf	21	24	25
30. Expand homeownership	18	18	4
31. Increase international economic development	5	46	41
32. Ensure an adequate energy supply	5	56	32
33. Strengthen the nation's airways system	6	47	11
34. Increase access to health care for low-income families	3	78	34
35. Improve elementary and secondary education	2	75	38

TABLE 2 (Continued)

Government Achievements	% Rated Very Successful	% Rated Very Important	% Rated Very Difficult
36. Reduce crime	3	45	48
37. Advance human rights and provide humanitarian relief	1	60	66
38. Make government more transparent to the public	3	46	27
39. Stabilize agricultural prices	11	18	13
40. Provide assistance for the working poor	3	60	27
41. Improve government performance	1	33	29
42. Reform welfare	3	31	43
43. Expand job training and placement	2	33	20
44. Increase market competition	13	13	11
45. Increase the supply of low-income housing	0	50	26
46. Develop and renew impoverished communities	<1	49	52
47. Improve mass transportation	1	61	41
48. Reform taxes	8	17	18
49. Control immigration	3	15	36
50. Devolve responsibility to the states	4	8	11

Note: This table is based on a July–October 2000 survey of 450 self-identified public policy experts selected from the membership directories of the American Historical Association and American Political Science Association. The paper-and-pencil survey instrument was mailed to an initial sample of 1,039 members, yielding a final response rate of 43 percent and a margin of error in all responses of plus-or-minus 5 percent.

goals. Nor did anyone have a defensible cost-benefit analysis to prove that these efforts would yield more in public value than they cost. Yet the nation endeavored nonetheless, often taking the moral high ground despite significant resistance.

Finally, achievement involves a readiness to invest over time. It is not enough merely to express a desire to solve persistent problems such as hunger, disease, or homelessness. Congress and the president must also provide the funding to honor the promises they make. Although there have been times when budget cuts were essential for economic growth, achievement often rests on a willingness to create balanced packages of budget cuts and revenue increases.

Achievements in Peril

Just as one can look back with considerable awe at what the federal government has tried to accomplish over the past half century, so, too, can one look forward with considerable doubt about whether government will ever be so bold again.

Indeed, as I write this, the most urgent threat we face may be the erosion of our past achievements.

Of the top twenty-five achievements listed in table 2, all but one, the Marshall Plan, are under siege. And I could easily argue that the current financial meltdowns in Greece, Portugal, Spain, and Turkey raise questions about the durable effect of even that great accomplishment. The top achievements and their current status are summarized in table 3. As that table suggests, there are many urgent threats on the horizon because of the benign and deliberate neglect of past attainments.

Congress added prescription drug coverage to government's long-standing effort to improve health security for older Americans, as well as a broad health insurance mandate to the stop-and-start effort to increase health care access for children and families, new regulations to strengthen control of

TABLE 3 Government Achievements Imperiled

Endeavor	Budget Cuts/ Failure to Maintain Investment	Inconsistent Regulation and Enforcement	Shifts in Global Dynamics (including technology, demographics, geopolitics, and the global recession)	Changes in National Priorities/ Partisanship
Expand the Right to Vote		X		X
Promote Equal Access to Public Accommodations	X	X		X
Reduce Disease	X	X	X	
Reduce Workplace Discrimination		X	X	
Ensure Safe Food and Drinking Water		X	X	
Strengthen the Nation's Highway System	X			
Increase Older Americans' Access to Health Care	X			X
Reduce the Federal Budget Deficit				X
Promote Financial Security in Retirement	X		X	X
Improve Water Quality	X	X		
Support Veterans' Readjustments and Training	X		X	

(*Continued*)

TABLE 3 (Continued)

Endeavor	Budget Cuts/ Failure to Maintain Investment	Inconsistent Regulation and Enforcement	Shifts in Global Dynamics (including technology, demographics, geopolitics, and the global recession)	Changes in National Priorities/ Partisanship
Promote Scientific and Technological Research	X			X
Improve Air Quality		X	X	
Enhance Workplace Safety		X		X
Strengthen the National Defense			X	
Reduce Hunger and Improve Nutrition	X			X
Increase Access to Postsecondary Education	X			
Enhance Consumer Protection		X		X
Expand Foreign Markets for US Goods			X	
Increase the Stability of Financial Institutions and Markets		X		X
Increase Arms Control and Disarmament			X	

TABLE 3 (Continued)

Endeavor	Budget Cuts/ Failure to Maintain Investment	Inconsistent Regulation and Enforcement	Shifts in Global Dynamics (including technology, demographics, geopolitics, and the global recession)	Changes in National Priorities/ Partisanship
Protect the Wilderness	X			X
Promote Space Exploration	X			X
Protect Endangered Species	X	X		X
Reduce Exposure to Hazardous Waste	X	X	X	
Enhance the Nation's Health Care Infrastructure	X			
Maintain Stability in the Persian Gulf			X	
Expand Homeownership			X	

the financial industry, and a burst of stimulus funding largely dedicated to rebuilding the transportation infrastructure. Congress also added the "war on terrorism" to the list of great endeavors.

Despite the hopes embedded in this mix of partisan and non-partisan expansions, the trend toward disinvestment and reversal applies to these additions, too, in no small part because Congress also enacted a massive tax cut in 2001 (and the nation launched along with the unfunded wars in Iraq and Afghanistan) that continues to constrain federal investment in problem solving.

Each expansion is facing its own backlash. Prescription drug coverage has become a significant driver of Medicare's financial crisis, the new health care law is under fire from Republicans and the courts, financial regulation is stalled as the financial industry pours vast resources into its lobbying effort, and the stimulus is long over. Coupled with the intense demand for fiscal austerity, the recent slate of across-the-board budget cuts in programs such as Medicaid, job training, education, and environmental protection suggests that the federal government's greatest achievements will be in peril for some time to come.

There are many threats to these impressive accomplishments, including the complacency that comes with time, the erosion of impact that occurs with the budget cutter's knife, and the bureaucratic sclerosis that weakens the implementation of promises made.

Americans too often take past achievements for granted. Many simply assume that their food and water are safe, their roads and bridges ready for traffic, their work free of harassment, their right to vote always guaranteed, and their airplanes up to code. As memories fade, so does public support for the achievements that made America and the world more equitable, healthy, educated, and tolerant, and the case for further action is easily denied as too costly or yet another example of tax-and-spend government.

Moreover, as budget cutting sweeps across the world, Americans have become enchanted with the promise of achievement on the cheap. There is nothing quite so alluring in Washington and state capitols today than replacing expensive social initiatives with innovative alternatives, especially if those alternatives are funded by private philanthropy or adopted as profit makers by private businesses.

This celebration of all things new often comes with a rejection of anything old. It is a common refrain referenced in the case for social entrepreneurship, which is a business-like version of the well-worn term "social innovation." Instead of giving a man a fish or teaching a man to fish, social entrepreneurs ask vaguely, why not change the fishing industry itself?

Social entrepreneurs bring great strengths to their efforts to create the new combinations of ideas for solving intractable problems such as hunger, disease, for solving. Unlike business entrepreneurs, who pursue new ideas for profits and glory, social entrepreneurs are clearly motivated by the desire to help others. Although some social entrepreneurs also make profits through social ventures, while others seem to seek glory, generally speaking, social entrepreneurs are motivated by a sense of social injustice that other entrepreneurs do not have. They are also convinced that there is no such thing as an intractable social problem.

At the same time, social entrepreneurs often dismiss past achievements as little more than distractions along the path to a new world. They are also convinced that business and social entrepreneurship are two sides of the same coin. Business entrepreneurship no doubt offers many important lessons for creating new endeavors and future achievements. But the analogy between business and social entrepreneurship can be stretched too far. Simply asked, are business and social entrepreneurship fundamentally alike in mostly unimportant respects?

The answer is mixed. On the one hand, business and social entrepreneurship both create "waves of creative destruction" as they advance toward achievement. Both also use many of the same disciplines for taking their ideas to "scale," including fundraising, research and development, and aggressive marketing.

However, even as both create waves of destruction, the destruction is not the same. When the waves crash ashore in business, whole industries are washed away for good. When the waves come ashore in social entrepreneurship, however, the industries of deprivation rarely disappear. Having reaped the profits of deprivation through poverty, disease, environmental degradation, and injustice, social entrepreneurs fight hard to regain power and reverse change. They do not control prevailing wisdom through the kind of complacency revealed in my downgrades of the federal government's past achievements—they prevail through the blunt exercise of power and control, crushing achievements through every means at their disposal.

Conclusion

Regardless of what we call them—social entrepreneurs, innovators, even public servants—these actors have a significant role to play in reversing the recent disinvestment in government's greatest achievements, whether through new ideas for revitalizing past endeavors, more effective tools for delivering on promises made, or new approaches for accelerating problem solving.

However, other problem solvers, including social stewards, explorers, and advocates, must also engage to work together against further erosion.

Consider social stewards as a first source of defense. The term "social steward" is particularly appealing as an alternative to the term "social service provider." Whereas service providers are often denigrated as little more than metaphorical cafeteria workers who serve the same tired food on metal trays each morning, social stewards have a much broader job description that includes the execution, defense, repair, innovation, and expansion of achievements. On the notion that the best offense is a good defense, social stewards must protect past gains and remedy past failures.

Consider social explorers as a second source. Social explorers are critical for providing the knowledge or intelligence for understanding the sources of past success and failure, anticipating alternative futures, and testing vulnerable assumptions. Their primary responsibility is to create strategies for achieving desired futures, even as they help entrepreneurs and stewards fine-tune their interventions. Social explorers are also essential for detecting trends that threaten past achievements and provide new opportunities for converting past and current endeavors into success.

Finally, consider social advocates as a third source. Social advocates provide the political muscle to fight the inevitable backlash against great achievements. They organize, lobby, campaign, poll, petition, and protest. They also help create the networks and alliances that pulse and swarm against the opposition. This work does not always involve the enactment or defeat of policies such as the 2001 tax cut. Social advocates also work to change public mind-sets, as do entrepreneurs, stewards, and explorers. They provide the energy to take new ideas to scale, fight disinvestment, and highlight key trends that block endeavors and undermine achievements. In a term, they provide the "shock and awe" that pushes back against the return of the old prevailing wisdom.

Each of these types of defender has its own role in creating and sustaining achievement. Social entrepreneurs face their greatest challenge in taking new ideas to scale, whether defined as growth or replication; social stewards face their greatest challenge in finding the resources to innovate under unrelenting pressure to deliver goods and services; social explorers hit their greatest obstacles when they tell inconvenient truths, especially when they confront the faddism that sometimes accompanies the latest new ideas; and social advocates are almost always under fire as too hot, too partisan, and too confrontational.

Nevertheless, each type has its own role in augmenting, fine-tuning, and defending achievement:

1. If the achievement requires a new combination of ideas for change, then social entrepreneurship is likely to be the preferred driver.

2. If the achievement demands protection, repair, maintenance, fine-tuning, expansion, and further innovation for sustained achievement, then social stewardship is likely to be the key.

3. If the achievement stands on an effort to anticipate key threats, monitor trends, and evaluate what does and does not work, then social exploring is likely to be the means to the end.

4. If the achievement acquires ultimate policy impact through lobbying, pressure, partisanship, and long-lasting social movement, then social advocacy must be engaged.

The four may have different roles, but they all share the same duty to fight disinvestment. The decision to call upon one or more of these defenders must reflect the hoped-for effects. Instead of working forward through a simplistic logic chain of inputs (urgent threats), activities (imagining, inventing, and so forth), outputs (social entrepreneurship), and outcomes (achievements), we might think about working backward from destination to driver by letting form follow function.

There will always be a role for social entrepreneurs in advancing endeavors and protecting achievements, but they must also make room for other forms of defense. And all four must accept the added burden of protecting the change they produce. It is the only way to prevent bygones from becoming bygones.

Rock and Roll Hall of Famer Joni Mitchell no doubt had it right decades ago when she sang "don't it always go to show that you don't know what you've got 'til it's gone." If the old way cannot work, replace it. If the old way needs repair, fix it. If the old way still works, defend it. And if it is being strangled by partisanship, austerity, or ignorance, fight for it. It takes decades to create an achievement, but only a moment to destroy it.

Notes

Preface

1. For the best one-volume survey of this anti-government attitude, see Garry Wills, *A Necessary Evil: A History of American Distrust of Government* (New York: Simon and Schuster, 1999).
2. Ibid., p. 320.

Chapter 1 Looking for Government in All the Wrong Places

1. Mike Brownfield, "Morning Bell: Big Government Rising?," September 6, 2011, The Foundry, http://blog.heritage. org/2011/09/06/morning-bell-big-government-rising/.
2. Proggirl, commenting on Beth Fouhy, "Carl Paladino Backs Welfare Prison Dorms, Hygiene Classes," August 21, 2005, www.huffingtonpost.com/2010/08/22/carl-paladino-backs-welfa_n_690284.html.
3. Suzanne Mettler, *The Submerged State: How Invisible Government Policies Undermine American Democracy* (Chicago: University of Chicago Press, 2011), 6.
4. Brian Balogh, *Government Out of Sight: The Mystery of National Authority in Nineteenth Century America* (New York: Cambridge University Press, 2009), 21.
5. Balogh, *Government Out of Sight*, 23; Max M. Edling, *A Revolution in Favor of Government: Origins of the U.S. Constitution and the Making of the American State* (New York: Oxford University Press, 2003),

40–41; Joseph J. Ellis, *Founding Brothers: Stories from the Early Republic* (New York: Knopf, 2000), 7; Andrew S. Trees, *The Founding Fathers and the Politics of Character* (Princeton, NJ: Princeton University Press, 2004), 1.

6. It was just such a conflation of the two that Paine challenged, writing, "Some writers have so confounded society with government, as to leave little or no distinction between them." Thomas Paine, "Common Sense," 1776, reprinted in Thomas Paine, *Common Sense* (Westminster, MD: Bantam Books, 2004) 3; Ellis, *Founding Brothers*, 14.

7. Benjamin Rush, "On the Defects of the Confederation," in *The Selected Writings of Benjamin Rush*, ed. Dagobert D. Runes (New York: Philosophical Library, 1947), 31, quoted in *Trees, Founding Fathers*, 3; John L. Larson, *Internal Improvement: National Public Works and the Promise of Popular Government in the Early United States* (Chapel Hill: University of North Carolina Press, 2001), 20; Peter S. Onuf, "Federalism, Democracy, and Liberty in the New American Nation" (lecture, Expansion of English Liberty Overseas, Cincinnati, November 1–3, 2007), 15–23. Balogh, *Government Out of Sight*, 24–25.

8. Alexander Hamilton, *Federalist Number 27*, December 25, 1787, as quoted in Balogh, *Government Out of Sight*, 3.

9. Ibid.; this phrase was suggested by Ed Ayers; Alexis De Tocqueville, *Democracy in America*, ed. J. P. Mayer, trans. George Lawrence (New York: HarperPerennial, 1989), 77, cited in Pauline Maier, "The Origins and Influence of Early American Local Self-Government," in *Dilemmas of Scale in America's Federal Democracy*, ed. Martha Derthick (New York: Cambridge University Press, 1999), 78; Balogh, *Government Out of Sight*, 4.

10. Zachary M. Schrag, "Transportation and the Uniting of the Nation," p. 27 of this volume.

11. Schrag, "Transportation," p. 22 of this volume.

12. Balogh, *Government Out of* Sight, 285–286.

13. Laura Phillips, "Contested Meanings of Freedom," *Journal of Gilded Age and Progressive* Era (forthcoming).

14. Julia Irwin, "Humanitarian Occupations: Foreign Relief and Assistance in America's International Progressive Era" (book manuscript, 2009, in author's possession), 31.

15. For an overview of the ways in which pluralist politics changed over the course of the twentieth century, see Brian Balogh, "Making Pluralism 'Great': Beyond a Recycled History of the Great Society," in *The Great Society and the High Tide of Liberalism*, ed. Sidney M. Milkis and Jerry Mileur (Amherst: University of Massachusetts Press, 2005), 145–182, and Elisabeth S. Clemens, "Lineages of the Rube

Goldberg State: Building and Blurring Public Programs, 1900–1949," in *Rethinking Political Institutions: The Art of the State*, ed. Ian Shapiro, Stephen Skowronek, and Daniel Galvin (New York: New York University Press, 2006), 187–215. For a penetrating analysis of the strengths and weakness of the American Medical Association, see Christy Chapin, "The AMA and the Institutional Intersection of Political and Market Power, 1945–1957," paper presented to the Institute for Applied Economics and the Study of Business Enterprise, Johns Hopkins University, Baltimore, October 2008. For a sophisticated discussion of the way in which the voluntary sector adapted to the rise of New Deal social service provision, see Andrew J. F. Morris, *The Limits of Voluntarism: Charity and Welfare from the New Deal through the Great Society* (New York: Cambridge University Press, 2009).

Kathleen Jill Frydl effectively demonstrates how prodigious spending for veterans was obscured by the institutional mechanisms through which it was delivered (in this case, the states and private contractors) at the very time it expanded federal authority in *The G.I. Bill* (New York: Cambridge University Press, 2009).

16. Citations to the literature on the hidden welfare state and the contractual state are in subsequent notes.

17. Women were more prone to seek government assistance at the state and local level than other members of the associative order. Elisabeth S. Clemens, *The People's Lobby: Organizational Innovation and the Rise of Interest Group Politics in the United States, 1890–1925* (Chicago: University of Chicago Press, 1997); Lorraine Gates Schuyler, *The Weight of the Their Votes: Southern Women and Political Leverage in the 1920s* (Chapel Hill: University of North Carolina Press, 2006). See also Balogh, "'Mirrors of Desires.'" The story of federal/voluntary relationships in social services is picked up in Morris, *The Limits of Voluntarism.*

18. The work of Christopher Loss has changed the way we think about universities in relationship to the state. Breaking out of the more traditional university research-military complex, Loss considers the ways in which universities reshape American citizenship, from the 1920s through the end of the Cold War. Christopher Loss, *Between Citizens and the State: The Politics of American Higher Education in the Twentieth Century* (Princeton, NJ: Princeton University Press, 2011).

19. Jonathan Zimmerman, "Uncle Sam at the Blackboard: The Federal Government and American Education," pp. 48–49 of this volume.

20. For a fascinating account of what the Social Security Administration was able to do once they *did* acquire computers, see Andrew Meade McGee, "'Please, Mr. Machine, Give This to a Human to Read':

Electronic Data Processing, Systems Management, and Great Society Idealism in the Social Security Administration, 1965–1974" (master's thesis, University of Virginia, August 2007).

21. For analytical histories of early Social Security and its administrators, see Martha Derthick, *Policymaking for Social Security* (Washington, DC: Brookings Institution Press, 1979); Edward Berkowitz, *Robert Ball and the Politics of Social Security* (Madison: University of Wisconsin Press, 2003); and Berkowitz, *Mr. Social Security: The Life of Wilbur J. Cohen* (Lawrence: University Press of Kansas, 1995).

22. Brian Balogh, Joanna Grisinger, and Philip Zelikow, "Making Democracy Work: A Brief History of Twentieth Century Executive Reorganization" (Miller Center of Public Affairs Working Paper, July 2002); Brian Balogh, *Chain Reaction: Expert Debate and Public Participation in American Commercial Nuclear Power, 1945–1975* (New York: Cambridge University Press, 1991).

23. Harold D. Lasswell, "The Garrison State," *American Journal of Sociology* 46, no. 4 (January 1941): 455–468. On "contract state," see Aaron L. Friedberg, *In the Shadow of the Garrison State: America's Anti-statism and Its Cold War Grand Strategy* (Princeton, NJ: Princeton University Press, 2000).

24. Thomas Sugrue, "The Right to a Decent Home," p. 115 of this volume. Suzanne Mettler, *Submerged State*; see also Juliana Koch and Suzanne Mettler, "Who Perceives Government's Role in Their Lives? How Policy Visibility Influences Awareness of and Attitudes about Social Spending," paper presented to the Miller Center Colloquia Series on Politics and History, October 7, 2011.

25. Suzanne Mettler, *Soldiers to Citizens: The G.I. Bill and the Making of the Greatest Generation* (New York: Oxford University Press, 2005).

26. David M. P. Freund, "Marketing the Free Market: State Intervention and the Politics of Prosperity," in *The New Suburban History*, ed. Kevin M. Kruse and Thomas J. Sugrue (Chicago: University of Chicago Press, 2006), 13, and 11–14 generally.

27. Peter F. Drucker, *The Unseen Revolution: How Pension Fund Socialism Came to America* (New York: Harper and Row, 1976), 46, quoted in Jacob S. Hacker, *The Divided Welfare State: The Battle over Public and Private Social Welfare Benefits in the United States* (New York: Cambridge University Press, 2002), 82; Hacker, *Divided Welfare State*, 11, 83. For other key interpretations of the hidden welfare state, see Chris Howard, *The Hidden Welfare State: Tax Expenditures and Social Policy in the United States* (Princeton, NJ: Princeton University Press, 1997), and Jennifer Klein, *For All These Rights: Business, Labor, and the Shaping of America's Public-Private Welfare State* (Princeton, NJ: Princeton University Press, 2003). For an excellent

example of the political culture that limited the kind and extent of taxation allowed, see Julian Zelizer, *Taxing America: Wilbur D. Mills, Congress, and the State, 1945–1975* (New York: Cambridge University Press, 1998).

28. Karen Kruse Thomas, "Solving the Nation's Number One Health Problem(s)," p. 119 of this volume.

29. Hacker, *Divided Welfare State.* On subsidies that have favored white middle-class constituents, see Ira Katznelson, *When Affirmative Action Was White: An Untold Story of Racial Inequality in Twentieth-Century America* (New York: Norton, 2005).

30. Philip Rucker, "SC Senator Is a Voice of Reform Opposition," *Washington Post,* July 28, 2009, www.washingtonpost.com/wp-dyn/content/article/2009/07/27/AR2009072703066.html; Timothy Noah, "The Medicare-Isn't-Government Meme," *Slate.com*, August 5, 2009, www.slate.com/id/2224350/.

Chapter 2   Transportation and the Uniting of the Nation

1. Jack Cady, "Kansas 5 A.M.," *Rolling Stone*, November 22, 1973, 63, 66. For the context of Cady's complaints and his perspective as an independent trucker, see Shane Hamilton, *Trucking Country: The Road to America's Wal-Mart Economy* (Princeton, NJ: Princeton University Press, 2008), chap. 7.

2. "Virginia-Maryland Boundary," n.d., www.virginiaplaces.org/boundaries/mdboundary.html; Richard B. Morris, "The Mount Vernon Conference: First Step toward Philadelphia," *This Constitution* 6 (Spring 1985): 38.

3. D. W. Meinig, *The Shaping of America: A Geographical Perspective on 500 Years of History*, vol. 2 (New Haven, CT: Yale University Press, 1993), 4.

4. James Madison, "Federalist No. 14: Objections to the Proposed Constitution from Extent of Territory Answered," November 30, 1787, http://thomas.loc.gov/home/histdox/fed_14.html.

5. John Lauritz Larson, "'Bind the Republic Together': The National Union and the Struggle for a System of Internal Improvements," *Journal of American History* 74, no. 2 (1987): 369.

6. US Department of the Treasury, *Report of the Secretary of the Treasury, on the Subject of Public Roads and Canals* (Washington, DC: R. C. Weightman, 1808), www.archive.org/details/reportofsecretar00unit.

7. Carter Goodrich, "The Gallatin Plan after One Hundred and Fifty Years," *Proceedings of the American Philosophical Society* 102, no. 5 (October 20, 1958): 440.

8. US Department of the Treasury, *Report of the Secretary of the Treasury, on the Subject of Public Roads and Canals*, 73.

9. Larson, "Bind the Republic Together," 377–380.

10. Goodrich, "The Gallatin Plan," 439.

11. Carter Goodrich, *Government Promotion of American Canals and Railroads, 1800–1890* (New York: Columbia University Press, 1960), 162. For the figure $1.34 trillion I have used "Measuring Worth," measuringworth.com, accessed September 2011.

12. John Haskell Kemble, "The Panamá Route to the Pacific Coast, 1848–1869," *Pacific Historical Review* 7, no. 1 (March 1, 1938): 3.

13. Pamela L. Baker, "The Washington National Road Bill and the Struggle to Adopt a Federal System of Internal Improvement," *Journal of the Early Republic* 22, no. 3 (Fall 2002): 462.

14. Robert Angevine, *The Railroad and the State: War, Politics, and Technology in Nineteenth-Century America* (Stanford, CA: Stanford University Press, 2004), 119–125.

15. James E. Vance, *The North American Railroad: Its Origin, Evolution, and Geography* (Baltimore: Johns Hopkins University Press, 1995), 107.

16. Ibid., 77, 110.

17. Ibid., 113.

18. George Washington Bates, *Sandwich Island Notes* (New York: Harper & Brothers, 1854), 492.

19. Franklin Ng, *The History and Immigration of Asian Americans* (New York: Taylor and Francis, 1998), 41.

20. T. J. Stiles, *The First Tycoon: The Epic Life of Cornelius Vanderbilt* (New York: Random House Digital, 2009), 215.

21. D. W. Meinig, *The Shaping of America: A Geographical Perspective on 500 Years of History*, vol. 3 (New Haven, CT: Yale University Press, 2000), 5.

22. Senator William Gwin, *Congressional Globe*, Senate, 33rd Congress, 1st session, April 10, 1854, 879, in "Congressional Globe Home Page: US Congressional Documents," n.d., 879, http://memory.loc.gov/ammem/amlaw/lwcg.html; Robert Royal Russel, *Improvement of Communication with the Pacific Coast as an Issue in American Politics, 1783–1864* (Cedar Rapids, Iowa: Torch Press, 1948), 199.

23. Meinig, *Shaping of America*, 3:12–15.

24. David Morris Potter, *The Impending Crisis, 1848–1861* (New York: HarperCollins, 1976), chap. 7.

25. Meinig, *Shaping of America*, 3:15–19.

26. Richard White, *Railroaded: The Transcontinentals and the Making of Modern America* (New York: Norton, 2011), 24.

27. Ibid., 107.

28. Meinig, *Shaping of America*, 3:260.
29. Gerald Berk, *Alternative Tracks: The Constitution of American Industrial Order, 1865–1917* (Baltimore, MD: Johns Hopkins University Press, 1997), 26.
30. White, *Railroaded*, 359.
31. Berk, *Alternative Tracks*, chap. 4.
32. John Steele Gordon, "R.I.P., ICC.," *American Heritage* 47, no. 3 (May 1996): 22.
33. Berk, *Alternative Tracks*, 106–107.
34. Colleen A. Dunlavy, *Politics and Industrialization* (Princeton, NJ: Princeton University Press, 1994), 251.
35. John Williams-Searle, "Risk, Disability, and Citizenship: U. S. Railroaders and the Federal Employers' Liability Act," *Disability Studies Quarterly* 28, no. 3 (Summer 2008), www.dsq-sds.org/article/view/113/113.
36. Mark Aldrich, *Death Rode the Rails: American Railroad Accidents and Safety, 1828–1965* (Baltimore, MD: Johns Hopkins University Press, 2006), 110–115.
37. Steven W. Usselman, *Regulating Railroad Innovation: Business, Technology, and Politics in America, 1840–1920* (New York: Cambridge University Press, 2002), 325.
38. Ari Arthur Hoogenboom and Olive Hoogenboom, *A History of the ICC: From Panacea to Palliative* (New York: Norton, 1976), 35–37.
39. Albro Martin, *Enterprise Denied: Origins of the Decline of American Railroads, 1897–1917* (New York: Columbia University Press, 1971), 345–348.
40. Mark H. Rose, Bruce Edsall Seely, and Paul F. Barrett, *The Best Transportation System in the World: Railroads, Trucks, Airlines, and American Public Policy in the Twentieth Century* (Columbus: Ohio State University Press, 2006), 8–9.
41. Ibid., 14.
42. Jim Cohen, "Private Capital, Public Credit and the Decline of American Railways, 1840–1940," *Journal of Transport History* 31, no. 1 (June 2010): 59.
43. Ibid., 52, 58.
44. Ibid., 61.
45. Warren Zimmermann, *First Great Triumph: How Five Americans Made Their Country a World Power* (New York: Farrar, Straus and Giroux, 2002), 424–435.
46. Tom D. Crouch, *The Bishop's Boys: A Life of Wilbur and Orville Wright* (New York: Norton, 1990), 140–141, 257–263.
47. Janet Rose Daly Bednarek, *America's Airports: Airfield Development, 1918–1947* (College Station: Texas A&M University Press, 2001), chap. 1.

48. Roger E. Bilstein, *Enterprise of Flight: The American Aviation and Aerospace Industry* (Washington, DC: Smithsonian Institution Scholarly Press, 2001), 22.

49. Nick A. Komons, *Bonfires to Beacons: Federal Civil Aviation Policy under the Air Commerce Act 1926–1938* (Washington, DC, 1978), 11, http://hdl.handle.net/2027/mdp.39015013920528.

50. Bilstein, *Enterprise of Flight*, 43.

51. Komons, *Bonfires to Beacons*, 17–18, 131.

52. F. Robert Van der Linden, *Airlines and Air Mail: The Post Office and the Birth of the Commercial Aviation Industry* (Lexington: University Press of Kentucky, 2002).

53. Rose, Seely, and Barrett, *Best Transportation System in the World*, 86.

54. *The Indiana Centennial, 1916; A Record of the Celebration of the Hundredth Anniversary of Indiana's Admission to Statehood*, n.d., 305, www.archive.org/details/indianacentennia1916indi.

55. D. W. Meinig, *The Shaping of America: A Geographical Perspective on 500 Years of History*, vol. 4 (New Haven, CT: Yale University Press, 2004), 13–22.

56. Bruce Edsall Seely, *Building the American Highway System: Engineers as Policy Makers* (Philadelphia: Temple University Press, 1987), 62, 67.

57. Richard F. Weingroff, "From Names to Numbers: The Origins of the US Numbered Highway System—Highway History—FHWA," 1987, www.fhwa.dot.gov/infrastructure/numbers.cfm.

58. Seely, *Building the American Highway System*, chaps. 4–6.

59. Rose, Seely, and Barrett, *Best Transportation System in the World*, 53, 72.

60. Dwight D. Eisenhower, "Special Message to the Congress Regarding a National Highway Program," February 22, 1955, www.presidency.ucsb.edu/ws/index.php?pid=10415&st=highways&st1=#axzz1QhJXkXFq.

61. Richard F. Weingroff, "Federal-Aid Highway Act of 1956: Creating the Interstate System," *Public Roads* 60, no. 1 (n.d.), www.fhwa.dot.gov/publications/publicroads/96summer/p96su10.cfm.

62. Lewis Mumford, "The Highway and the City," *Architectural Record*, April 1957, 179.

63. Raymond A. Mohl, "The Interstates and the Cities: The US Department of Transportation and the Freeway Revolt, 1966–1973," *Journal of Policy History* 20, no. 2 (2008): 193–226; Brian D. Taylor, "Public Perceptions, Fiscal Realities, and Freeway Planning: The California Case," *Journal of the American Planning Association* 61, no. 1 (1995): 43.

64. Rose, Seely, and Barrett, *Best Transportation System in the World*, 99.

65. Robert J. Dilger, *American Transportation Policy* (Westport, CT: Praeger, 2002), 77–84.

66. Hamilton, *Trucking Country*, 115–117.

67. Meinig, *Shaping of America*, 4:74–78.

68. Robert Jay Dilger, "TEA-21: Transportation Policy, Pork Barrel Politics, and American Federalism," *Publius* 28, no. 1 (January 1, 1998): 49–69.

69. Tad DeHaven, "Amtrak Subsidies: Downsizing the Federal Government," n.d., www.downsizinggovernment.org/transportation/amtrak/subsidies; Randal O'Toole, "Urban Transit: Downsizing the Federal Government," n.d., www.downsizinggovernment.org/transportation/urban-transit. To be fair, such critics also question the wisdom of subsidies to highways. See John Robert Meyer, John F. Kain, and Martin Wohl, *The Urban Transportation Problem* (Cambridge, MA: Harvard University Press, 1965), 349; Gabriel Roth, "Federal Highway Funding Downsizing the Federal Government," n.d., www.downsizinggovernment.org/transportation/highway-funding.

70. Robert Jay Dilger, "TEA-21," 69; Shailagh Murray, "For a Senate Foe of Pork Barrel Spending, Two Bridges Too Far," *Washington Post*, October 21, 2005.

71. Rose, Seely, and Barrett, *Best Transportation System in the World*, chaps. 4–6.

72. Hamilton, *Trucking Country*, 229; Andrew R. Goetz and Timothy M. Vowles, "The Good, the Bad, and the Ugly: 30 Years of US Airline Deregulation," *Journal of Transport Geography* 17, no. 4 (July 2009): 251–263; Marc Levinson, "Two Cheers for Discrimination: Deregulation and Efficiency in the Reform of US Freight Transportation, 1976–1998," *Enterprise and Society* 10, no. 1 (March 1, 2009): 178–215.

73. Clifford Winston, *Last Exit: Privatization and Deregulation of the US Transportation System* (Washington, DC: Brookings Institution Press, 2010), 23, 35–37.

74. K. Bhatt, T. Higgins, and J. T. Berg, "US and Worldwide Experience with Congestion Pricing: An Overview," *TR News*, no. 263 (2009); "Virginia HOT Lanes," n.d., http://virginiahotlanes.com/faqs/.

75. Richard F. Weingroff, "Backbone: Creation of the National Highway System—Highway History—FHWA," n.d., www.fhwa.dot.gov/infrastructure/backbone.cfm.

76. Robert Jay Dilger, "TEA-21," 59.

77. Barack Obama, "Remarks by the President in State of Union Address," January 25, 2011, www.whitehouse.gov/the-press-office/2011/01/25/remarks-president-state-union-address.

78. William R. Childs, "State Regulators and Pragmatic Federalism in the United States, 1889–1945," *Business History Review* 75, no. 4 (December 1, 2001): 704.

Chapter 3   Uncle Sam at the Blackboard

1. David Tyack, Thomas James, and Aaron Benavot, *Law and the Shaping of Public Education, 1785–1954* (Madison: University of Wisconsin Press, 1987), 22.

2. John R. Thelin, *A History of American Higher Education* (Baltimore: Johns Hopkins University Press, 2004), 75–77, 135–146; Williamjames Hoffer, *To Enlarge the Machinery of Government: Congressional Debates and the Growth of the American State, 1858–1891* (Baltimore: Johns Hopkins University Press, 2007), 61.

3. Hoffer, *To Enlarge the Machinery of Government*, 19, 35; Thelin, *History of American Higher Education*, 75; Homer D. Babbidge Jr. and Robert M. Rosenzweig, *The Federal Interest in Higher Education* (New York: McGraw-Hill, 1962), 5–7; Jonathan Zimmerman, *Innocents Abroad: American Teachers in the American Century* (Cambridge, MA: Harvard University Press, 2006), 84.

4. Sidney W. Tiedt, *The Role of the Federal Government in Education* (New York: Oxford University Press, 1966), 24; David Tyack, Robert Lowe, and Elisabeth Hansot, *Public Schools in Hard Times: The Great Depression and Recent Years* (Cambridge, MA: Harvard University Press, 1984), 105; Kevin P. Bower, "'A Favored Child of the State': Federal Student Aid at Ohio Colleges and Universities, 1934–1943," *History of Education Quarterly* 44, no. 3 (Fall 2004): 364; Jonathan Zimmerman, *Small Wonder: The Little Red Schoolhouse in History and Memory* (New Haven, CT: Yale University Press, 2009), 102.

5. Tyack et al., *Public Schools in Hard Times*, 129; Charles Dorn, *American Education, Democracy, and the Second World War* (New York: Palgrave, 2007), 134; Ann Cooper and Lisa M. Holmes, *Lunch Lessons: Changing the Way We Feed Our Children* (New York: HarperCollins, 2006), 34; Americo D. Lapati, *Education and the Federal Government: A Historical Record* (New York: Mason/Charter, 1975), 22.

6. Dorn, *American Education, Democracy, and the Second World War*, 141, 157; Cooper and Holmes, *Lunch Lessons*, 35; Susan Levine, *School Lunch Politics: The Surprising History of America's Favorite Welfare Program* (Princeton, NJ: Princeton University Press, 2008), 81–82.

7. Thelin, *History of American Higher Education*, 262–265; Rupert Wilkinson, *Aiding Students, Buying Students: Financial Aid in America* (Nashville: Vanderbilt University Press, 2005), 48; Wilson Smith and Thomas Bender, *American Higher Education Transformed, 1940–2005* (Baltimore: Johns Hopkins University Press, 2008), 394; Christopher P. Loss, "'The Most Wonderful Thing Has Happened to Me in the Army': Psychology, Citizenship, and American Higher Education in

World War II," *Journal of American History* 92, no. 3 (December 2005): 889.

8. Wilkinson, *Aiding Students, Buying Students*, 53–54; Lapati, *Education and the Federal Government*, 26; Smith and Bender, *American Higher Education Transformed*, 398; David Gamson, "From Progressivism to Federalism: The Pursuit of Equal Educational Opportunity, 1915–1965," in *To Educate a Nation: Federal and National Strategies of School Reform*, ed. Carl F. Kaestle and Alyssa E. Lodewick (Lawrence: University of Kansas Press, 2007), 192–193.

9. Hugh Davis Graham and Nancy Diamond, *The Rise of American Research Universities: Elites and Challengers in the Postwar Era* (Baltimore: Johns Hopkins University Press, 1997), 47, 34–36; Roger L. Geiger, *Research and Relevant Knowledge: American Research Universities since World War II*, 2nd ed. (New Brunswick, NJ: Transaction, 2004 [1993]), 182, 173, 163.

10. Lapati, *Education and the Federal Government*, 80; Hugh Davis Graham, *The Uncertain Triumph: Federal Education Policy in the Kennedy and Johnson Years* (Chapel Hill: University of North Carolina Press, 1984), xiv–xv, 223.

11. Patrick McGuinn and Frederick Hess, "Freedom from Ignorance? The Great Society and the Evolution of the Elementary and Secondary School Act of 1965," in *The Great Society and the High Tide of Liberalism*, ed. Sidney Milkis and Jerome Mileur (Amherst: University of Massachusetts Press, 2005), 294, 298; Lyndon B. Johnson, "Remarks in Johnson City, Texas, Upon Signing the Elementary and Secondary Education Bill, April 11, 1965," www.lbjlib.utexas.edu/johnson/archives.hom/speeches.hom/650411.asp, accessed May 17, 2011; Zimmerman, *Small Wonder*, 134.

12. Maris A. Vinovskis, "Federal Education Policy and Politics," in *The Columbia History of Post–World War II America*, ed. Mark C. Carnes (New York: Columbia University Press, 2007), 473; Lapati, *Education and the Federal Government*, 36; Stephen K. Bailey and Edith K. Mosher, *ESEA: The Office of Education Administers a Law* (Syracuse, NY: Syracuse University Press, 1968), 167–168.

13. Lee W. Anderson, *Congress and the Classroom: From the Cold War to "No Child Left Behind"* (University Park: Penn State University Press, 2007), 67–69; McGuinn and Hess, "Freedom from Ignorance?," 299; Gareth Davies, "Towards Big-Government Conservatism: Conservatives and Federal Aid to Education in the 1970s," *Journal of Contemporary History* 43, no. 4 (2008): 627; Gareth Davies, *See Government Grow: Education Politics from Johnson to Reagan* (Lawrence: University Press of Kansas, 2007), 282.

14. Christopher Cross, *Political Education: National Policy Comes of Age* (New York: Teachers College Press, 2004), 69; Davies, *See Government Grow*, 143, 151.

15. Davies, *See Government Grow*, 167–171; Davies, "Towards Big-Government Conservatism," 631.

16. Susan Ware, *Title IX: A Brief History with Documents* (New York: Bedford/St. Martin's, 2007), 1–3; Amanda Ross Edwards, "Why Sport? The Development of Sport as a Policy Issue in Title IX of the Education Amendments of 1972," *Journal of Policy History* 22, no. 3 (2010): 305.

17. Cross, *Political Education*, 29–30.

18. Davies, *See Government Grow*, 273–274.

19. Patrick McGuinn, *No Child Left Behind and the Transformation of Federal Education Policy, 1965–2005* (Lawrence: University of Kansas Press, 2006), 7; McGuinn and Hess, "Freedom from Ignorance?," 311.

20. Jonathan Zimmerman, "What Are Schools For?," *New York Review of Books*, October 14, 2010, 29–31.

21. Davies, *See Government Grow*, 106–107, 324n55; Zimmerman, "What Are Schools For?," 29.

22. Phone conversation with US Office of Education representative, Washington, DC, September 7, 2011; Center on Budget and Policy Priorities, "An Update on State Budget Cuts," February 9, 2011, www.cbpp.org/cms/index.cfm?fa=view&id=1214; "Recovery Funds Stabilize State Education Budgets," November 25, 2009, www.recovery.gov/News/featured/Pages/Education-SFSFnumbers.aspx.

Chapter 4   Banking on Government

1. Thomas M. Doerflinger, *A Vigorous Spirit of Enterprise: Merchants and Economic Development in Revolutionary Pennsylvania* (Chapel Hill: University of North Carolina Press, 1986); Clarence L. VerSteeg, *Robert Morris, Revolutionary Financier* (New York: Octagon Books, 1976); Stephen Mihm, "Funding the Revolution: Monetary and Fiscal Policy in Eighteenth-Century America," in *Oxford Handbook of the American Revolution,* ed. Jane Kamensky and Edward Gray (Oxford: Oxford University Press, forthcoming).

2. Bray Hammond, *Banks and Politics in America from the Revolution to the Civil War* (Princeton: Princeton University Press, 1990), 40–88, 144–196.

3. Quoted in H. Wayne Morgan, "The Origins and Establishment of the First Bank of the United States," *Business History Review* 30 (December 1956): 472–492, esp. 479 and 478.

4. John C. Miller, *The Federalist Era, 1789–1801* (New York: Harper, 1960), 55–63; Benjamin B. Klubes, "The First Federal Congress and the First National Bank: A Case Study in Constitutional Interpretation," *Journal of the Early Republic* 10 (Spring 1990): 19–41, quoted in H. Wayne Morgan, "The Origins and Establishment of the First Bank of the United States," *Business History Review* 30 (December 1956): 472–492, esp. 479 and 478.

5. Hammond, *Banks and Politics in America from the Revolution to the Civil War*, 227–285.

6. Andrew Jackson, "First Annual Message," December 8, 1829, www.presidency.ucsb.edu/ws/index.php?pid=29471#axzz1eaC0uSwU; Andrew Jackson, "Bank Veto," July 10, 1832, millercenter.org/scripps/archive/speeches/detail/3636; Edwin J. Perkins, "Lost Opportunities for Compromise in the Bank War: A Reassessment of Jackson's Veto Message," *Business History Review* 61 (Winter 1987): 531–550; Robert Remini, *Andrew Jackson and the Bank War* (New York: Norton, 1967); Thomas P. Govan, *Nicholas Biddle: Nationalist and Public Banker, 1786–1844* (Chicago: University of Chicago Press, 1959).

7. Richard Sylla, "Forgotten Men of Money: Private Bankers in Early U.S. History," *Journal of Economic History* 36 (1976): 173–188.

8. Eugene Nelson White, *The Regulation and Reform of the American Banking System, 1900–1929* (Princeton: Princeton University Press, 1983): 10–38.

9. Ibid.

10. James Livingston, *Origins of the Federal Reserve System: Money, Class, and Corporate Capitalism, 1890–1913* (Ithaca: Cornell University Press, 1986), 33–48.

11. Martin J. Sklar, *The Corporate Reconstruction of American Capitalism: 1890–1916: The Market, the Law, and Politics* (Cambridge: Cambridge University Press, 1988); James Weinstein, *The Corporate Ideal in the Liberal State, 1900–1918* (Boston: Beacon Press, 1968);

12. Federal Reserve Bank of Boston, *Panic of 1907* (Boston: Federal Reserve Bank of Boston, [undated]), www.bos.frb.org/about/pubs/panicof1.pdf.

13. Livingston, *Origins of the Federal Reserve System*, 217–225; quoted in Federal Reserve Bank of Boston, *Panic of 1907*, 11.

14. White, *Regulation and Reform of the American Banking System*.

15. William J. Barber, *From New Era to New Deal: Herbert Hoover, the Economists, and American Economic Policy, 1921–1933* (Cambridge: Cambridge University Press, 1985).

16. Jordan Schwarz, *The New Dealers: Power Politics in the Age of Roosevelt* (New York: Knopf, 1993), 59–95, esp. 60–62; quoted on 214 and 61.

17. Dr. Max Winkler, "Deposit Guarantee Looms," *Los Angeles Times*, April 11, 1933, 12; "Bankers Oppose Deposit Insurance," *New York Times*, May 21, 1933, N7 & N9; Jill M. Hendrickson, "The Long and Bumpy Road to Glass-Steagall Reform: A Historical and Evolutionary Analysis of Banking Legislation," *American Journal of Economics and Sociology* 60 (October 2001): 849–879; Kenneth Weiher, "The Rise and Fall of Glass-Steagall," *Essays in Economic and Business History* 19 (2001): 209–219.

18. Ibid.; "To Provide a Guaranty Fund for Depositors in Banks," House Subcommittee of the Committee on Banking and Currency, March 14, 23, 24, 25, 26, 29, 30, April 1, 2, 6, 8, 1932, esp. 174, 177, 181; "Bankers Oppose Deposit Insurance."

19. Quoted in "Roosevelt 'Won' to Banking Insurance," *New York Times*, October 27, 1936, 14; Franklin Delano Roosevelt, First Fireside Chat, March 12, 1933, http://historymatters.gmu.edu/d/5199/.

20. Vincent Carosso, "Washington and Wall Street: The New Deal and Investment Bankers, 1933–1940," *Business History Review* 44 (Winter 1970): 425–445; Weiher, "The Rise and Fall of Glass-Steagall."

21. Judith Stein, *Pivotal Decade: How the United States Traded Factories for Finance in the Seventies* (New Haven: Yale University Press, 2010), 1–22; John Steele Gordon, "Understanding the S&L Mess," *American Heritage* 42 (February/March 1991), http://search.ebscohost.com/login.aspx?direct=true&db=ahl&AN=9103251097&site=ehost-live.

22. Quoted in Elizabeth Tandy Shermer, *Creating the Sunbelt: Phoenix and the Political Economy of Metropolitan America* (Philadelphia: University of Pennsylvania Press, forthcoming), chap. 8; Milton Friedman and Anna Jacobson Schwartz, *A Monetary History of the United States, 1867–1963* (Princeton: National Bureau of Economic Research, 1963), 437; Clifford F. Thies and Daniel A. Gerlowski, "Deposit Insurance: A History of Failure," *Cato Journal* 8 (Winter 1989): 677–693, esp. 678, 688; F. Stevens Redburn, "Never Lost a Penny: An Assessment of Federal Deposit Insurance," *Journal of Policy Analysis and Management* 7 (1988): 687–702, esp. 687, 690.

23. Sandra Sundra and Robin Kolodny, "Paving the Road to 'Too Big to Fail': Business Interests and the Politics of Financial Deregulation in the United States," *Politics and Society* 39 (March 2011): 74–100, quoted on 85; quoted in Gordon, "Understanding the S&L Mess."

24. Weiher, "The Rise and Fall of Glass-Steagall"; Hendrickson, "The Long and Bumpy Road to Glass-Steagall Reform"; Sundra and Kolodny, "Paving the Road to 'Too Big to Fail'"; Michael A. Bernstein, "The Contemporary Banking Crisis in Historical Perspective," *Journal of American History* 80 (March 1994): 1382–1396.

25. Evan Thomas, "Paulson's Complaint," *Newsweek*, May 15, 2009, www.newsweek.com/id/197810/page/2; Suárez and Kolodny, "Paving the Road to 'Too Big to Fail,'" 74–100.

26. Joe Nocera, "Sheila Bair's Bank Shot," *New York Times Magazine*, July 9, 2011, www.nytimes.com/2011/07/10/magazine/sheila-bairs-exit-interview.html?_r=1&pagewanted=all; Eric Dash, "As Bank Failures Rise, F.D.I.C. Fund Falls into the Red," *New York Times*, November 24, 2009, www.nytimes.com/2009/11/25/business/economy/25fdic.html; Eric Dash, "As Bank Woes Ease, the F.D.I.C.'s Fund Is Building Up," *New York Times Dealbook*, May 24, 2011, http://dealbook.nytimes.com/2011/05/24/with-bank-troubles-easing-f-d-i-c-fund-almost-positive/.

27. "Bureau of Consumer Financial Protection," *New York Times*, December 8, 2011, http://topics.nytimes.com/top/reference/timestopics/organizations/c/consumer_financial_protection_bureau/index.html?inline=nyt-org.

28. Eric Dash, "Banks Quietly Ramping Up Costs to Consumers," *New York Times*, November 13, 2011, www.nytimes.com/2011/11/14/business/banks-quietly-ramp-up-consumer-fees.html; Neil M. Barofsky, "Where the Bank Bailout Went Wrong," March 29, 2011, http://www.nytimes.com/2011/03/30/opinion/30barofsky.html.

29. Ben Protess, "Consumer Watchdog Builds Up Its Ranks," *New York Times Deal Book*, January 6, 2011, http://dealbook.nytimes.com/2011/01/06/consumer-watchdog-builds-up-its-ranks/; Nia-Malika Henderson, "Ron Paul Bashes Fed and Supercommittee," *Washington Post*, November 16, 2011, www.washingtonpost.com/blogs/election-2012/post/ron-paul-bashes-fed-and-supercommittee/2011/11/16/gIQAwxYKRN_blog.html; Nocera, "Sheila Bair's Bank Shot."

Chapter 5   Twenty-Nine Helmets

1. Massey Energy Company, "Preliminary Report of Investigation, Upper Big Branch Mine Explosion," June 2, 2011, 22, *Wall Street Journal*, June 4, 2011, online edition; Governor's Independent Investigation Panel, "Upper Big Branch, the April 5, 2010 Explosion: A Failure of Basic Coal Mine Safety Standards," May 2011, 14–15, 76–90, 108, *New York Times*, May 19, 2011, online edition.

2. Bartolomeo Vanzetti, *The Story of a Proletarian Life* (Boston: Sacco-Vanzetti Defense Committee, 1923), 5, 8–9.

3. Vanzetti, *The Story of a Proletarian Life*, 9–10; Bartolomeo Vanzetti to Luigina Vanzetti, January 12, 1911, reprinted in *Non piangete la mia*

morte: Lettere ai familiari, ed. Cesare Pillon and Vincenzina Vanzetti, (Editori Riuniti, 1962), 49.

4. Kevin Boyle, "Work Places: The Economy and the Changing Landscape of Labor, 1900–1920," in *Perspectives on Modern America: Making Sense of the Twentieth Century,* ed. Harvard Sitkoff (New York: Oxford University Press, 2001), 102.

5. Jeffry Frieden, *Global Capitalism: Its Fall and Rise in the Twentieth Century* (New York: Norton, 2006), chap. 1; John Bodnar, *The Transplanted: A History of Immigrants in Urban America* (Bloomington: Indiana University Press, 1985), chap. 1; James Cobb, *The Most Southern Place on Earth: The Mississippi Delta and the Roots of Regional Identity* (New York: Oxford University Press, 1992), 99.

6. Daniel Rodgers, *Atlantic Crossings: Social Politics in a Progressive Age* (Cambridge, MA: Harvard University Press, 1998), 49–50; Peter Gavrilovich and Bill McGraw, *The Detroit Almanac* (Detroit: Detroit Free Press, 2000), 289 ; US Census Bureau, "Nativity of the Population for the 50 Largest Urban Places, 1870–1990," www. census.gov/population/www/documentation/twps0029/tab19.html, accessed July 21, 2011.

7. Robert Hunter, *Poverty* (New York: Macmillan, 1904), 29; James Patterson, *America's Struggle against Poverty in the Twentieth Century,* 4th ed. (Cambridge, MA: Harvard University Press, 2000), 11.

8. Davitt McAteer, *Monongah: The Tragic Story of the 1907 Monongah Mine Disaster, the Worst Industrial Accident in US History* (Morgantown: West Virginia University Press, 2007); "Chicago's Horrible Crib Disaster," *Popular Mechanics* 11 (March 1909): 193; David Von Drahle, *Triangle: The Fire That Changed America* (New York: Grove Press, 2003); Michael B. Katz, *In the Shadow of the Poorhouse: A Social History of Welfare in America* (New York: Basic Books, 1986), 191–192; Hunter, *Poverty,* 37.

9. James Barrett, *Work and Community in the Jungle: Chicago's Packinghouse Workers, 1894–1922* (Urbana: University of Illinois Press, 1987), 75; Olivier Zunz, *The Changing Face of Inequality: Urbanization, Industrial Development, and Immigrants in Detroit, 1880–1920* (Chicago: University of Chicago Press, 1982), 376; Ric Burns and James Sanders, *New York: An Illustrated History* (New York: Knopf, 1999), 246; Thomas Philpot, *The Slum and the Ghetto: Immigrants, Blacks, and Reformers in Chicago, 1880–1930* (New York: Oxford University Press, 1978), 27; S. J. Kleinberg, *The Shadow of the Mills: Working-Class Families in Pittsburgh, 1870–1907* (Pittsburgh: University of Pittsburgh Press, 1988), 97–98.

10. Lizabeth Cohen, *Making a New Deal: Industrial Workers in Chicago, 1919–1939* (Cambridge: Cambridge University Press,1990), 64–66; Rodgers, *Atlantic Crossings,* 216–220; Vanzetti, *Story of a Proletarian Life,* 10.

11. Rodgers, *Atlantic Crossings*, 212–213; Katz, *In the Shadow of the Poorhouse*, 73;

12. Progressivism has an enormous literature. There are no better starting places than Robert Wiebe's classic, *The Search for Order, 1877–1920* (New York: Hill and Wang, 1967); Rodgers's brilliant *Atlantic Crossings;* and Michael McGerr', *A Fierce Discontent: The Rise and Fall of the Progressive Movement in America, 1870–1920* (New York: Oxford University Press, 2003).

13. Theda Skocpol, *Protecting Soldiers and Mothers: The Political Origins of Social Policy in the United States* (Cambridge, MA: Harvard University Press, 1992), 58–60; Alice Kessler-Harris, *In Pursuit of Equity: Women, Men, and the Quest for Economic Citizenship in 20th-Century America* (New York: Oxford University Press, 2001), 29–34; Shelton Stromquist, *Reinventing "The People": The Progressive Movement, the Class Problem, and the Origins of Modern Liberalism* (Urbana: University of Illinois Press, 2006), 93–96; Alan Dawley, *Struggles for Justice: Social Responsibility and the Liberal State* (Cambridge, MA: Harvard University Press, 1991), 282.

14. Roy Lubove, *The Progressives and the Slums: Tenement House Reform in New York City, 1890–1917* (Pittsburgh: University of Pittsburgh Press, 1962); Kathryn Kish Sklar, *Florence Kelley and the Nation's Work: The Rise of Women's Political Culture, 1830–1900* (New Haven: Yale University Press, 2005); "The Needed Child Labor Law," *Journal of Education* 81 (April 22, 1915): 430; Rodgers, *Atlantic Crossings*, 245–250.

15. Rodgers, *Atlantic Crossings*, 240; Linda Gordon, *Pitied but Not Entitled: Single Mothers and the History of Welfare, 1890–1935* (Cambridge, MA: Harvard University Press, 1994), chaps. 2–4.

16. David Kennedy, *Freedom from Fear: The American People in Depression and War, 1929–1945* (New York: Oxford University Press, 1999), chaps. 2–4; Patterson, *America's Struggle against Poverty*, 41; Cohen, *Making a New Deal*, 227–234; Richard Lowitt and Maurine Beasley, eds., *One Third of a Nation: Lorena Hickok Reports on the Great Depression* (Urbana: University of Illinois Press, 1981), 28.

17. Arthur Schlesinger Jr., *The Crisis of the Old Order, 1919–1933* (Boston: Houghton Mifflin, 1957), 7; Rodgers, *Atlantic Crossings*, 409–416; William Leuchtenburg, *Franklin Roosevelt and the New Deal, 1932–1940* (New York: Harper and Row, 1963), 143–146; Kennedy, *Freedom from Fear*, 469–470.

18. Kennedy, *Freedom from Fear*, 144–147, 252–257. For a vigorous critique of the Keynesian turn, see Alan Brinkley's challenging *The End of Reform: New Deal Liberalism in Recession and War* (New York: Knopf, 1995).

19. Cynthia Griggs Fleming, *In the Shadow of Selma: The Continuing Struggle for Civil Rights in the Rural South* (New York: Rowman and Littlefield, 2004), 71; Dennis Nordin and Roy Scott, *From Prairie Farmer to Entrepreneur: The Transformation of Midwestern Agriculture* (Bloomington: Indiana University Press, 2005), 82; Patterson, *America's Struggle against Poverty*, 65–73; Gordon, *Pitied but Not Entitled*, chaps. 8–9. For insightful treatments of the labor movement's great surge forward, see Robert Zieger, *The CIO, 1935–1955* (Chapel Hill: University of North Carolina Press, 1995), and David Brody, "Workplace Contractualism: A Historical/Comparative Analysis," in Brody, *In Labor's Cause: Main Themes on the History of the American Worker* (New York: Oxford University Press, 1993), 221–250. The data on Chrysler workers comes from Kevin Boyle, "Auto Workers at War: Patriotism and Protest in the American Automobile Industry, 1939–1945," in *Autowork,* ed. Robert Asher and Ronald Edsforth (Albany: State University of New York Press, 1995), 103–107.
20. Kennedy, *Freedom from Fear*, 269, 363–364; Leuchtenberg, *Franklin Roosevelt and the New Deal*, 137–141.
21. Michael Edelstein, "War and the American Economy in the Twentieth Century," in *The Cambridge Economic History of the United States: The Twentieth Century,* ed. Stanley Engerman and Robert Gallman (Cambridge: Cambridge University Press, 2000), 347; Thomas McGraw, "The New Deal and the Mixed Economy," in *Fifty Years Later: The New Deal Evaluated,* ed. Harvard Sitkoff (New York: Knopf, 1985), 44; US Bureau of Labor Statistics, "Employment Status of the Civilian Non-institutional Population, 1940 to date," ftp://ftp.bls.gov/pub/special.requests/lf/aat1.txt, accessed July 22, 2011; Kennedy, *Freedom from Fear*, 641, 644.
22. James Patterson, *Grand Expectations: The United States, 1945–1974* (New York: Oxford University Press, 1996), particularly chaps. 3 and 11; Patterson, *America's Struggle against Poverty*, 77.
23. Patterson, *Grand Expectations*, 562; Patterson, *America's Struggle against Poverty*, chaps. 8 and 10; Robert Dallek, *Flawed Giant: Lyndon Johnson and His Times, 1961–1973* (New York: Oxford University Press, 1998), particularly chap. 4.
24. Doris Kearns, *Lyndon Johnson and the American Dream* (New York: Harper and Row, 1976), 391.
25. US Bureau of Labor Statistics, *Employment and Earnings: United States, 1909–1970*, Bulletin 1212–1217 (Washington, DC: Government Printing Office, 1971), 232–233; US Bureau of Labor Statistics, "City Workers' Family Budget for a Moderate Standard of Living," Bulletin 1570–1 (Washington, DC: Government Printing Office, 1967).

26. Bennett Harrison and Barry Bluestone, *The Great U-Turn: Corporate Restructuring and the Polarizing of America* (New York: Basic Books, 1988), chap. 1; Clifford L. Broman et al., "The Impact of Unemployment on Families," *Michigan Family Review* 2 (Winter 1996–97), http://quod.lib.umich.edu/m/mfr/4919087.0002.207? rgn=main;view=fulltext; Judith Stein, *Pivotal Decade: How the United States Traded Factories for Finance in the Seventies* (New Haven, CT: Yale University Press, 2010), chaps. 10 and 11; Kim Phillips-Fein, *Invisible Hands: The Making of the Conservative Movement from the New Deal to Reagan* (New York: Norton, 2009), chaps. 8–11.

27. Patterson, *America's Struggle against Poverty*, chaps. 14–16; Ron Haskins, "Welfare Reform, Success or Failure? It Worked," *Policy and Practice* 64 (2006), www.brookings.edu/articles/2006/0315welfare_ haskins.aspx, accessed July 22, 2011; Deepak Bhargava et al., "Battered by the Storm: How the Safety Net Is Failing Americans and How to Fix It" (Washington, DC: Foreign Policy in Focus, December 7, 2009). For a powerful exploration of the poor in modern America, see David Shipler, *The Working Poor: Invisible in America* (New York: Knopf, 2004).

28. Boyle, "Work Places," 122; Nelson Lichtenstein, *State of the Union: A Century of American Labor* (Princeton, NJ: Princeton University Press, 2002), chaps. 6–7; "Study Finds Exploitation of Day Laborers," *New York Times*, January 9, 2011.

29. US Social Security Administration, "Basic Facts," www.ssa.gov/ pressoffice/basicfact.htm, accessed July 22, 2011; "GOP Seeks Dramatic Changes in Medicare and Medicaid," *USA Today*, April 6, 2011; "Kaiser Poll: Half of Americans Report Personal Ties to Medicaid," *Wall Street Journal*, May 25, 2011; United States Department of Labor, Employment and Training Administration, "Unemployment Insurance Weekly Report," March 1, 2012, www. dol.gov/opa/media/press/eta/ui/current.htm, accessed March 4, 2012; "Congress Restructures Unemployment Benefits," *CNN Money*, February 17, 2011, http://money.cnn.com/2012/02/16/news/ economy/congress_unemployment_benefits/index.htm, accessed March 4, 2012; "Number of Americans on Unemployment Reaches Two-Year High," *Wall Street Journal*, November 29, 2007. Polls show that 55 percent of Americans believe that today's children are unlikely to have better lives than their parents. That's the highest percentage holding a pessimistic opinion of the future since the pollsters began asking the question. See Ellizabeth Mendes, "In US, Optimism for Youth Reaches an All-Time Low," May 2, 2011, www.gallup.com/ poll/147350/optimism-future-youth-reaches-time-low.aspx, accessed July 22, 2011.

30. Barack Obama remarks, April 25, 2010, www.whitehouse.gov/blog/2010/04/25/families-big-branch-mine-our-hearts-ache-alongside-you, accessed July 16, 2011. Also see Rachel Martin, "Obama Pays Respect to West Virginia Miners," April 25, 2011, http://abcnews.go.com/WN/west-virginiacoal-miners-memorial/story?id=10472987, accessed July 22, 2011. For visuals of the ceremony, see www.necn.com/04/25/10/In-memory-of-W-Va-miners-The-lights-that/landing_nation.html?blockID=223056&feedID=4207, accessed July 22, 2011.

Chapter 6   The Right to a Decent Home

1. *Walt Whitman: Complete Poetry and Selected Prose and Letters*, ed. Emory Holloway (New York: Nonesuch Press, 1938), 607; "The Presidency: Home Sweet Home," *Time*, December 14, 1931.

2. Eric Larrabee, "The Six Thousand Houses Levitt Built," *Harper's* 197 (December 1948): 84.

3. William J. Clinton, "Remarks on the National Homeownership Strategy," June 5, 1995, in *The American Presidency Project,* ed. John T. Woolley and Gerhard Peters, www.presidency.ucsb.edu/ws/?pid=51448.

4. George W. Bush, "Remarks in St. Cloud, Minnesota," September 16, 2004, in *The American Presidency Project,* ed. John T. Woolley and Gerhard Peters, www.presidency.ucsb.edu/ws/?pid=72749.

5. D'Vera Cohn, "No Place Like Home—Even If the Value Is in the Tank," *Pew Research Center Publications*, February 19, 2009, http://pewresearch.org/pubs/1126/home-buy-sell-comfort-burden-polling.

6. US Census Bureau, Housing and Household Economic Statistics Division, *Historical Census of Housing Tables*, September 4, 2004, www.census.gov/hhes/www/housing/census/historic/owner.html.

7. Quoted in Lendol Calder, "Hard Payments: Consumer Credit and Thrift," in *Thrift and Thriving in America: Capitalism and Moral Order from the Puritans to the Present,* ed. Joshua J. Yates and James Davison Hunter (New York: Oxford University Press, 2011), 308.

8. Lendol Calder, *Financing the American Dream: A Cultural History of Consumer Credit* (Princeton, NJ: Princeton University Press, 1999), 64–70.

9. John Taylor Boyd Jr., "Recent Developments in Housing Finance, Part I," *Architectural Record* 48 (December 1920): 428.

10. John Hancock, "The Apartment House in Urban America," in *Buildings and Society: Essays on the Social Development of the Built Environment,* ed. Anthony D. King (Oxford: Routledge and Kegan Paul, 1980), 151–192.

11. David L. Mason, *From Buildings and Loans to Bail-Outs: A History of the American Savings and Loan Industry, 1831–1995* (Cambridge: Cambridge University Press, 2004), 78–84.

12. C. Lowell Harriss, *History and Policies of the Home Owners Loan Corporation* (Washington, DC: National Bureau of Economic Research, 1951); Kenneth T. Jackson, *Crabgrass Frontier: The Suburbanization of the United States* (New York: Oxford University Press, 1985), 190–218.

13. Franklin Delano Roosevelt, "Message to Congress on the State of the Union," January 11, 1944, in *The Public Papers and Addresses of Franklin D. Roosevelt,* vol. 13 (New York: Harper, 1950), 41.

14. US Census Bureau, *Historical Census of Housing Tables*; Jackson, *Crabgrass Frontier*; Lizabeth Cohen, *A Consumer's Republic: The Politics of Mass Consumption in Postwar America* (New York: Knopf, 2003), 123.

15. Gail Radford, *Modern Housing for America: Policy Struggles in the New Deal Era* (Chicago: University of Chicago Press, 1996).

16. David M. P. Freund, "Marketing the Free Market: State Intervention and the Politics of Prosperity in Metropolitan America," in *The New Suburban History,* ed. Kevin M. Kruse and Thomas J. Sugrue (Chicago: University of Chicago Press, 2006), 28.

17. Mel Scott, *American City Planning since 1890* (Berkeley: University of California Press, 1971), 351.

18. Jackson, *Crabgrass Frontier*, 190–218; Arnold R. Hirsch, "Choosing Segregation: Federal Housing Policy between *Shelley* and *Brown*," in *From Tenements to the Taylor Homes: In Search of an Urban Housing Policy in Twentieth-Century America,* ed. John Bauman et al. (University Park: Penn State University Press, 2000).

19. See Charles Abrams, *Forbidden Neighbors: A Study of Prejudice in Housing* (New York: Harper and Brothers, 1955), 156.

20. Douglas S. Massey and Nancy A. Denton, *American Apartheid: Segregation and the Making of the Underclass* (Cambridge, MA: Harvard University Press, 1993).

21. Arnold R. Hirsch, "The Inner City, Suburbs, and State-Sanctioned Segregation in the Era of Brown," in *The New Suburban History,* ed. Kevin M. Kruse and Thomas J. Sugrue (Chicago: University of Chicago Press, 2006), 33–56.

22. Thomas J. Sugrue, *Sweet Land of Liberty: The Forgotten Struggle for Civil Rights in the North* (New York: Random House, 2008), 282–283, 422–425.

23. Robert B. Avery, Kenneth P. Brevoort, and Glenn B. Canner, "The 2006 HMDA Data," *Federal Reserve Bulletin* 93 (2007): A73–A109.

24. United States Census Bureau, "Net Worth and Asset Ownership of Households: 1998 and 2000," *Current Population Reports: Household Studies*, May 2003, 12. On the black-white gap, see Thomas M. Shapiro, *The Hidden Cost of Being African American: How Wealth Perpetuates Inequality* (New York: Oxford University Press, 2004); Dalton Conley, *Being Black, Living in the Red: Race, Wealth, and Social Policy in America* (Berkeley: University of California Press, 1999); and Melvin L. Oliver and Thomas M. Shapiro, *Black Wealth, White Wealth: A New Perspective on Racial Inequality* (New York: Routledge, 1997). Darrick Hamilton and William Darity Jr., "Race, Wealth, and Intergenerational Poverty," *American Prospect On-Line*, August 19, 2009, www.prospect.org/cs/articles?article=race_wealth_and_intergenerational_poverty.

25. Viral V. Acharya et al., *Guaranteed to Fail: Fannie Mae, Freddie Mac, and the Debacle of Mortgage Finance* (Princeton, NJ: Princeton University Press, 2011).

26. Algernon Austin, "Subprime Mortgages Are Nearly Double for Hispanics and African Americans," Economic Policy Institute, June 11, 2008, www.epi.org/economic_snapshots/entry/webfeatures_snapshots_20080611/; Andrew Jakabovics and Jeff Chapman, "Unequal Opportunity Lenders? Analyzing Racial Disparities in Big Banks' Higher Priced Lending," Center for American Progress, September 2009, www.americanprogress.org/issues/2009/09/pdf/tarp_report.pdf; Jennifer Wheary, Tatjana Meschede, and Thomas M. Shapiro, "The Downside before the Downturn: Declining Economic Security among Middle-Class African Americans and Latinos, 2000–2006," Brandeis University, Institute on Assets and Social Policy and Demos, n.d. [2009], http://iasp.brandeis.edu/pdfs/batfive.pdf.

27. "Mortgage Clinic Restructures Loans for Homeowners," Associated Press, August 11, 2009.

28. Comprehensive data on real estate foreclosures are compiled by Realty Trac: www.realtytrac.com. The 1 out of 355 figure for August 2009 was widely reported. See, for example, "Foreclosures Reach Record Numbers again in July," *Daily Finance*, August 13, 2009, www.dailyfinance.com/2009/08/13/foreclosures-reach-record-numbers-again-in-july/.

29. National Foundation for Credit Counseling, "Survey Reveals Long-Term Implications of Mortgage Meltdown," June 23, 2009, www.nfcc.org/newsroom/newsreleases/files09/HomeownershipSurvey.pdf.

Chapter 7   Solving the Nation's Number One Health Problem(s)

1. Gary W. Shannon and Gerald F. Pyle, *Disease and Medical Care in the United States: A Medical Atlas of the Twentieth Century* (New York: Macmillan, 1993), 3–4.

2. Shannon and Pyle, *Disease and Medical Care in the United States;* Allan M. Brandt, *The Cigarette Century: The Rise, Fall, and Deadly Persistence of the Product That Defined America* (New York: Basic Books, 2007), 126.

3. Oscar Ewing, speech to the FSA Regional Staff Meeting, December 10, 1951, Oscar Ewing Papers, box 41, Harry S. Truman Presidential Library, Independence, MO.

4. Rosemary Stevens, *In Sickness and in Wealth: American Hospitals in the Twentieth Century* (New York: Basic Books, 1989), 55–59.

5. Alexander D. Langmuir, "The Surveillance of Communicable Diseases of National Importance," *New England Journal of Medicine* 268, no. 4 (1963): 182.

6. John Duffy, *The Sanitarians: A History of American Public Health* (Champaign: University of Illinois Press, 1992), 159–161.

7. John Ettling, *The Germ of Laziness: Rockefeller Philanthropy and Public Health in the New South* (Cambridge, MA: Harvard University Press, 1981); Duffy, *The Sanitarians*, 221–234; Fitzhugh Mullan, *Plagues and Politics: The Story of the United States Public Health Service* (New York: Basic Books, 1989), 54–58, 63–65.

8. US Public Health Service, National Office of Vital Statistics, *Vital Statistics Rates in the United States, 1900–1940* (Washington, DC: Government Printing Office, 1947), 330–331.

9. *Report of the President on the Emergency Relief Appropriations Acts, 1935–1941* (Washington, DC: Government Printing Office, 1941), 32; Frederick Dodge Mott and Milton I. Roemer, *Rural Health and Medical Care* (New York: McGraw-Hill, 1948), 385, 392; Florence Kerr, "Health Conservation and the WPA" (speech, October 21, 1939), WPA Papers, RG 69, series 737, box 7, National Archives; Mullan, *Plagues and Politics*, 102, 121; Margaret Humphreys, *Malaria: Poverty, Race, and Public Health in the United States* (Baltimore: Johns Hopkins University Press, 2001), 49–68; Martin V. Melosi, *The Sanitary City: Urban Infrastructure in America from Colonial Times to the Present* (Baltimore: Johns Hopkins University Press, 2000), 224–229.

10. E. H. Beardsley, *A History of Neglect: Health Care for Blacks and Mill Workers in the Twentieth-Century South* (Knoxville: University of Tennessee Press, 1987), 41, 127–129, 156–185; Mullan, *Plagues and*

Politics, 104, 107; Thomas Parran, "Annual Report of the Surgeon General of the Public Health Service," *American Journal of Public Health* 27, no. 5 (1937): 214–215; "Government Services," *Journal of the American Medical Association* 112, no. 5 (1939): 457.

11. Michael M. Davis, *America Organizes Medicine* (New York: Harper and Brothers, 1941), 278–279; Alan Derickson, *Health Security for All: Dreams of Universal Health Care in America* (Baltimore: Johns Hopkins University Press, 2005), 44, 79.

12. Paul Starr, *TheSocial Transformation of American Medicine* (New York: Basic Books, 1982), 180–197.

13. Carl V. Reynolds, "Coordination of Public Health and Related Agencies," *North Carolina Medical Journal* 1, no. 1 (1940): 24–25.

14. Congress, Senate, Committee on Education and Labor, Subcommittee on Wartime Health and Education, *Interim Report* (Washington, DC: Government Printing Office, 1945), 1–2, 5–6, 22; "How Sick Is the South?" *Southern Patriot* 3 (May 1945): 2; "North Carolina's Draft Rejection Figures," *North Carolina Medical Journal* 6, no. 1 (1945): 39–40; Mott and Roemer, *Rural Health and Medical Care*, 117–121, 131, 135.

15. Patricia Sullivan, *Lift Every Voice: The NAACP and the Making of the Civil Rights Movement* (New York: Free Press, 2009), 228–229; Congress, Senate, Committee on Education and Labor, *To Establish a National Health Program: Hearings on S. 1620* (Washington, DC: Government Printing Office, 1939), 237–243, 285–290, 891–898; Congress, Senate, Committee on Education and Labor, *Construction of Hospitals: Hearings on S. 3230* (Washington, DC: Government Printing Office, 1940), 78–91; Congress, House, Committee on Interstate and Foreign Commerce, *Hospital Construction Act: Hearings on S.191* (Washington, DC: Government Printing Office, 1946), 184–188; Karen Kruse Thomas, *Deluxe Jim Crow: Civil Rights and American Health Policy, 1935–1954* (Athens: University of Georgia Press, 2011).

16. Thomas Parran, quoted in Karen Ferguson, *Black Politics in New Deal Atlanta* (Chapel Hill: University of North Carolina Press, 2002), 112.

17. Mullan, *Plagues and Politics*, 116.

18. Leo Slater, *War and Disease: Biomedical Research on Malaria in the Twentieth Century* (Piscataway, NJ: Rutgers University Press, 2009), 7–13, 50–57, 123–155, 170–171; Randall M. Packard, *The Making of a Tropical Disease: A Short History of Malaria* (Baltimore: Johns Hopkins University Press, 2007), 140–141; Donald Burke and David Sullivan, "A Brief History of Malaria Research at Johns Hopkins," Johns Hopkins Malaria Research Institute, Malaria: Progress, Problems and Plans in the Genomic Era, conference proceedings, January 27–29, 2002, Baltimore.

19. Stevens, *In Sickness and in Wealth*, 49; E. Walls, "Hot Springs Waters and the Treatment of Venereal Diseases: The U.S. Public Health Service Clinic and Camp Garraday," *Journal of the Arkansas Medical Society* 91 (1995): 437; Raymond A. Vonderlehr, "Are We Checking the Great Plague?," *Survey Graphic* 29, no. 4 (1940): 217; "VD Balance Sheet," *Time,* September 30, 1946.

20. The full scope of the Tuskegee Syphilis Study and its ethical implications are beyond the scope of this essay, but they are ably discussed in Susan M. Reverby, *Examining Tuskegee: The Infamous Syphilis Study and Its Legacy* (Chapel Hill: University of North Carolina Press, 2009). On the role of race in the Public Health Service and federal health policy, see Thomas, *Deluxe Jim Crow.*

21. Beardsley, *History of Neglect,* 172–174; Allan M. Brandt, *No Magic Bullet: A Social History of Venereal Disease in the United States since 1880,* expanded ed. (New York: Oxford University Press, 1987), 161–170.

22. "VD Balance Sheet"; US Public Health Service, *1945 Annual Report* (Washington, DC: Government Printing Office, 1946), 295–301; M. A. Waugh, "History of Clinical Developments in Sexually Transmitted Diseases," in *Sexually Transmitted Diseases,* 2nd ed., ed. K. K. Holmes, P. Märdh, P. F. Sparling, and P. J. Wiesner (New York: McGraw-Hill, 1990), 13; "Rapid Treatment Center Closes," *American Journal of Public Health* 40, no. 8 (1950): 1056–1057.

23. Brandt, *No Magic Bullet,* 176–179.

24. Harry M. Marks, *The Progress of Experiment: Science and Therapeutic Reform in the United States, 1900–1990* (New York: Cambridge University Press, 2000), 53–59, 105–128, 98–135; Starr, *Social Transformation of American Medicine,* 335–344; Joseph Earle Moore, J. F. Mahoney, Walter Schwartz, Thomas Sternberg, and W. Barry Wood, "The Treatment of Early Syphilis with Penicillin: A Preliminary Report of 1,418 Cases," *Journal of the American Medical Association* 126, no. 1 (1944): 67–72; Joseph Earle Moore, *Penicillin in Syphilis* (Springfield, IL: Charles C. Thomas, 1947), 4; M. Merrell, "Results of the Nationwide Study of Penicillin in Early Syphilis; Amorphous Penicillin in Aqueous Solution," *American Journal of Syphilis, Gonorrhea, and Venereal Diseases* 33, no.1 (1949): 12–18; Daniel Carpenter, *Reputation and Power: Organizational Image and Pharmaceutical Regulation at the FDA* (Princeton, NJ: Princeton University Press, 2010).

25. *Congress and the Nation 1945–1964* (Washington, DC: Congressional Quarterly, 1965), 1114; US Department of Health, Education, and Welfare, *1955 Annual Report* (Washington, DC: Government Printing Office, 1956), 30–31, 53–56; US Department of Health, Education, and Welfare, *1960 Annual Report* (Washington, DC: Government Printing

Office, 1961), 12–13; US Department of Health, Education, and Welfare, *1964 Annual Report* (Washington, DC: Government Printing Office, 1965), 76–77; Abraham Bergman et al., "A Political History of the Indian Health Service," *Milbank Memorial Fund Quarterly* 77, no. 4 (1999): 571–604.

26. John L. Thurston, "More Opportunities for All through Social Security," April 9, 1952, Federal Security Agency-General Correspondence, box 29, Oscar Ewing Papers; William Shonick, *Government and Health Services: Government's Role in the Development of U.S. Health Services, 1930–1980* (New York: Oxford University Press, 1995), 92; Abraham M. Lilienfeld and B. Pasamanick, "The Association of Maternal and Fetal Factors with the Development of Cerebral Palsy and Epilepsy," *American Journal of Obstetrics and Gynecology* 70 (1955): 93–101.

27. Beardsley, *History of Neglect*, 13–14; "The Symptoms," *Southern Patriot* 3, no. 5 (May 1945): 3; Mott and Roemer, *Rural Health and Medical Care*, 290, 306.

28. US Senate, Committee on Labor and Public Welfare, Subcommittee on Health, *Hill-Burton Hospital Survey and Construction Act: History of the Program and Current Problems and Issues* (Washington, DC: Committee Print, 1973), 11–13.

29. Karen Kruse Thomas, "The Hill-Burton Act and Civil Rights: Expanding Hospital Care for Black Southerners, 1939–60," *Journal of Southern History* 72, no. 4 (2006): 860–861.

30. Lewis E. Weeks and Howard J. Berman, *Shapers of American Health Care Policy: An Oral History* (Ann Arbor: University of Michigan Press, 1985), 39; Bruce Schulman, *From Cotton Belt to Sunbelt: Federal Policy, Economic Development, and the Transformation of the South, 1938–1980* (Durham, NC: Duke University Press, 1994), 118–119; "The Republican Welfare States," *Atlantic Monthly,* March 2004, 48.

31. Mullan, *Plagues and Politics*, 121; Federal Security Administration, *1950 Annual Report*, 115–116, 127, 129, 163; Health, Education, and Welfare (HEW), *1955 Annual Report*, 13, 134, 140–141, 190–191; HEW, *1960 Annual Report*, 174–175, 271–272; HEW, *1964 Annual Report*, 228–229; Alexander D. Langmuir, "The Epidemic Intelligence Service of the Center for Disease Control," *Public Health Reports* 95, no. 5 (1980): 473.

32. Langmuir, "The Epidemic Intelligence Service of the Center for Disease Control," 473; Alexander D. Langmuir, "The Surveillance of Communicable Diseases of National Importance," *New England Journal of Medicine* 268, no. 4 (1963): 182–192; Amy L. Fairchild, Ronald Bayer, and James Colgrove, *Searching Eyes: Privacy, the State,*

and Disease Surveillance in America (Berkeley: University of California Press, 2007), xviii, 17, 22, 247.

33. John B. Hozier, "Responsibilities of the Public Health Service in Civil Defense," *Journal of the American Medical Association* 160, no. 14 (1956): 1206–1208; HEW, *1955 Annual Report*, 13.

34. Stephen P. Strickland, *The Story of the NIH Grants Programs* (Lanham, MD: University Press of America, 1989), 78–79.

35. "Achievements in Public Health, 1900–1999: Tobacco Use—United States, 1900–1999," *Morbidity and Mortality Weekly Report* 48, no. 43 (1999): 986–993.

36. Brandt, *The Cigarette Century*, 211–239.

37. Congress, Senate, Committee on Government Operations, Subcommittee on Reorganization and International Organizations, *The United States and the World Health Organization* (Washington, DC: Committee Print, 1959), 121–141.

38. Sunil S. Amrith, *Decolonizing International Health: India and Southeast Asia, 1930–1965* (New York: Palgrave McMillan, 2006), 146; Timothy D. Baker, "Malaria Eradication in India: A Failure?," *Science* 319. no. 5870 (2008), 1616.

39. John J. Hanlon, *Principles of Public Health Administration* (Maryland Heights, MO: C. V. Mosby, 1950), 295–297; Hanlon, *Principles of Public Health Administration*, 3rd ed. (Maryland Heights, MO: C. V. Mosby, 1960), 362–368; Maurice Pate, "UNICEF Goals in Maternal and Child Health," *American Journal of Public Health* 50, no. 6 (1960): 8–12.

40. John J. Hanlon, *Principles of Public Health Administration*, 5th ed. (Maryland Heights, MO: C. V. Mosby, 1969), 235–240.

41. "USAID History," www.usaid.gov/about_usaid/usaidhist.html, accessed September 2, 2011.

42. "A Record of Achievement," www.usaid.gov/about_usaid/accompli. html, accessed September 2, 2011.

43. "About PEPFAR," www.pepfar.gov, accessed September 2, 2011.

44. Jill Quadagno and Steve McDonald, "Racial Segregation in Southern Hospitals: How Medicare 'Broke the Back of Segregated Health Services,'" in *The New Deal and Beyond: Social Welfare in the South since 1930,* ed. Elna C. Green (Athens: University of Georgia Press, 2003), 120–122.

45. Colleen M. Grogan, "A Marriage of Convenience: The Persistent and Changing Relationship between Long-Term Care and Medicaid," in *History and Health Policy in the United States: Putting the Past Back In,* ed. R. A. Stevens, C. E. Rosenberg, and L. R. Burns (New Brunswick, NJ: Rutgers University Press, 2006), 202–228.

46. "Understand the Law," www.healthcare.gov, accessed September 2, 2011.

47. Derickson, *Health Security for All*, 140–143.
48. "Times Topics: American Medical Association," http://topics. nytimes.com/topics/reference/timestopics/organizations/a/american_ medical_association/index.html, accessed September 2, 2011; Michael D. Maves to Harry Reid, December 1, 2009, www.ama-assn.org/ resources/doc/washington/hsr-ama-reid-hr3590.pdf, accessed September 2, 2011.

Chapter 8   Culture for the People

1. I have taken some of the following information and quotes from the exhibition catalogue by Bruce Bustard, *A New Deal for the Arts* (Washington, DC: National Archives and Records Administration in association with the University of Washington Press, 1997), especially 1–23.
2. Quoted in Bustard, *A New Deal for the Arts*, 7.
3. It is worth remembering that Ronald Reagan's father and brother both worked for the New Deal in Illinois. Neither lifted any shovels, but they were among the bureaucrats who doled out money for projects. Reagan's recollections of how his family was supported by the New Deal, like so much else, were hopelessly muddled, as Lou Cannon, Gary Wills, and others have shown.
4. Quoted in Bustard, *A New Deal for the Arts,* 18.
5. Quoted in Bustard, *A New Deal for the Arts,* 23.
6. For an engaging review of some of this recent scholarship, see Louis Menand, "Unpopular Front," *New Yorker*, October 17, 2005.
7. Quoted in James Standifer, "The Complicated Life of *Porgy and Bess*," *Humanities* 18, no. 6 (November/December 1997): n.p.
8. Quoted in William Safire, ed., *Lend Me Your Ears: Great Speeches in History* (New York: W. W. Norton, 2004), 228.
9. Quoted in Donna M. Binkiewicz, *Federalizing the Muse: United States Arts Policy and the National Endowment for the Arts, 1965–1980* (Chapel Hill: University of North Carolina Press, 2004), 160.
10. Donna M. Binkiewicz, *Federalizing the Muse: United States Arts Policy and the National Endowment for the Arts, 1965–1980*, 218.
11. James Heilbrun and Charles M. Gray, *The Economics of Art and Culture* (Cambridge: Cambridge University Press, 2001), 279.
12. See Donna M. Binkiewicz, *Federalizing the Muse: United States Arts Policy and the National Endowment for the Arts, 1965–1980,* especially the final chapter.
13. These are all recent grants awarded by the NEA, listed on its Web site: www.nea.gov, accessed July 5, 2011.

14. For the best short history of this, see Peter Dobkin Hall, *Inventing the Nonprofit Sector* (Baltimore: Johns Hopkins University Press, 1992), 1–83.
15. The following figures come from the GivingUSA Foundation report for 2009: www.givingusa.org/press_releases/gusa/GivingReaches300billion.pdf. See also Stephanie Strom, "Charitable Giving Declines, a New Report Finds," *New York Times*, June 9, 2009.
16. This episode is related in Livingston Biddle, *Our Government and the Arts: A Perspective from the Inside* (New York: ACA Books, 1988).

Chapter 9   From Franklin to Facebook

1. Paul Starr, *The Creation of the Media: Political Origins of Modern Communications* (New York: Basic Books, 2004), 73–82.
2. Richard R. John, *Spreading the News: The American Postal System from Franklin to Morse* (Cambridge, MA: Harvard University Press, 1995), 37–44.
3. Cited in John, *Spreading the News*, 33.
4. John, *Spreading the News*, 38.
5. David Nord, "The Evangelical Origins of Mass Media in America, 1815–1835," *Journalism Monographs* 88 (1984): 1–30.
6. Steven Lubar, "The Transformation of Antebellum Patent Law," *Technology and Culture* 32 (October 1991): 932–959.
7. Richard R. John, *Network Nation: Inventing American Telecommunications* (Cambridge, MA: Harvard University Press, 2010), chap. 2.
8. John, *Network Nation*, 182.
9. James L. Baughman, *Same Time, Same Station: Creating American Television, 1948–1961* (Baltimore: Johns Hopkins University Press, 2007), chap. 4.
10. Paul E. Ceruzzi, "The Internet before Commercialization," in *The Internet and American Business*, ed. William Aspray and Paul E. Ceruzzi (Cambridge, MA: MIT Press, 2008), 9.
11. Janet Abbate, *Inventing the Internet* (Cambridge, MA: MIT Press, 1999).
12. Fred Turner, *From Counterculture to Cyberculture: Stewart Brand, the Whole Earth Network, and the Rise of Digital Utopianism* (Chicago: University of Chicago Press, 2006).
13. Kimberly A. Zarkin and Michael J. Zarkin, *The Federal Communications Commission: Front Line in the Culture and Regulation Wars* (Westport, CT: Greenwood Press, 2006), 104.

Index

A Nation at Risk, 59
Adams, Abigail, 141
Adams, Charles Francis, 31
Adams, John, 141, 142, 161
"Advancing American Art"
    exhibition, 147
Affordable Care Act, 138
African Americans, 62, 89, 95, 113,
    147
    and health, 123, 125
    and housing, 110–114
Age Discrimination Act, 181
Aid for Dependent Children
    (ADC), 94, 96, 99
Aldrich, Nelson, 75
American Bankers Association, 78
American Historical Association,
    183
American Medical Association,
    124, 138
American Political Science
    Association, 183
American Red Cross, 11, 122
American Telephone and Telegraph
    (AT&T), 165, 170
Americans with Disabilities Act, 181

Angelou, Maya, 147
Annapolis (Naval Academy), 48
Armed Forces Epidemiological
    Board, 126
Articles of Confederation, 23, 68
Astor, John Jacob, 24

Baker, James, 151
Baltimore & Ohio Canal, 27
Bank of America, 65, 82, 83, 84,
    115
Bank of the United States (BUS),
    69
Barr, Albert, 146
Bell, Alexander Graham, 162, 164
Bell Laboratories, 166
Bellow, Saul, 144
Biddle, Nicholas, 71–72, 80
Bilingual Education, 45, 56, 58, 62
Bilingual Education Act, 56
Bimson, Walter, 80
Borah, William, 37
Bretton Woods Agreement, 181
"Bridge to nowhere" (Alaska), 40
Brown, Walter Folger, 43
Brown University, 48

Brown v. Board of Education, 62
Buchanan, James, 48
Bureau of Public Roads, 36, 37
Burns, Ken, 152
Bush, George H. W., 59
Bush, George W., 60, 103,
    113, 136

Calhoun, John, 26
Carter, Jimmy, 41, 82
Centers for Disease Control
    (CDC), 119, 131–133
Central Intelligence Agency (CIA),
    146
Chaffee, Suzy, 57
Chesapeake & Delaware Canal, 27
Chesapeake & Ohio Canal, 26
child labor, 91
Civil Rights Act, 62, 112, 137, 181
Civil War, 8, 22, 28, 30, 48, 73,
    142, 152, 162
Civil Works Administration, 143
Clark, William, 25
Clay, Henry, 26
Clinton, William J., 59–60, 82,
    102, 113
Cold War, 15, 152
    and communications, 169–170
    and culture, 145–148, 149
    and education, 51–52
    and housing, 102
    and public health, 131–135
Conant, James B., 51
Confederacy, 8
Conrail, 40
Constitution, US, 22, 23, 24, 26,
    47, 157–158, 170
    and First Amendment, 158
Consumer Financial Protection
    Bureau, 84
Continental Congress, 67
"Continentals," 67
Contras, 150

Coors, Joseph, 150, 155
Cornell University, 47

Democratic Party, 14, 183
Department of Agriculture, 36, 50
Department of Commerce, 35, 80
Department of Defense, 52
Department of Education, 44, 56,
    59, 63
Department of Health and Human
    Services (also Health,
    Education and Welfare; also
    Federal Security Agency), 119
Department of Homeland Security,
    132, 182
Department of Housing and Urban
    Development (HUD), 112,
    113
Department of Justice, 166
Department of Labor, 82
Department of State, 45, 135, 146,
    147, 148
Department of Transportation, 21,
    39, 41
Department of Treasury, 69, 70, 71,
    73, 76, 82, 83, 114
Dodd-Frank Wall Street Reform
    and Consumer Protection
    Act, 84
Dondero, George, 148
Douglas, Stephen, 30
Drucker, Peter, 17

earned income tax credit, 20
Education for All Handicapped
    Children Act, 56, 57
Eisenhower, Dwight D., 38, 43,
    112
Elementary and Secondary
    Education Act (ESEA),
    54–55, 56, 58
    and Title I, 54, 55, 59
    and Title II, 55

and Title III, 55
and Title VII, 56
and Title IX, 45, 57–58
Emergency Education Program
    (EEP), 49
Epidemiological Intelligence
    Service, 131
Erie Canal, 26
Ewing, Oscar R., 119

Farm Security Administration,
    143, 145
Federal-Aid Highway Act, 36
Federal Children's Bureau, 122
Federal Communications
    Commission (FCC), 167, 171
Federal Deposit Insurance
    Corporation (FDIC), 65–66,
    79, 82, 83, 84
Federal Emergency Relief
    Administration (FERA), 49
Federal Highway Administration,
    36
Federal Home Loan Bank Act,
    105–106
Federal Housing Administration
    (FHA), 106, 108, 110
Federal National Mortgage
    Association (Fannie Mae),
    106, 112, 113, 116
Federal Reserve Act, 76
Federal Reserve System, 66, 76, 79,
    82, 84
Federal Savings and Loan
    Insurance Corporation, 82
Federalist, 6–7, 24
Filipinos, 48–49
Financial Services Modernization
    Act, 82
Food and Drug Administration
    (FDA), 119, 121
Fourteenth Amendment, 10, 130,
    158

Franklin, Benjamin, 158
French and Indian War, 5, 25
Friedman, Milton, 80
Fulbright Program, 45

Gallatin, Albert, 25, 26, 28, 35, 43
Gingrich, Newt, 1, 151
Glass-Steagall, 66, 67, 78, 79, 80,
    82
Gore, Al, 60
Great Depression, 77, 104, 117,
    122, 130, 142, 143, 174
Great Recession, 99
Great Society, 2, 96, 137, 148, 149,
    184

Hacker, Jacob, 17
Hamilton, Alexander, 6, 9, 69
Harrison, Benjamin, 32, 142
Harvard University, 51
Hatch Experimental Station, 13
Heritage Foundation, 1, 150
Heston, Charlton, 150, 154, 155
Higher Education Act (HEA), 53
Higher Education Facilities Act, 53
Highway Trust Fund, 38
Hill-Burton Hospital Survey
    Construction Act, 130–131
HIV/AIDS, 119, 136
Home Loan Bank Board, 108
Home Mortgage Disclosure Act,
    114
Home Owners' Loan Corporation,
    106, 110
Hoover, Herbert, 33, 35, 77, 102,
    105, 106, 143
Hopkins, Harry, 143
housing discrimination, 110–112
Hutchins, Robert, 51
Hygienic Laboratory, 120, 133

Individuals with Disabilities
    Education Act, 57

industrial accidents, 89–90
infant mortality, 118
Inglis, Robert, 19
Intermodal Surface Transportation
    Efficiency Act (ISTEA), 40
International Cooperation
    Administration (ICA), 135
Interstate Commerce Act, 31
Interstate Commerce Commission
    (ICC), 31, 32, 33
Interstate Highway System, 36, 38,
    40, 42

Jackson, Andrew, 26, 27, 71, 159
Jay, John, 161
Jefferson, Thomas, 24, 25, 26, 69,
    70, 142, 161, 162
Johns Hopkins University, 16, 44
Johnson, Lyndon B., 20, 53,
    54, 56, 96, 112, 137, 148,
    149, 184
Jones, Jesse, 78
Kennedy, Edward, 41, 60
Kennedy, John F., 112, 136,
    148–149
Kennedy, Robert F., 58
Keynesianism, 94, 95

land grants, federal, 30, 47
Langley, Samuel Pierpont, 34
Lange, Dorothea, 143
Langmuir, Alexander, 131
Lanham Act, 50
Lasswell, Harold D., 15
Lawrence, Jacob, 144, 148
Lee, Russell, 145
L'Enfant, Pierre, 142
Levitt, William, 102
Lewis, Meriwether, 25
Lincoln, Abraham, 43, 142
Lincoln Highway Association, 37
Louisiana Purchase, 24, 25, 28
Luce, Henry, 146

McDonald, Thomas, 37
Madison, James, 24, 26, 28, 43
Maher, Bill, 19
malaria, 122–123, 126, 128, 131,
    135, 137
Mapplethorpe, Robert, 151, 152
Marshall, E. G., 144
Marshall Plan, 184, 188
Massey Energy Corporation, 85
Medicaid, 96, 100, 137–138, 192
Medicare, 18, 19, 20, 96, 100,
    137–138
Merchants Association of New
    York, 78
Mexican-American War, 29, 54
Miller, George, 60
Mississippi River, 24
Missouri Compromise, 30
Monetary History of the United States,
    80
Morgan, James Pierpont, 75
Morrill Land Grant Act, 13,
    47–48
Morris, Robert (also "Morris
    notes"), 67–68, 69
Morse, Samuel F. B., 162–163, 164
Mumford, Lewis, 39

National Advisory Committee for
    Aeronautics, 35
National Aeronautics Space
    Administration, 53
National Association of Real Estate
    Boards, 111
National Banking Acts, 73
National Banking System (NBS),
    74
National Broadcasting Corporation
    (NBC), 168
National Cancer Act, 134
National Cancer Institute, 134
National Defense Education Act
    (NDEA), 51–52, 53

National Endowment for the Arts
(NEA), 149–152
National Endowment for the
Humanities (NEH),
149–152
National Homeownership
Day, 102
National Institute of Child Health
and Human Development,
129
National Institutes of Health
(NIH), 52, 133–134
National Interregional Highway
Committee, 38
National Railroad Passenger
Corporation, 39
National School Lunch Program
(NSLP), 50
National Science Foundation, 53
National System of Interstate and
Defense Highways, 38
National Tuberculosis Association,
122
National Venereal Disease Control
Act, 127
National Youth Agency (NYA), 49
Native Americans, 48
New Deal, 2, 45, 64, 67, 77, 80,
93–94, 97, 117, 126, 149
    and African Americans, 95
    and the arts, 143–145, 155
    and banking, 66
    and education, 49–50, 54
    and health, 122–124
    and housing, 106–107, 117
New York Telegraph Act, 163
Nixon, Richard M., 56, 149–150
No Child Left Behind Act
(NCLB), 60–61
North, Oliver, 150
North American Free Trade
Agreement, 181
Northwest Ordinance, 47

Obama, Barack, 19, 42, 84, 117,
138, 139
Office of Management and Budget
(OMB), 81
Ohio River, 25, 28
Omnibus Crime Control and Safe
Streets Act, 181
Organized Crime Control Act, 181

Pacific Railroad Act, 30
Paladino, Carl, 1
Panama Canal, 34
Panic of 1907, 75
Parran, Thomas, 125, 126–127
Paulson, Henry, 83
Peace Corps, 63
Pell Grants, 53
Peña, Federico, 41
Penn Central Railroad, 40
Pershing, John, 36
Pike, Zebulon, 25
Planning Profitable Neighborhoods,
109
Polio Vaccination Assistance Act,
181
Pollock, Jackson, 145–146
Porgy and Bess, 146–147
Post Office Act, 158–160, 161, 162,
170
Post Office Department, 163–164.
168, 170
Postal Service, 15, 35, 39
Progressive-era reform, 91–93
    and health, 120–122
Public Health Service (PHS), 119,
121, 122, 123, 126, 127, 128,
129, 132, 133
public housing, 94, 108, 115
Pure Food and Drug Act, 121

Radio Act, 167, 168
Railroad Administration, 33
Rayburn, Sam, 37

Reagan, Ronald, 59, 98, 99, 150, 151, 152, 155
Reconstruction Finance Corporation (RFC), 33, 77, 78
Report of the Secretary of the Treasury on the Subject of Roads and Canals, 26
"republican ideology", 5–6
Republican Party (GOP), 55, 56, 183, 184, 192
Research, federal funding of, 13, 36, 52, 58, 119, 126, 127, 128, 129, 132, 133–135, 154, 170, 181
Reserve Officer Training Corps, 63
Revolutionary War (War of Independence), 5, 8, 15, 157, 158
Reynolds, Carl V., 124
Rockefeller Foundation, 121
Roosevelt, Franklin Delano (FDR), 14, 20, 33, 38, 78, 79, 93, 94, 106, 123, 143, 149
Roosevelt, Theodore, 34, 43
Route 66, 36
Rush, Benjamin, 6

Safety Appliance Act, 32
Sanitary Commission, 121
savings & loans (S&Ls), 72, 77, 81, 82
Second Bank of the United States (SBUS), 71–72, 84
Securities and Exchange Commission (SEC), 79–80, 82
Serrano, Andres, 151
Servicemen's Readjustment Act (GI Bill), 16–17, 45, 46, 51–52, 53

Shahn, Ben, 143, 148
Sheppard-Towner Act, 12, 13
Slater, Rodney, 42
Smith, Sydney, 140, 155
Smithsonian Institution, 34
Social Security Act, 14, 20, 94, 123, 124, 128, 129, 137
and Titles V and VI, 123
Social Security Administration, 15, 18, 47, 95, 96, 97, 100
Spanish-American War, 8
Sputnik, 51, 52, 59
state-chartered banks, 66, 68, 72, 73, 74, 76, 84
Stiles, Charles Wardell, 121
suburbs, growth of, 107–109
Supreme Court, 10, 32, 91, 93, 110
Surgeon General's Report on Smoking and Health, 134
Switzer, Katherine, 57–58
syphilis, 119, 123, 126–128

tax exempt organizations, 153
taxation, resistance to, 6, 9
Tea Party, 4, 6
Tocqueville, Alexis de, 7, 159
Trade and Tariff Act, 181
Trade Expansion Act, 181
Trail of Tears, 8
Triangle Shirtwaist Factory fire, 89
Trident submarine, 152
Troubled Asset Relief Program (TARP), 83
Truman, Harry, 80, 184
tuberculosis, 87, 119, 122, 127, 128, 135, 137
Tuskegee Study of Untreated Syphilis, 127

Union Pacific Railroad, 30, 31
United Automobile Workers, 95

United Nations International Children's Emergency Fund (UNICEF), 135
United States Capitol, 142
United States Patent Office, 163
University of California, Berkeley, 48, 53
University of Chicago, 51, 80
University of Michigan, 47, 53, 123
US Agency for International Development (USAID), 135, 136, 137
US President's Emergency Plan for AIDS Relief (PEPFAR), 136–137
USAPATRIOT Act, 182

Vanzetti, Bartolomeo, 86–87, 89, 91
venereal disease (VD), 126–128
Veterans Administration (VA), 45, 46, 106, 110, 125

Wagner-Murray-Dingell National Health Bill, 124
War of 1812, 70, 72

War on Poverty, 54, 98
Washburn, Israel, 28
Washington, George, 6, 23, 48, 69, 142
Wayland, Francis, 48
West Point, 7, 27, 48
Western Union, 164, 166
Wilson, Woodrow, 32, 36, 43
Works Progress Administration (WPA), 49, 50, 122, 123, 143–145
    And Federal Project Number One, 144
World Health Organization (WHO), 135
World Trade Center, 15
World War I, 32, 55, 106, 158
World War II, 15, 16, 17, 22, 36, 37, 45, 48, 50, 80, 95, 96, 97, 109, 133, 135, 146, 169, 173, 174, 175, 184
    and health, 124–128
Wright, Richard, 144
Wright brothers, 34, 35